Coastal Walks in Andalucía

The Best Walks close to Andalucía's Mediterranean and Atlantic Coastlines

Guy Hunter-Watts

SANTANA BOOKS

COASTAL WALKS IN ANDALUCÍA

Published by Ediciones Santana, S.L.

Apartado 41
29650 Mijas-Pueblo (Málaga)
Spain

Tel: (0034) 952 48 58 38
EMail: info@santanabooks.com

www.santanabooks.com

Photos by Guy Hunter-Watts

Cartography: 1:50000 Maps reproduced with permission of Instituto Geográfico Nacional

Cartografía Original: Instituto Geográfico Nacional

1:50000 Maps L Series for La Axarquía reproduced with thanks to Servicio Geográfico del Ejercito

Design: Cheryl Gatward   Layout: Sarah Gatward

Printed in Spain by Industrias Gráficas Solprint, S.L.

ISBN: 978-84-89954-93-9
Depósito Legal: MA 2360 - 2011

Acknowledgements

When researching this book I looked to many sources in both English and Spanish.

When it came to Spanish literature the brochures produced by the town halls of Istán, Casares and Mijas were a starting point if somewhat perfunctory. The map of the Sierra de Ojén compiled by the Refugio de Juanar was a help as was the walking guide *Guía de la Sierra de Mijas* compiled by the young Spanish walker Juan Antonio Gómez Alarcón. His unexplained disappearance in these same mountains serves to remind us that there will always be inherent dangers should you set out alone to explore uncharted terrain.

The German guide *Andalusien Sud* by Bernd Plikat gave me a few clues as to which routes to explore as did my friend Jürgen Paeger's book *Wandern in Andalusien.* And when deciding on which walks to list in the Vejer de la Frontera and Caños de Meca region, James Stuart from Casa del Califa shared his knowledge of the local footpaths.

As far as guide books in English go, Charles Davies' *Walk! Axarquía* was a very useful pointer. I much enjoy C.D.'s highly personal approach to describing walks – I've followed his notes in the Tramuntana mountains of Mallorca and on La Gomera – and recommend his book if you're looking for more challenging trails in the mountains close to Nerja or out from the more remote villages of the *Costa* hinterland. Elma Thompson's leaflets about walking in the Axarquía were also a great help. I first used them more than a dozen years back and was delighted to run into this indomitable lady of the hills when taking a break with a group in the Chillar canyon.

Thanks are also due to Mona and Stefan Crites who lent me their Puerto Banus apartment when I was researching routes in the Sierra de Ojén as well as to Pierre and Isabel from El Águila close to Mijas for being generous hosts when I was in the Mijas area.

I also owe gratitude to Peter Jones and Martin Jacoby for providing the check lists for birds and plants that you'll find at the end of this book and to the National Geographical Institute for granting me permission to use their cartography. Much more of the same is due to Cheryl and Sarah Gatward of New Image for fielding my documents, maps and photographs and transforming them into the book that's now between your hands.

And, as always, my thanks to Tiki for your constant support.

Photography
All photographical images are by the author apart from the three ornithological images which are courtesy of Spanish Nature.

Cartography
1:50000 Maps reproduced with permission of Instituto Geográfico Nacional

This book is dedicated to my oldest friend Andy Waterer with whom I've shared many an adventure, and misadventure, in Morocco, Colombia, South Africa, Greece, Sweden, Switzerland, Tanzania, Ecuador and many other parts of the planet.

Contents

Foreword

The first time I get a glimpse of the sea on a walk my step feels lighter. It's as if the vastness of an ocean view offers the perfect counterpoise to the immediacy and physical effort of walking a mountain trail. And who doesn't feel more in touch with the Big Picture than when walking beside the ocean? If walking is good for body, soul and mind one senses that *coastal* walking is even more so.

A few years back, whilst researching another book, I came across the stunning footpath along the Atlantic coast close to Tarifa along with other trails close to Gibraltar. Later that year I explored the Sierra de Mijas and was again bowled over by the beauty of its footpaths. If these walks were new to me, I already knew many of the trails in the Almijara mountains close to Nerja and others in the Sierra de Ojén above Marbella. These walks were the kernel from which this guide was born, a book whose aim is to describe the best walking trails close to Andalucía's southern seaboard.

It was a surprise to discover how few books existed about walks in this area. Most of those I came across were written several years ago, at a time when those in charge of promoting tourism seemed unaware that not all visitors to the *Costa* wish to spend their time lazing on a beach or by a hotel pool. The good news is that the past decade has seen a radical change in perception and many local councils have invested time, along with considerable municipal and regional funds, in marking out local footpaths. Whilst these initiatives are to be applauded they haven't made that simple act of going out on a new walk that much easier. Even in areas where waymarking and signposting have been created there's a dearth of literature about the newly marked trails: the few sketchy pamphlets that describe the local network of paths are ludicrously short on detail.

This guide aims to bridge that gap and describe a full week of walking in the 7 most beautiful Natural Parks along Andalucía's Atlantic and Mediterranean coasts. The routes chosen are close to some of the region's prettiest villages and most are circular itineraries. All the walks described are within the capabilities of anyone in good health who walks on a regular basis. That said, most routes involve steep ascents and descents and just a few have sections which might be described as challenging. The Subbética chain is a grandiose and rumpled swathe of *sierra*: it was never my aim to skirt round these mountains to create easier walks but rather to take you to the heart of the matter.

If you're resident in the area covered by the guide you won't be more than a two hour drive from most trailheads and often much closer. And if you plan to travel to southern Spain for a walking holiday within these pages you'll find the makings of a memorable walking holiday in any one of the seven listed Parks.

The compilation of this book has been a journey of discovery and the magnificence of the trails which lie so close to the Andalucían seaboard has been a genuine inspiration. Not to walk out and discover these oceanside paths, gorges, river pools, high passes and peaks would be to miss out on one the biggest experiences that this multifaceted region of Iberia has to offer.

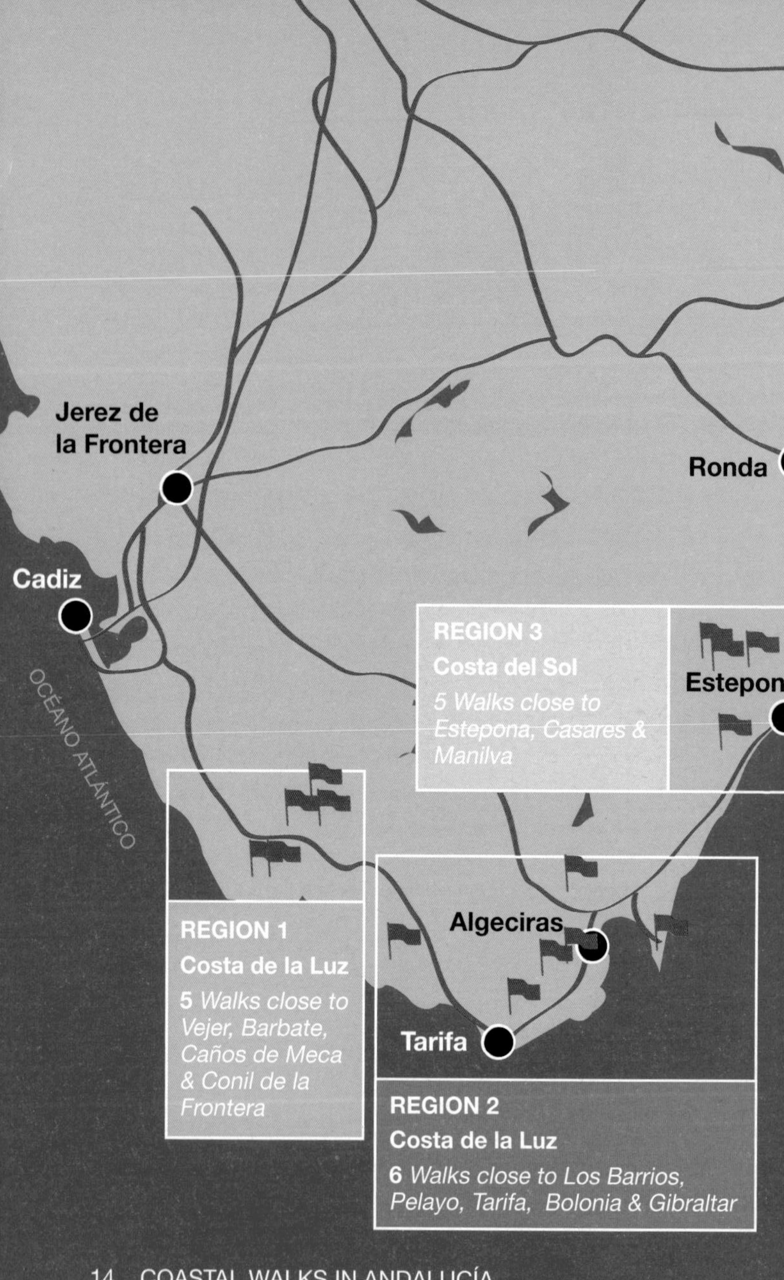

Jerez de
la Frontera
Ronda
Cadiz
OCÉANO ATLÁNTICO
REGION 3
Costa del Sol
5 Walks close to
Estepona, Casares &
Manilva
Estepona
REGION 1
Costa de la Luz
5 Walks close to
Vejer, Barbate,
Caños de Meca
& Conil de la
Frontera
Algeciras
Tarifa
REGION 2
Costa de la Luz
6 Walks close to Los Barrios,
Pelayo, Tarifa, Bolonia & Gibraltar

Coastal Walks in Andalucía

43 walks in 7 different coastal regions

Introduction

Talk to most people about the coast of Andalucía and they'll picture the small swathe of seaboard that runs from Torremolinos to Estepona, the heartland of what is commonly sold as the *Costa del Sol*. First associations are of crowded beaches, busy coastal roads and blocks of holiday apartments. Few amongst them will conjure up visions of the mighty chain of mountains, the tail end of the Sierra Subbética, which rises up a few kilometres back from the sea. Nor do they tend to evoke the wilder beaches of the Costa de la Luz or the footpaths that run just a few metres from the Atlantic surf.

Since Iberian times these paths have seen the passage of livestock, charcoal, fruit and vegetables, dried fish, lime, ice from the high *sierras*, silks and spices from distant lands, contraband coffee and tobacco along with muleteers and shepherds, itinerant workers, fortune seekers and armies on the march. These footpaths were created with practicality to the fore and even when you set out on a walk for the first time you get a sense of where a path will lead you. Ancient byways have their own logic and when researching this book I was constantly struck by a sense of *Times Past*, not only when a section of ancient paving or a finely cobbled path suggested Roman or Arabic origins. This sense of history, and at the same time of continuity, gives nearly all the walks described in this book an added appeal. It's as if these ancient byways serve to reconnect us with something that has been around since Time immemorial but which we rarely experience.

If the areas described in the book share a common historical thread the different parts of the *Costa* have their own unique character. The cliffs, pine forests and marshlands close to Vejer are very different in feel to the wooded slopes of the Algeciras hinterland with its unique *canuto* (glossary) ecosystem. The lunaresque landscapes of the Sierra Bermeja stand in marked contrast to the wooded mountainsides behind Marbella and Mijas, whilst the cliffs and crumpled massif of the *sierras* between Nerja and Almuñecar have a beauty all of their own. Each region is described in greater detail in its corresponding section but, have it from me, there's superb walking in every one of them.

There are many terms to describe a protected area in Andalucía: *Unesco Biosphere Reserve, Parque Natural, Paraje Natural* and so on. All seven coastal regions described fall into one of these categories apart from the Sierra de Mijas which is soon to gain protected status: in practical terms it has been in place for several years since the radical change in the Andalucían rural development laws. All of these areas now have some form of waymarking in place although it doesn't cover all the routes in this book, and in many cases marker posts are damaged or missing. But with the map sections and walking notes you should have no problems in navigating your way through the *sierras.*

The one other area that naturally belongs within these pages is the Cabo de Gata Natural Park at the eastern end of Andalucía. The park has a unique beauty and is a great destination for winter walking. It is absent from this book because space was limited and because it has a more remote geographical location. That said, the Cabo de Gata coastal path - it runs from Agua Amarga all the way to the western end of the Park - is an easy trail to follow and clearly waymarked. There are also waymarked trails just back from the coast close to Rodalquilar and its defunct gold mines. Anyone resident in Andalucía with a love of walking should visit this remarkable Park at some point. Cabo de Gata is a great destination for walking in winter with its scant rainfall and long hours of sunshine.

Coastal Walking: a definition of terms

The walks in this book are generally one of three types. There are walks which link different coastal villages, others which are circular itineraries which involve some walking at the ocean's edge and a third group of inland circuits and gorge walks a few kilometres back from the sea. At some point during all of the walks you'll be treated to vistas of the Atlantic or Mediterranean.

A brief introduction to the 7 different regions

The different walking areas are arranged in 7 chapters which correspond to different Natural Parks and protected areas, or combinations of them. In just a few instances the walks described fall just outside of official park boundaries.

You'll almost certainly be amazed at just how different the landscapes are in each of the different regions. At the beginning of each section I give a more detailed overview of each area but a brief description follows of the kind of walking & terrain you can expect to encounter:

1 Costa de la Luz: Parque Natural de la Breña & las Marismas

The five walks listed are all close to the towns of **Vejer, Conil, Caños de Meca and Zahara de los Atunes**. Most walks follow footpaths very close to the ocean apart from the Marismas circuit, a marsh walk just a few kilometres inland and the Santa Lucía circuit which is a fifteen minute drive from the ocean and explores the hills north of Vejer. Gradients are generally gentle in the coastal hinterland whilst sea breezes help make even summer walking enjoyable.

2 Costa de la Luz: Parque Natural de Los Alcornocales & del Estrecho

The six walks described are close to **Los Barrios, Pelayo, Tarifa, Bolonia and Gibraltar**. I've listed a Gibraltar walk in a southern Spanish walking guide because it's a stunning excursion and easy to access. Three walks follow footpaths along the ocean's edge whilst the other two, which involve more climbing, introduce you to the beautiful southern flank of the Alcornocales park and its unique *canuto* (glossary) ecosystem.

3 Costa del Sol: Paraje Natural de Sierra Bermeja & Sierra Crestellina

Of five walks listed, two lead out from **Casares**, one from close by to the village, another from a point just north of **Manilva** whilst the Pico Reales circuit involves a short drive north from **Estepona**. Although all walks lie a few kilometres inland you can expect incredible views of the Mediterranean, Morocco and Gibraltar. Be prepared for sections of steepish climbing on all walks although none are graded 'difficult'.

4 Costa del Sol: La Sierra de Ojén in the Parque Natural Sierra de las Nieves

Of the seven walks I describe one leads out from **Ojén**, another from the just north of **Marbella**, two from **El Refugio de Juanar** whilst three circuits lead out from the pretty mountain village of **Istán**. Most walks involve steep sections of climbing though two are quite short in distance. The magnificent Concha ascent is one of the few walks within these pages for which a head for heights is required though I wouldn't describe it as dangerous.

5 Costa del Sol: Sierra de Mijas

The six walks described lead out from the villages of **Mijas, Benalmádena, Alhaurín de la Torre and Alhaurín el Grande** and lead you to the most beautiful corners of the compact, yet stunningly varied landscape of the Sierra de Mijas. The *sierra* is essentially one big massif at the tail end of the Subbetica chain and all walks involve sections of steep climbing. However, the local network of footpaths are pretty well maintained and iron out a lot of the difficulty.

6 Costa Tropical: Western Sierra de Tejeda, Almijara & Alhama

Although the villages of **Cómpeta, Canillas, Sedella and Alcaucín** are situated just back from the sea high on the southern flank of the Sierra de Almijara, all four of them look out to the Mediterranean and their history and economy have always been inextricably linked to that of the coast. The Maroma ascent and the Blanquillo circuit are big, full day walks whilst the other four routes are less demanding. All walks are easily accessed from the Costa Tropical and you'll get beautiful views south to the ocean on all of the hikes.

7 Costa Tropical: Eestern Sierra de Tejeda, Almijara & Alhama

Were I to choose one area of the Andalucía coast for a great week of walking in southern Spain the swathe of mountains surrounding **Frigiliana, Nerja, Maro and Almuñecar** would be high on the list. The trails listed here include canyon and cliffside walks and exhilarating high mountain footpaths. Being linear up-and-down walks you can decide how far you'd like go along the canyon trails. The circuits listed are mostly *Medium* grade walks whilst the Maro to Frigiliana walk is a reasonably challenging day hike but a great one at that.

When to walk in Andalucía

As a general rule the best time to walk in Andalucía is from late April through to early June and from mid September to the end of October when you're almost guaranteed mild, sunny weather and the chances of rain are slight. Wild flowers tend to be at their best in late April/early May and this is the time when many walking companies tend to plan their walks.

The months most walkers avoid are July and August when temperatures can climb to as high as 40 degrees Celsius. But if you're in good physical shape, get going really early and take plenty of water you can still enjoy walking in summer.

If you're prepared to risk rain then winter is a wonderful time to be out walking, especially from December to February when rainfall is generally less than in November, March and April. *Generally* means just that: rainfall statistics for the past century confirm all of the above but the past two decades, with the prolonged drought of the nineteen-nineties followed by some unusually wet winters, provide no steady yardstick against which to base your predictions.

How to use the walking notes

These notes, together with the individual route map, should allow you to follow these walks without difficulty. But I recommend that you always have a compass and the 1:50000 I.G.N. map of the area, in addition to the one provided in this book.

A handheld GPS device can also be a useful.

Distances: rounded off to the nearest kilometre

Rating: each walk has been graded in one of four brackets

Easy/Medium: shorter walks with little height gain
Medium: mid length walks with some sections of climbing
Medium/Difficult: longer walks with longer sections of climbing
Difficult: more challenging full day walks with a number of steep climbs

Time required
This is an estimation of how long you should set aside for each walk and includes time for rest stops. **This is different to the bracketed timing of the notes themselves** which is my timing for each route without breaks at a steady walking pace. Your

pace may be slower or faster than mine but the timings should give you a good idea of how far into any particular walk you might be.

Total Height Gain

This is the total height gain across the whole of the walk and includes any height gain on the return leg of a linear walk. Figures given are to the nearest 25m.

Water

For each itinerary I've listed the springs you pass with a Ⓦ symbol. Be aware that in dry years these springs can slow to little more than a trickle, or even dry up, so always carry plenty of water.

Maps

Lists the Instituto Geográfico Nacional 1:50000 series map(s) for each walk. The series has recently been updated and is a reliable reference but remember that the grid on these maps is in UTM European 1950 format. The route is also covered by the 1:25000 series should you wish to have more detailed cartography. You may be surprised, as I was, at how many of the tracks and paths of the walk are visible on Google Maps. I found G.M. to be a useful tool on my iphone when researching these routes.

At the back of this book you'll find a bilingual order form which could make the process of ordering maps much easier from within Spain. All places listed will send maps *contra reembolso*, i.e. you pay when the maps are delivered to you.

In Andalucía the best place to order maps from are:

MAPAS Y COMPAÑIA
Calle Compañia 33, Málaga
952 608 815
info@mapasycia.es

www.mapasycia.es

As well as most 1:50000 maps, and some of the 1:25000 I.N.G. series, this bookshop stocks a wide selection of walking guides in both English and Spanish.

L.T.C.
Avenida Menéndez Pelayo 42-44, Sevilla
954 425 964
ltc@ltcideas.com
www.ltcideas.com

L.T.C. have scanning facilities and normally have the 1:50000 series in stock.

In Madrid the best places to order maps are:

Centro Nacional de Información Geográfica
General Ibánez de Ibero 3, 28010 Madrid
91 597 9453
consulta@cnig.es
www.cnig.es

La Tienda Verde
Calle Maudes 23 & 38, 28003 Madrid
91 533 0791
info@tiendaverde.org
www.tiendaverde.org

In the U.K. the best place for maps, which can be ordered on line, is:

Stanfords
12-14 Long Acre, London, WC1
Tel: 0207 836 1321 Fax: 0207 836 0189
Email: sales@stanfords.co.uk
www.stanfords.co.uk

Stanfords also stock a huge range of walking guides including my other two walking books Walking in Andalucía and The Andalucían Coast to Coast Walk.

Definition of terms: I've tried to make these route notes as unambiguous as possible. When describing the walks I've used *track* for any thoroughfare wide enough to permit vehicle access and *path* to describe one that is wide enough only for pedestrians and animals.

GPS references

I've provided full GPS references for each walk which are all accurate to within 20 metres and nearly all to within 5 metres. I can send these to you as a set of GPX files should you wish to load them straight into your Garmin/hand-held device.

Please email me at the address below. Bear in mind that references given are those that correspond to WGS 84 Datum which is the data used on the grid of the IGN maps reproduced in this book. GPX files from: info@rondatejar.com

Compass

When it seems to help I include approximate compass bearings in the walking notes. You should always have one in your pack.

G.R. & P.R.

You'll see several references in these route notes to G.R. and P.R.

G.R. signifies *Gran Recorrido* or Long Distance footpath and these routes are marked with red and white waymarking. P.R. signifies *Pequeño Recorrido* or Short Distance footpath and these routes are marked with yellow and white waymarking.

WALKING CHECK LIST

The two most important things to have along when you walk in Andalucía are:

- **Water:** carry a minimum of 1 litre and preferably more. During the warmer months the greatest potential danger facing you is heat exhaustion and dehydration. Wear loose-fitting clothing, a hat and keep drinking
- **Comfortable, broken-in walking boots:** no walk is enjoyable with blisters

You should also remember the following (this list compiled with maximum safety in mind):

- **Water bottle** (*Sigg* bottles are excellent)
- **Hat & sun block**
- **Map & compass**
- **Swiss army knife** or similar
- **Torch & whistle**
- **Mobile phone:** coverage is patchy in the mountains but if you have a mobile phone it would be silly not to take it along
- **Waterproofs** according to season
- **Fleece or jumper:** temperatures can drop rapidly at the top of the higher passes
- **Picnic**
- **First aid kit** to include antihistamine cream, plasters, bandage, plastic skin etc for blisters
- **Water purifying tablets**
- **Walking stick(s):** many hikers are now using light weight aluminium walking sticks, the best of which have shock-absorbing tips. Evidence shows that they reduce the possibility of injury whilst conserving energy
- **Chocolate/sweets** or glucose tablets

Things to remember when walking in Andalucía

- **Close all gates.** You'll come across some gate closing devices which can require patience to open and to close

- **Ganado bravo.** The sign designates an area where you could find fighting bulls though none of the walks described here take you through these areas. A sign saying *Coto* or *Coto Privado de Caza* designates an area where hunting is permitted in season. It doesn't mean you're walking on private property. Cotos are normally marked by a small rectangular sign divided into a white and black triangle.

- **Fire.** In the dry months the hillsides of southern Spain become a vast tinder-box. Be careful if you smoke or use camping stoves.

- **Springs/Water.** I've only mentioned those springs which I believe run all year. On some walks you'll be passing farmhouses where you may well find water in extremis.

Safety when walking

Let at least one person know where you're headed and at what time you expect to reach your destination.

Numbers you should have in your mobile:

- 112 Emergency services: general number
- 062 *Guardía Civil*
- 061 Medical emergencies
- 080 Fire Brigade

Bibliography of Fauna and Flora

Ornithology

The species check list at the end of this book was kindly provided by Peter Jones of the Andalucía Bird Society which organises birding trips in Spain and other parts of the world (see check list for Peter's contact details).

The classic field guides are:

A Field Guide to the Birds of Britain & Europe
Peterson, Mountfort & Hollom (ISBN 0-00-219900-9)

Bird Guide
Mullarney, Svennsson, Zetterström & Grant
(ISBN 0-00-219728-6)

Where to Watch Birds in Southern Spain
García & Paterson (ISBN 0-71363859-1)

An interesting reference book but too large for the field is:

Birds of Iberia
Finlayson & Tomlinson (ISBN 84-88127-08-1)

Botany

The plant list at the end of the guide was kindly provided by Martin Jacoby. Although he is now retired Martin continues to be involved in conservation in Andalucía and is a leading expert on the Doñana National Park. References quoted in his plant list correspond to the classic field guide:

Wildflowers of the Mediterranean
Marjorie Blamey & Christopher Grey-Wilson (ISBN 0-7136-7015-0)

Other recommended flower guides:

Flowers of Southwest Europe: A Field Guide

Oleg, Polunin & Smythies (ISBN: 0-19-288178-7)
Very comprehensive: this is a classic botanical must-have.

Wildflowers of Southern Spain
Betty Molesworth Allen (ISBN 84-88127-06-5)
The book not only gives you the botanical information but also describes medicinal and culinary uses of the plants. It also lists the common Spanish names.

A Field Guide to the Wild Flowers of Southern Europe
Davies & Gibbons (ISBN 1-85223-659-0)
A more comprehensive work than the above and of manageable size.

Best Sleeps

Price brackets quoted are meant to be a rough guideline:

€	**€50 or less for a double**
€€	**€50 to €100 for a double**
€€€	**€100 or more for a double**

I've listed hotels and simple places in the villages close to where the walks described begin or end and others which could easily be reached by car or taxi. The places included all have one thing in common: they are clean and welcoming.

Many are listed in much greater detail in my guide:
Small Hotels & Inns of Andalucía. www.santanabooks.com
IBSN: 978-89954-87-8

Be aware that hotels in Andalucía make extensive use of marble and ceramic tiles. They make perfect materials for the searing heat of the summer whilst in winter it means that floors can be icy cold. So pack a pair of slippers. And when travelling in the colder months it's a good idea to ring ahead and request that heating be switched on *before* your arrive.

Updates by Email

I've tried to be as accurate as possible in describing the routes in this book. But paths are constantly changing: new signs or buildings appear, tracks are bulldozed, trees chopped down and fires can occur. I'd be grateful for your feedback on any changes you encounter. These can be incorporated in subsequent printings of this guide.

All updates are listed under *Discussions* on my page *Walking in Andalucia* on www.facebook.com It's worth having a quick look before you set out.

You'll also find updates to the walks included in *Walking in Andalucía* as well as *The Andalucían Coast to Coast Walk.*

Contact: Guy Hunter-Watts info@rondatejar.com

Costa de la Luz: Parque Natural de la Breña & las Marismas

Walks close to Vejer, Barbate, Caños de Meca & Conil de la Frontera.

Costa de la Luz

Costa de la Luz: El Parque Natural de la Breña & las Marismas

The Parque Natural de la Breña & las Marismas covers an area of 5077 hectares of which a little over 1000 fall within the marine park which stretches a kilometre out into the Atlantic. If this makes it the smallest of Andalucía's Natural Parks the ecosystems found within its limits are surprisingly varied and the walks described here aim to introduce you to its three principal habitats.

Most notable is the swathe of stone pines or *pinos pinoñeros* (Pinus Pinea) of La Breña. The trees were planted in the 19th century as a means of halting the advance of the coastal dune system which until then had little protection against the force of the *levante* winds. An added bonus came in the annual harvest of nuts from the pine cones of the trees. The network of footpaths which cut through the forest are enjoyable even in summer thanks to the trees' dense, umbrella-like canopies.

The ecosytem of the cliffs between Barbate and Caños de Meca is very different in feel. Here the flora and fauna are born of the interplay of ocean spray and the sweet water springs which rise at the base of its sand and limestone cliffs: these are the *Caños* after which the village was named. The cliffs rise to 100m and the path which runs along their edge is a highlight of any visit to the area. The path cuts past the Torre del Tajo, one of a string of watch towers built in the 16th century as a deterrent to the frequent raids by Turkish and North African corsairs. Next to the tower are two of the finest *miradors* of the Andalucían seaboard: on clear days you'll see Jebel Musa across the Strait. The cliffs are home to large colonies of gulls and are a favoured nesting site of cattle egrets. And this is one of the few places on the Atlantic coast where you've a chance of spotting peregrine falcons.

The third natural jewel of the park are the wetlands of the Marismas del Río Barbate. The marshes are on the main migratory route to Africa and are also home to a large population of resident wading birds: the dykes that crisscross the *marismas* are perfect ornithological viewing platforms. Stretches of the marshes were drained in the last century to create grazing for livestock but much of this land has been returned to its natural state.

The area is blessed with one of Andalucía's most exquisite towns, Vejer de la Frontera, which fans out along a ridge 7kms back from coast: it's unique amongst the *pueblos blancos* in that it looks to both *sierra* and *mar*. The old town is an architectural arabesque and home to several excellent hotels and restaurants. Barbate is very different in feel, a modern town with some dingy suburbs and one of the highest unemployment rates in Spain. The town has one of the largest fishing fleets in Spain and is best known for the annual *almadraba* or netting that take place when shoals of tuna are making their way from the Atlantic to the warmer waters of the Mediterranean: the fish are caught in much the same way as they were in Roman times. If you plan to stay close to the ocean Caños de Meca should be first choice. Home to a multi-ethnic crowd of New Agers the village is quiet in all but the summer months and has a couple of good places to stay and decent fish restaurants.

A further treat comes in the form of some of the finest beaches along the Costa de la Luz. To either side of the Trafalgar lighthouse, near the spot where the naval battle took place in 1805, are long stretches of fine sand where even in summer you can escape the crowds. The latter section of the walk from Vejer to Caños leads you along its beach whilst the Trafalgar to Conil walk is nearly all at the ocean's edge.

BEST SLEEPS

Vejer de la Frontera

La Casa de Califa €€
Tel: 956 447 730 Email: info@lacasadelcalifa.com
www.lacasadelcalifa.com
Beautiful bedrooms and a restaurant offering a mix of Med' and Eastern cuisine.

Siete Balcones €€
Tel: 956 447 732 Email: info@sietebalcones.com
www.sietebalcones.com
Another excellent choice at the heart of the old town with four stylish rooms and great serve-yourself breakfasts.

Caños de Meca

Hotel Madreselva €€
Tel: 956 437 255 Email: madreselva@grupocalifa.com
www.madreselva.grupocalifa.com
Spruce little hotel with pool and courtyard-facing rooms with good deals in low season.

Hotel La Breña €€
Tel: 956 437 368 Email: info@hotelbrena.com
www.hotelbrena.com
Friendly hotel close to the start of the Caños to Barbate cliff path with one of the village's best restaurants.

Taxis: Vejer de la Frontera 956 450 185, 956 450, Conil de la Frontera 956 445 039, 956 440 975, Caños de Meca (nearest taxis in Barbate) 956 43 10 84

Distance: 11 kms **Time Required:** 4 hours **Rating:** Medium
Total Height Gain: 275m **Map:** IGN 1:50000 Barbate 1073 (12-47)
Ⓦ **Water:** no springs along the way so take plenty

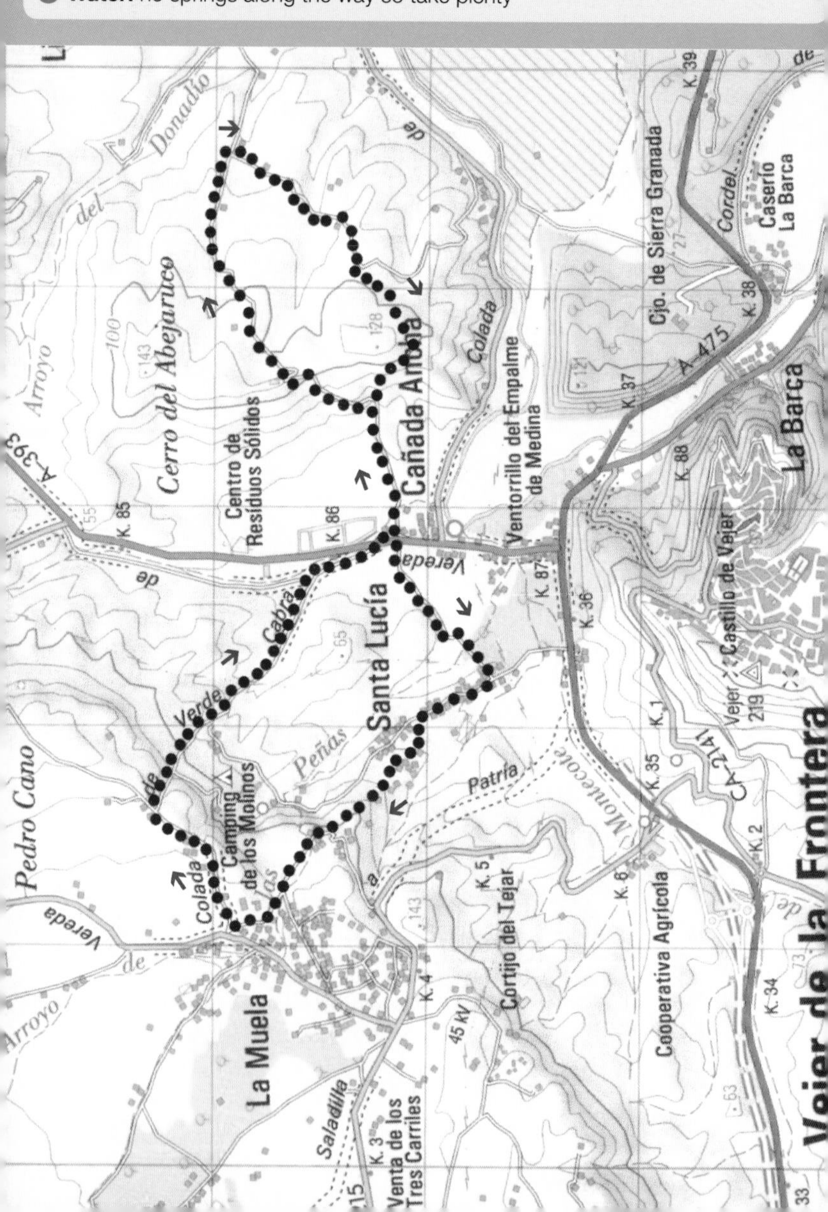

1 Vejer de la Frontera: Santa Lucía & El Abejaruco Circuit

Overview

This figure-of-eight route combines two of the prettiest walks close to Vejer, *The Route of the Watermills* and *The Route of the Bee-eaters*. The walk begins in the sleepy hamlet of Santa Lucía where, since Roman times, the waters of the Peñas stream have been channeled into the races of a series of millhouses. The first section of the walk is deeply bucolic as you climb a pretty path up past the 16th century aqueduct. After a short section of quiet tarmac road, farm tracks lead you down from La Muela then steeply up round the southern flank of the Abejaruco peak. From here you follow ancient bridleways lined with hedgerows as you make your way once more east and back to your point of departure. The views are contantly changing: south to Vejer and its rice paddies and east towards the Grazalema mountains. Try to set out by 10.30 in the morning which ensures that you get back to Santa Lucía in time for a leisurely lunch in one of the hamlets three restaurants: Venta El Toro would be my first choice.

Getting to the beginning of the walk

From the Cepsa petrol station just northeast of Vejer head along the N340 towards Cádiz. Continue past the turning for Medina Sidonia then after 350m turn right at a small sign for Santa Lucía. Follow a narrow road for just over 900m to Venta El Toro, to the right of the road, where the walk begins.

The Walk

The walk begins outside Venta El Toro in Santa Lucía (1). With your back to the restaurant turn right up the hill past two enormous palm trees. Passing a cross you reach a signboard

Ruta Molinos del Agua. Keeping straight ahead you'll shortly see signs for a camp site. Reaching a water deposit to your left (and a second camp site sign) cut left up a track which leads to a signboard about *El Acueducto de Santa Lucía* which lies in front of you 2.

Here cut right up a narrow path which leads up the right side of the aqueduct to reach an old mill fronted by a post-and-rail fence. Pass right of the building, angle right beneath a cast iron pipe, then continue up a narrow, leafy path which climbs to a flat area with a picnic bench 3. From here head straight on along a quiet minor road towards La Muela. After 450m you reach a fork. Here branch right 4 away from the tarmac along a sandy track which arcs round the boundary fence of a quarry. Passing the quarry's entrance you reach a point where the fence cuts right by another sign *Ruta Molinos del Agua* 5. Here turn right. After 30m the track merges with a broader one which climbs in an easterly direction as views open out towards the mountains of the Grazalema park. Bearing slightly right and levelling the track reaches another junction next to a house with a line of cypress trees at its boundary 6. **(30 mins)**

Here turn right along a track which descends across farmland in a southeasterly direction. Vejer comes into view. Bearing right the track runs parallel to the A396 (marked A393 on the I.N.G.map) passing a signboard about drover's paths like the one you're following: *Los Caminos Históricos y las Cañadas.* 250m beyond the sign the track angles left to meet the A396 7. Cross the road and turn right. After 75m angle through a gap in the crash barrier and continue on along a dirt track. Just past a villa marked *Muñoz de Begines* cut left along a track which soon crossses a stream via a concrete bridge 8 then reaches a fork. Take the left branch. The track runs gently up towards the Cerro del Abejaruco (named after the bee-eaters which nest here). Adopting a northerly course it climbs more steeply to reach a

point where a track leads straight towards a farm 9. **(1hr 10 mins)**

Here, cutting right, you pass a sign *Ruta El Abejaruco*. The track drops down before climbing once again to another junction. Here bear slightly right along the main track to reach a third junction next to a pylon 10. Cut left between two *Coto* signs down a less distinct track which is rougher underfoot. Bearing right, left, then right again the track runs across an open field before crossing a (dry) stream 11 then meets with the track you were following earlier (which has been diverted to avoid an overgrown stretch of hedgerow). Here angle right and continue down the old track which runs on between hedgerows. Passing a building surrounded by cypress trees the track becomes clearer as you follow a line of pylons eastwards. Passing a farmhouse then another sign *Ruta El Abejaruco* you reach a junction 12. **(1 hr 30 mins)**

Here turn right along a leafy dirt track lined by cactii and wild olives. Angling sharply right you reach a junction. Ignoring a sign pointing right to El Abejaruco angle left and follow the track down through a thick stand of bamboo then cross a (dry) stream 13. Beyond the stream the track climbs steeply past a modern house where it angles right, left, then right again as it passes the entrance to the villa, *La Valdesa*. From here there are views down to the rice paddies to either side of the Río Barbate. Crossing a ridge Vejer again comes into view. 500m past *La Valdesa* the track begins to angle gently right and reaches another house with a sign *Propiedad Privada* 14 where you reach a fork. Keep left and follow the track round the house's perimeter fence, passing a second house to your left. After descending steeply down an ancient cobbled track, eroded in parts, you reach the track you followed earlier in the walk 15. **(1 hr 55 mins)**

From here retrace your footsteps back to the A396. Hop over the crash barrier then angle left across the road to a signboard *Rutas Molinos del Agua* 16 **(2 hrs 5 mins)** then continue westwards along a farm track across open countryside. Descending, then angling left then right, you come to the first buildings of Santa Lucía. Crossing a bridge over the Arroyo de las Peñas 17 the track meets the road you followed earlier up to Venta El Toro 18. Turn right and climb back to your point of departure 1. **(2 hrs 40 mins)**

Distance: 10 kms **Time Required:** 3 hours **Rating:** Easy
Total Height Gain: 5m **Map:** IGN 1:50000 Barbate 1073 (12-47)
Ⓦ **Water:** no springs along the way so take plenty

2 Vejer de la Frontera: Las Marismas de Barbate Circuit

Overview

Since 1994 the flat delta at the mouth of the Río Barbate river, *Las Marismas de Barbate*, has formed part of the Natural Park of La Breña. These low-lying marshlands, crisscrossed by water canals, streams and raised tracks, have a bewitching beauty and are home to a richly diverse flora and fauna. This is one of the best places on the Atlantic coast for birding: the marshes lie on one of the major migratory routes between northern and central Europe and Africa and are used by birds as a half-way house before and after the journey across the Strait. The birds, both sedentary and migratory, feed on the abundant molluscs and crustaceans of its tidal reedbeds and it's easy to spot egrets, mallards, grebes and herons as well as several different warblers amongst the reeds and tamarisk. The walk is particularly memorable early on an autumn day when the low-lying flora of the *Marismas* is taking on its autumnal colours and Vejer hovers above the early morning mist.

Getting to the beginning of the walk

From the N340 at La Barca, just to the east of Vejer, take the A314 (marked on the map A393) towards Barbate for approx. 3 kms until you reach a sign 'Sendero Marismas de Barbate'. Cut left into a parking area where the walk begins.

The Walk

The walk begins in the car parking area to one side of the A314 (1). *There's a waste treatment plant is to one side of it so you'll be keen to get moving as quickly as possible.* From the car park go through a small black gate to one side of a larger green one, next to a signboard *Sendero Marismas de Barbate.*

Bearing right and adopting a southerly course you'll immediately begin to spot all kinds of wading birds out in the marshes.

Reaching a fork next to a sign *Parque Natural* 2 turn left along a track which cuts due east across the marshes for a little over 700m then, just before it reaches the Río Barbate, angles right 3 and runs on close to the looping course of the river. From here there are fine views back across the floodplain to Vejer. Eventually the track, bearing left, crosses a bridge 4 **(1 hr)** then reaches a signboard listing the most common birds found in the marshes. The track passes by twin rusting metal posts (ignore a track which cuts right unless you wish to shorten the walk) sticking close to the bank of the Río Barbate before reaching a fork just beyond a sluice gate which is to your right 5. Here cut right and head back to the western edge of the marshes and a group of farm buildings. Crossing a cattle grid then a small brick bridge **(1 hr 30 mins)** you reach a junction with a broader

track 6. Turn right and head on towards Vejer. Passing beneath power lines the track arcs left then passes through an enclosure with a group of ramshackle animal pens, passing through gates at either end. Angling right through a grove of eucalyptus trees you reach a fork. Here keep right, sticking to your same course. Soon you pass over a cattle grid where you reach more open countryside.

The track narrows down as it runs on between beds of reeds, still heading towards Vejer. Soon the track arcs hard right 7 **(2 hrs 5 mins)** then once more left. Adopting its former course it passes through thicker undergrowth where there are stands of bamboo and mimosa. Crossing a cattle grid 8 the track runs on to reach the junction where, earlier in the walk, you cut across to the eastern side of the marsh 2. From here retrace your footsteps back to the car park 1. **(2 hrs 30 mins)**

Distance: 17.5 kms **Time Required:** 5/5.5 hours **Rating:** Medium/Difficult
Total Height Gain: 50m **Map:** IGN 1:50000 Barbate 1073 (12-47)
Ⓦ **Water:** Hotel Palomar de la Breña, waypoint 13 @ 1 hr 25 mins

3 Vejer to Cape Trafalgar via El Palomar de la Breña

Overview

The route from Vejer to Cape Trafalgar (from where you can organise a taxi back for just €15) makes for a fascinating day of walking. After winding through the old town you cut along a high ridge past twin rows of wind turbines: how much you enjoy this part of the walk will depend on where you stand in the aeolic debate. Leaving the turbines behind you cut across open fields then follow a hedgerow-lined drover's path to the edge of the Breña Reserve where you pass Hotel Palomar de la Breña. From here sandy tracks, a short section of road, then another of firebreak, lead you through the reserve to the Caños-Barbate cliff path where you cut west towards Trafalgar. From Caños you follow the ocean all the way to the lighthouse: it feels like a natural end point to the walk but access is blocked to vehicles so there's a final section of road walking before you reach the A2233. The walk could be shortened by breaking off at Hotel Palomar de la Breña (almost halving the total distance) or at Hotel La Breña (reducing it by some 5kms). Both hotels have restaurants/bars open to outside guests.

The Walk

The walk begins next to a fountain in front of the Casa del Califa hotel in the pretty Plaza de España at the eastern side of Vejer ①. With your back to the hotel pass left of a kiosk, angle right and pass beneath an arch. Climbing past the Vera Cruz restaurant the street angles right then left then reaches a sign *Arco de la Segur*. Here cut right and continue parallel to a line of battlements. Passing beneath the arch of Puerta de la Segur drop down Calle Marqués de Tamarón which soon becomes

Nuestra Señora de la Oliva to reach the Plazuela square. Here angle left along Calle Juan Relinque following a sign *Teatro de San Francisco*. Reaching house 22A cut right up Calle San Ambrosio to a *Stop* sign ② then turn left along the palm-lined Avenida de Andalucía. At the end of the street, reaching a supermarket, cut right ③ and climb. Leaving the last of the town's houses behind you pass a sign *Ruta del Interior 1.4* ④. **(15 mins)**

From here head along a sandy footpath, just right of the tarmac road, which runs towards a line of wind turbines atop a ridge. Reaching a fork ⑤ angle left back towards the road then once more right through low-growing shrub. You shortly pass to the right of a radar installation used by civil aviation. Views open out towards Conil and Zahara de los Atunes. Passing a picnic area the path once more meets with the road ⑥. Continuing for 300m you reach a junction by group of buildings. Ignoring the track that cuts down to the right continue for 10m to a second junction then angle right following a sign *Consorcio de Aguas de la Zona Gaditana* ⑦. The track climbs then passes the first turbine. Heading on past several turbines you reach a sign *Via Pecuaria Collada de Buena Vista y los Carrascales*. 125m past this sign you come to a signboard for *El Bosque y El Matorral Mediteraneo* ⑧. **(50 mins)**

Here cut left along a narrow track. After 40m it arcs right and runs on parallel to a second line of turbines. Just beyond the last turbine the track reaches a wire-and-post gate ⑨. Go through the gate then, angling right, continue on towards the sea. Ahead you'll now see the building marked on your map as *Cortijo y Ermita de la Porquera* (later in the walk you'll see it's been reborn as *Hotel Palomar de la Breña*). After some 350m you reach a group of buildings and a breeze block wall. Here angle right then left, passing west of the buildings. Reaching a fork just beyond an odd dwelling with a caravan grafted to one side ⑩ angle

left and after 75m go through a wire-and-post gate. Continue along a sandy track which soon angles right towards the sea then passes through another wire-and-post gate. From here head straight on (ignoring a track to the left). Passing through yet another wire-and-post gate 11 head along the left edge of a huge field. After 650m the track loops hard right and descends between thick hedgerows. Sandier and more eroded it narrows to become a path that shortly crosses a (dry) streambed 12 . Beyond the stream, climbing steeply, you reach a track and a sign *El Palomar de la Breña* 13 .

(1 hr 25 mins)

Here bear right and climb a broad sandy track which leads to the edge of the *Pinar de la Breña*, the protected area of stone pines. Crossing a cattle grid the track arcs to the right then merges with a broader track 14 . Continuing in a westerly direction the track becomes tarmacked as it angles left then passes an 8T weight limit sign. Heading due south past the *Área Recreativa El Jarillo*, you reach a junction with the A2233 15 . **(2 hrs)**

Cross the road to a metal gate and climb through a style to its right then continue along a broad fire break towards the sea: the going is less tiring on a path which runs a few metres in to its right, even though it's overgrown in parts. 1.4kms after crossing the A2233 the firebreak runs up to a broad path by a marker post 16 . **(2 hrs 20 mins)**

Here turn right *(unless you wish to visit the Torre del Tajo in which case you could cut left: the tower is about 800m to your east)* along a path running parallel to the cliff edge and the sea. Reaching a three way junction 17 head straight on as indicated by marker posts. Your destination, the Cape Trafalgar lighthouse, come into view through the pines before you reach an information board about *Pinares Costeros* 18 . Here angle down left then once more right towards Caños and Hotel Mar de Frente. Passing behind the hotel you reach a sign for *Sendero Acantilado de Barbate* 19 . **(2 hrs 40 mins)**

Beyond the sign you reach a concrete road. Turn left and pass between Hotel Mar de Frente and Hotel La Breña. Heading on parallel to the sea for 300m then, opposite house no. 26, cut left down a narrow path 20 which leads down to the ocean. Here turn right along the beach towards Trafalgar. Reaching the second of two ramps which angle away from the beach 21 leave the sand and follow a promenade past a house with a porthole window. At its far end 22 climb back down to the beach via a staircase made of rocks and continue along the ocean's edge. At the far end of the beach, reaching a sign *Zona Peligrosa, Prohibido El Baño* take the second of two paths which angle away from the beach. Passing above a ruin it winds through the dunes before dropping back down to the beach. At its far end you come to a signboard *La Isla de Trafalgar*. Here cut up a wooden walkway to the lighthouse 23. **(3hrs 25 mins)**

From here follow a tarmac road (closed to traffic) northeast past a signboard explaining how the *Tombola de Trafalgar* was formed. Head on past a barrier then a roundabout. After some 600m pass a second barrier then a series of bars and restaurants to reach the A2233 opposite the Hostal MiniGolf. This is an ideal point to rendezvous with a taxi to take you back up to Vejer 24. **(3 hrs 40 mins)**

Distance: 19 kms **Time Required:** 5 hours **Rating:** Medium/Difficult
Total Height Gain: 225m **Map:** IGN 1:50000 Barbate 1073 (12-47)
W **Water:** no springs so take plenty

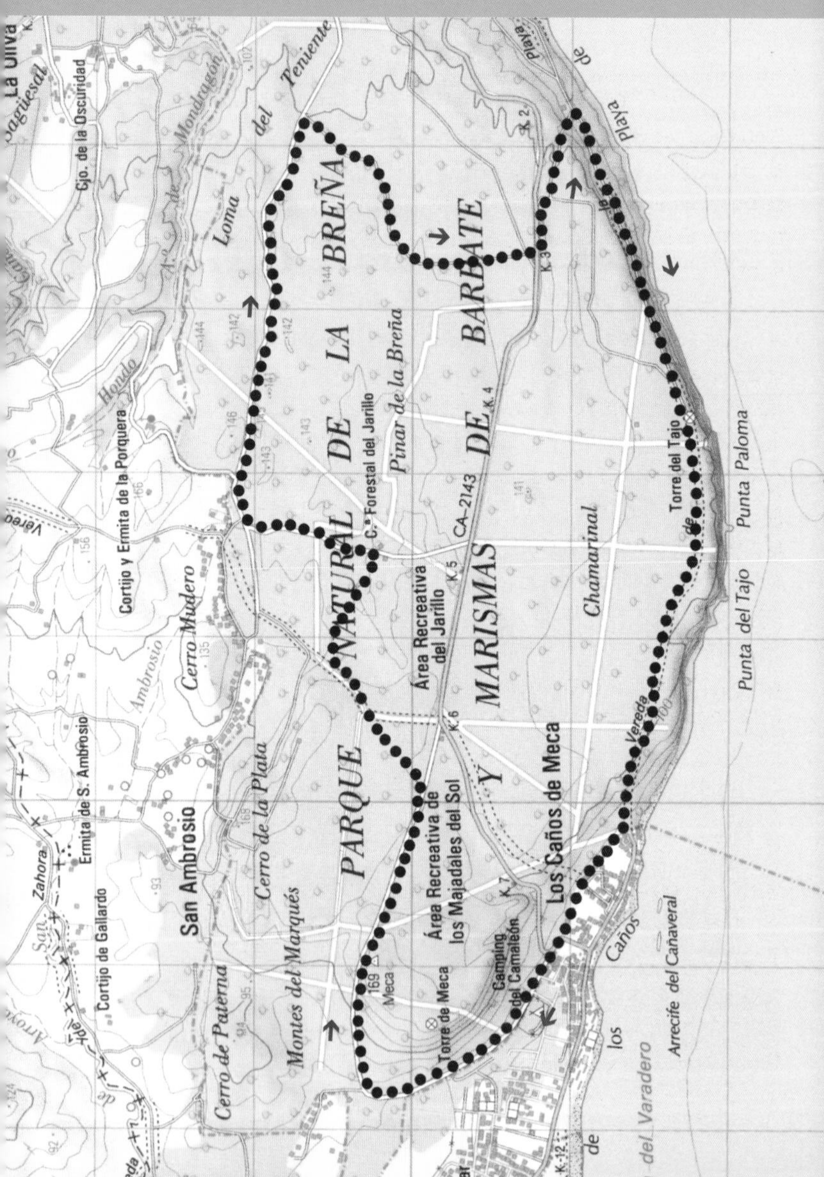

4 Caños de Meca: La Breña & Los Acantilados Circuit

Overview

This wonderful circular walk gives you the chance to sample the twin natural habitats that make the Parque Natural de la Breña such a special treat, introducing you to its vast forest of stone pines as well as to the spectacular cliffs which rise 100m above one of the best beaches in Andalucía. The walk begins with a section of forest walking as you follow sandy paths and tracks towards San Ambrosio. After heading on towards Barbate via a broad forestry track you cut south through the stone pines to reach the A2233. From here you angle down a sandy gully to reach the cliff path that leads back to Caños past the *Torre del Tajo*. The cliff path is the highlight of the walk and I recommend building in time for a leisurely picnic at one of the viewing points just beyond the tower. I've graded the walk *Medium/Difficult* not so much for the distance covered but rather because of the additional effort required when walking on sandy paths. *You could shorten the walk by taking a taxi from Caños to the Punto de Información that is to your right as you arrive in Barbate coming from Caños along the A2233. You'll see signs here marking the beginning of the cliff path.*

The Walk

The walk begins outside Hotel Madreselva (1) which you pass as you head east through the village on the A2233. From here head east past a row of palm trees. Reaching a *3.5T* sign turn left (2). The road soon arcs left. Just past the *km14* sign cut left along a sandy track following a sign *Sendero Caños-Torre de la Meca* (3). After running west the road contours right as it passes beneath the Torre de Meca. Reaching a 3 way junction (4) bear right past

a chain that blocks vehicle access. The track climbs gently as it runs eastwards: views open out above the treetops. Shortly beyond the top of the rise you pass a sign 5 marking the path up to the Torre de la Meca. **(35 mins)**
*** Should you choose to climb up and down add 35/40 minutes to these timings.*

The track runs on due east. Just before reaching a metal gate and the *Majadales del Sol* picnic area 6 cut hard left along a sandy track. Marker posts lead you on through the forest. Reaching twin posts, one marked *31* 7 angle right and continue in an easterly direction. Passing a firebreak the path runs downhill, adopting a northeasterly course, and eventually leads through a green gate **(1 hr 10 mins)** 8 beyond which you reach a picnic area. Angling slightly left you pass a sign *Sendero Torre de Meca* then, passing stone tables and benches, you reach a tarmac road 9. Cutting left along to the road you cross a cattle grid then after some 650m reach a junction where a sign points left for San Ambrosio. Ignoring the sign carry on along the track which arcs right, passes a sign prohibiting access to lorries, then reaches a fork 10. **(1 hr 25 mins)**

Keep right along the main track (ignoring a sign left for *Palomar de la Breña*) which you'll now follow without bifurcating for a little over 2kms. At first you follow a line of pylons but these soon angle away to the left. Reaching a junction by an information board about *El Pinar de Pinos Piñoneros* 11 **(1 hr 45 mins)** turn right away from the main track.

Passing a line of animal pens the track runs on through the pines before crossing a cattle grid then reaching the A2233 12. Angle right across the road, cross a stile then cut left along a broad sandy track parallel to the road. After 300m the track angles right. After 50m you reach a junction 13. Angle left and continue on parallel to the A2233. Just as the track angles

back towards the road you reach a cattle grid 14. Here angle 45 degrees to the right then after 75m cut right through the scrub and drop down to the sandy bed of a gully. Here cut left and follow a narrow, sandy path down towards the sea. The gully widens: head on down the easiest path to reach the Barbate-Caños cliff path 15. **(2hrs 20 mins)**

From here head west past a steep cliff face, parallel to the sea: you'll occasionally see white and green waymarking. Soon a rail and post barrier runs between you and the ocean. The path leads on past a sign 16 explaining about the *Pinares Costeras*, or the coastal pine forest: it was planted between 1895-1926 to stabalise the dune system. 200m past the sign you reach the Torre del Tajo. **(2 hrs 50 mins)** Be sure to visit the two miradors to its left and right for the finest cliff views of the walk.

Continuing towards Caños you reach a junction where the pole fence that has been to your left comes to an end. Head straight on. The sandy path now runs slightly further from the sea. As Cape Trafalgar and its lighthouse come into view the path divides 17. Take the higher option which leads past a second sign about *Pinares Costeros*. Here angle down left then once more right towards Caños and Hotel Mar de Frente. Passing behind the hotel you reach a signboard 18 describing the path to the Torre del Tajo. Here cut right up a stony track which bears left along the northern edge of the village before descending to the A2233 19. Turn left then right to return to the start point of the walk 1. **(3 hrs 45 mins)**

Distance: 13.5 kms **Time Required:** 3.5 hours **Rating:** Medium
Total Height Gain: 25m **Map:** IGN 1:50000 Barbate 1073 (12-47)
Ⓦ **Water:** bars/restaurants in El Palmar at approx. 1 hr 15 mins

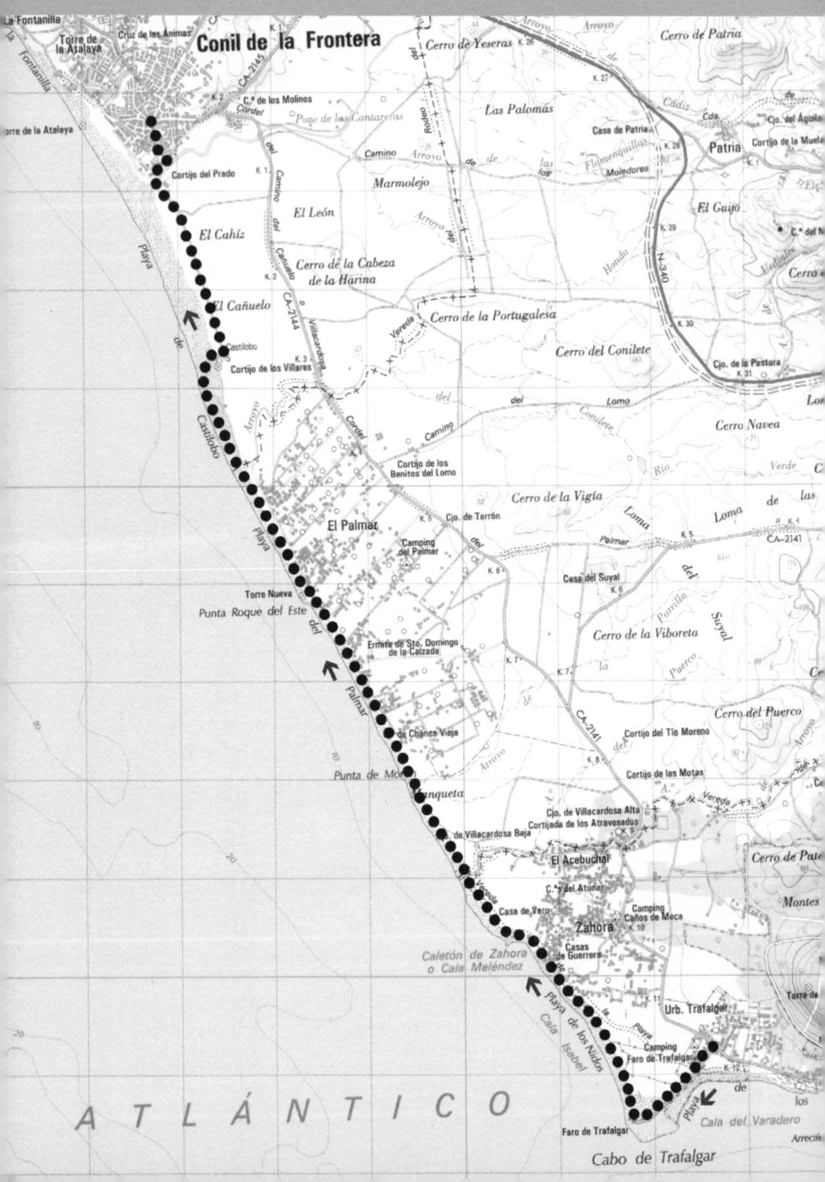

5 From Cape Trafalgar to Conil via the Castilnovo Tower

Overview

This linear walk takes in one of the finest sweeps of sand in southern Spain as you pass from Trafalgar to Conil via the beaches of Los Nidos, El Palmar and Castilobo. From the starting point just west of Caños de Meca you follow a road, blocked to vehicles, out to the Trafalgar lighthouse before dropping down to the Atlantic which you'll be following most of the way to Conil. This is a great walk for birdlife with plenty of ornithological action at the ocean's edge and in the marshes that you cross on the approach to Conil. Take a wind check before setting out: a strong *Levante* whips sand hard across the beaches and can turn the walk into an ordeal rather than a pleasure. If you set out before 11am you could end the walk with lunch in Conil: Bar Rincón de la Villa in the corner of Plaza de España is a perfect spot for alfresco *tapas or raciones*. If you prefer a shorter walk you could break off in El Palmar - it also has several beachside bars and restaurants - or simply walk part of the way then return by the same route.

Getting to the beginning of the walk

From Vejer take the CA2233 (marked on ING maps as CA2141) towards Caños de Meca. Approx. 1.5kms before reaching the village park on the left side of the road next to Hostal Restaurante MiniGolf.

The Walk

The walk begins outside Hostal Restaurante MiniGolf (1). Cross the road and head towards the lighthouse following a sign *Faro de Trafalgar*. Pass a line of bars and restaurants then a white and yellow barrier blocking vehicle access. Approaching the lighthouse head across a roundabout then pass a plaque commemorating the 1805 naval battle. 30m beyond a second barrier 2 cut right along a wooden walkway past a signboard explaining how the *Tómbolo de Trafalgar* was formed. Just before the walkway ends a second one 3 cuts left to the lighthouse: it's worth the diversion. Otherwise continue straight ahead then turn right along La Playa de los Nidos where the firmer sand at the ocean's edge makes for easier walking. At the far end of the beach you pass the beach bar *Chiringuito Sajorami* 4 . **(30 mins)**

Head on towards a ruin on a headland. Reaching the rocks at the end of the beach continue past a sign *Zona Peligrosa de Baño* 5 and pass beneath the ruin. Beyond the headland you reach the Playa del Palmar. Follow the path which runs just above the beach at the edge of the dunes until it drops back to the beach and return to the firmer sand at the ocean's edge. The white tower of Torre Nueva, between El Palmar and the sea, comes into view.

Passing just left of Torre Nueva 6 **(1 hr 25 mins)** after some 750m you reach the Playa de Castilobo: there's no clear demarcation between the two beaches. A square tower, La Torre de Castilnovo, is shortly visible to the right of the beach. Cut away from the beach to the tower 7 **(2 hrs)** where a signboard tells of its history: it has served both as watchtower against raiding corsairs as well as a lookout post for the annual *Almadraba (tuna catch).*

From the tower head on across the marshes via a sandy track which runs straight towards Conil, parallel to the beach. This is a great place for ornithology: you'll almost certainly see marsh harriers hunting above the flats. As the track reaches a concrete trig point marked *DPMT* you reach a fork. Bear left 8 and continue on with a fence now just to your right. Passing the

buildings of Cortijo del Prado, which are over to your right, cross a footbridge over the Río Salado 9. **(2 hrs 30 mins)**

Beyond the bridge cut right parallel to the northwest bank of the river. Reaching a damaged signboard cut left across the street and, passing a small *kiosko* and a football pitch, head straight 10 past a *No Entry* up Calle Azorín. At the top of the street bear left then take the next right in front of the Moorish-looking door of house no.8. At the next junction turn left along Calle José then take the next right to reach Plaza de Andalucía. Here, bearing left then right, you reach Plaza de España next to Bar Rincón de la Villa 11. **(2 hrs 40 mins)**

From Plaza de España head up the hill, pass beneath an arch, then turn right to reach the taxi rank. The fare back from Conil to the walk's starting point is less than €20.

Costa de la Luz: Parque Natural de Los Alcornocales & del Estrecho

Walks close to Los Barrios, Pelayo, Tarifa, Bolonia & Gibraltar

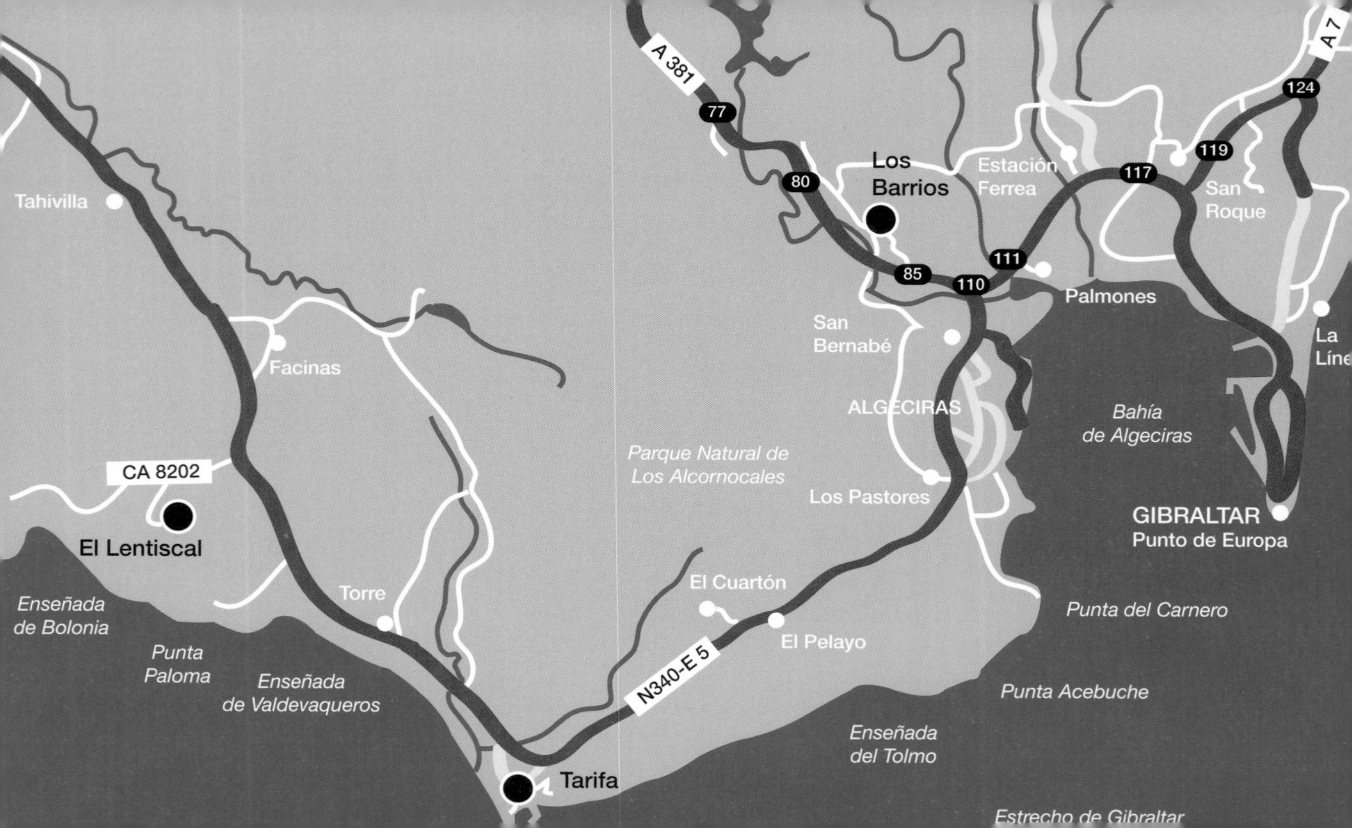
A 381
77
80
Los Barrios
85
110
111
Estación Ferrea
117
119
124
A 7
San Roque
Palmones
La Líne
Tahivilla
Facinas
San Bernabé
ALGECIRAS
Bahía de Algeciras
Parque Natural de Los Alcornocales
Los Pastores
GIBRALTAR
Punto de Europa
CA 8202
El Lentiscal
Torre
El Cuartón
El Pelayo
Punta del Carnero
Enseñada de Bolonia
Punta Paloma
Enseñada de Valdevaqueros
N340-E 5
Punta Acebuche
Enseñada del Tolmo
Tarifa
Estrecho de Gibraltar

Costa de la Luz: Parque Natural de Los Alcornocales & del Estrecho

The Parque Natural del Estrecho is one of the most recently created protected areas in southern Spain. Fanning out to both sides of Tarifa as far as Bolonia to the west and Algeciras to the east it encompasses a 19,000 hectare slice of Andalucía's Mediterranean and Atlantic coast. This is the southernmost tip of western Europe where just 10.5 kilometres separate the continent from Africa: on a clear day on any walk in the area you'll be rewarded with the sight of the Moroccan Rif rising above the Strait whilst yachts, tankers and ferries plough the waters between the two coastlines.

The main protagonist here is the *levante* wind which blows hard from the east for much of the year. Funnelled down as it passes through the Strait the wind's cutting edge has been responisble for the creation of high dune systems: these rise to over 30m in height at the end of Bolonia's beautiful arc of sand. The region is host to one of the most extraordinary natural events of the Andalucían year, the Spring and Autumn migration between Europe and Africa. It's been estimated that a mind-boggling 30 million birds cross the Strait during the autumn passage and the sight of the migration is never to be forgotten.

The comparative lack of development along the Costa de la Luz, thanks in part to the military bases that have long existed along Spain's southern border, make this coastal strip very different in feel to parts of the Costa del Sol whilst the creation of the Natural Park has effectively put an end to the developers' dreams of creating more coastal resorts. The walks described in this section to either side of Tarifa lead past hidden coves and long sandy beaches which feel a world away from the crowded ones that are just a few dozen kilometres to the east. You will, however, see a lot of action out on the waves: the kite surfing community has made Tarifa its adopted home and for much of the year you'll be treated to an amazing display of acrobatics off the beaches of Los Lances and Valdevaqueros where international competitions sometimes take place.

Two of the walks described in this section lie within the Parque Natural de los Alcornocales which runs up to the northern boundary of the Parque del Estrecho. This fringe of the park is home to one of its most beautiful tracts of cork oak forest and to lush laurisilva (laurel forest) in its *canutos*, an ecosytem unique to this part of Andalucía born of the warm and humid conditions present in the park's southernmost gulleys. The walk from close to Los Barrios to El Pelayo cuts through this wonderful swathe of woodland as does the Prisioneros circuit which has the added attraction of leading you past a series of idyllic rock pools along the course of the Río de la Miel.

I've also included a circular walk on Gibraltar. Even if the Rock is not politically a part of Andalucía it's very much present on most of these walks, rising lion-like in the distance above the bay of Algeciras. The circuit described, which leads up the Mediterranean Steps then along its knife-like ridge, is a thrilling half day excursion and should not be missed provided that you have a reasonable head for heights.

Most visitors to the area tend to gravitate towards the hotels of the old town of Tarifa or those close to the beach of Los Lances where you'll find accommodation for all budgets. Bolonia also has a number of cheap-and-cheerful hostals and the added attraction of the exquisite Roman site of Baelo Claudio and its state-of-the-art museum.

BEST SLEEPS

Bolonia

La Hormiga Voladora €–€€
Tel: 956 688 562 Email: hostalhormigavoladora@yahoo.es
Simple and enchanting hostal right at the ocean's edge.

Hostal Ríos €–€€
Tel: 956 688 586 Email: hostalrios@terra.es
www.hostalriosbolonia.com
Another cheap-and-cheerful *pensión* with a number of ocean-facing rooms.

El Pelayo €–€€
Tel: 608 483 458 Email: reservas@huertagrande.com
www.huertagrande.com
Log cabins hidden in amongst cork oaks, a great base for any the walks.

Tarifa

Hostal Alameda €€
Tel: 956 681 181 Email: reservas@hostalalameda.com
www.hostalalameda.com
Clean and friendly hostal with restaurant at the edge of the old town.

Taxis: Bolonia/Tarifa 956 439 233, Pelayo 956 606 060, Los Barrios 956 621 872

Distance: 12.5 kms **Time Required:** 3.5 hours **Rating:** Medium
Total Height Gain: 250m **Map:** IGN 1:50000 Tarifa 1077 (13-48)
Ⓦ **Water:** no springs along the way so take plenty

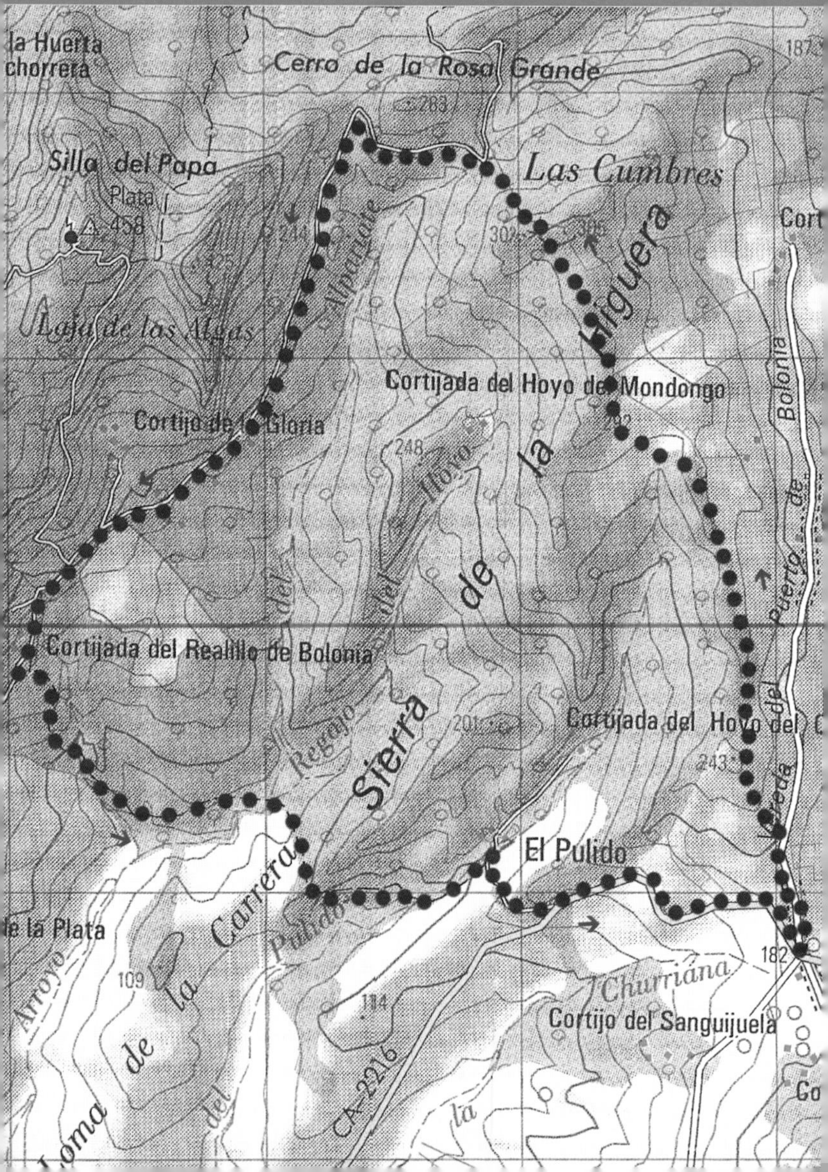

1 Bolonia: Laja de la Zarga Observatory Circuit

Overview

This stunning half day walk, with panoramic coastal and mountain views for most of the way, describes a big loop behind the beautiful beach of Bolonia and the Roman ruins of Baelo Claudio. The footpath isn't that clear for the first hour or so of the walk but provided you stick more or less to the ridge top with eyes peeled for the clearest path you can't go wrong. The middle section of the walk makes for much easier walking as you follow a broad farm track past the jagged ridge of Laja de la Zarga. From the bird hide at the base of this rocky outcrop - it's an ideal spot to break for your picnic - you're guaranteed great sightings of griffon vultures. Beyond the hide you continue towards the ocean along farm tracks before cutting east, back towards the start point of the walk, along the drover's path which led from Realillo de Bolonia to the small settlement of Betis then on towards Tarifa. Parts of the early section, as you climb northwest up the ridge, are quite overgrown so pack long trousers.

Getting to the beginning of the walk

Exit from the N340 at Hotel Valle de San José for Bolonia/Baelo Claudio. Follow the CA8202 (marked on the I.N.G. map as CA2216) for 2.5km to Venta El Tropezón. Here turn right up a dirt track where there's plenty of space to park to your left.

The Walk

The walk begins on the opposite side of the road to Venta El Tropezón, just back from signs for *Parque Natural del Estrecho* and *Observatorio de Bolonia* ①. With your back to the signs turn right up a broad track passing a sign *Cortijo de la Lapa/*

Las Cumbres. After 350m ❷ cut left along a less distinct track which narrows to become a path. Keeping parallel to the left side of a fence go through a metal gate. Maintaining your course you pass remains of a military bunker then pass well to the left of a stone ruin. Reaching a second ruin continue past two stone benches then pass to the left of a third ruin. Where the fence cuts left, maintaining your course along the ridge, you go through a second green gate (sometimes left open) ❸. **(15 mins)**

Beyond the gate the footpath angles slightly to the right of the ridge, now running parallel to a fence which is down to your right. Views open towards Facinas and southeast to the craggy ridge of Loma de San Bartolomé. Returning to the ridge top you pass through a third metal gate with a sign for *Coto* ❹. Beyond the gate the path divides. Take the left option which again runs close to the fence. The path now climbs more steeply before passing two benches and a tethering rail. Crossing an open swathe of ground, running between two fences along the ridge top, you go through a fourth gate ❺. **(25 mins)**

Stick to your same course. The fence to your left ends to be replaced by a stone wall. Continuing parallel to the wall you reach a swathe of denser vegetation where the path becomes rockier as it cuts through a fifth gate (sometimes left open) ❻. With the fence to its right after 125m the path braids. Keep straight on, sticking to the top of the ridge. Crossing more open terrain the path passes two more benches and another tethering rail ❼. **(45 mins)**

Continue on up, close to the fence and a wall. Follow the wall as it angles left: after some 50m you pick up a clearer path which, passing through a gap in the lentiscus, runs steeply downwards. The wind turbines in front of Facinas come into view. Merging with a broader path you descend to another green metal gate ❽

Beyond the gate, bearing right then left, continue your descent between two walls to a broad track where there are twin benches in the shade of a wild olive ⑨. **(55 mins)**

Bearing slightly left follow the track towards the transmitter masts atop the Silla del Papa. After 350m the track bears right before it angles hard left and descends parallel to the jagged edge of the Laja de la Zarga. On a clear day Morocco will now

be visible. The track leads to a wooden bird hide **(1 hr 15 mins)** ⑩ and a signboard about griffon vultures and the *Laja de la Zarga*. It's a great spot to break for some raptor spotting and a picnic.

From the hut continue down the track towards the sea. Reaching Cortijo de la Gloria you pass through a gate ⑪. The track becomes better surfaced as it runs past a number of houses. After climbing for a short section it descends to a point where it becomes tarmacked ⑫. **(1 hr 30 mins)**

Running on down after 450m you reach the houses of Cortijada del Realillo de Bolonia. Some 150m after passing a wooden sign for *La Semilla* you reach the last houses of the hamlet. Here cut left ⑬ and descend parallel to the wall of the house which is to your left. Holding a southeasterly course you pick up a stony path which drops steeply down, deeply eroded in parts, before it crosses the Realillo stream ⑭. The path, much clearer now, climbs, bears right then descends to cross another (dry) stream. Angling slightly left it passes through a swathe of thick shrub before it crosses a third (dry) stream ⑮. **(2 hrs 5 mins)**

Angling right along the clearest path you reach a fence and a wire-and-post gate. Don't go through the gate but continue on along a sandy path with the fence to your right which leads you over a low rise. A fence now runs to your left. Crossing the (dry) boulder-strewn bed of Arroyo del Pulido the path bears left and climbs, passes through a wire-and-post gate then merges with a track ⑯. Bearing right for 75m you reach a junction with the tarmac road leading to Cortijo El Pulido ⑰. Here cut right and follow the road up and over a rise where, reverting to dirt, it descends to meet with the CA8202 ⑲. Here cut left and follow the road for 1100m back to the start point of the walk ①. **(2 hrs 45 mins)**

Distance: 20 kms **Time Required:** 5.5 hours **Rating:** Medium
Total Height Gain: 50m **Map:** IGN 1:50000 Tarifa 1077 (13-48)
Ⓦ **Water:** close to waypoint 16 @ 3 hrs 45 mins

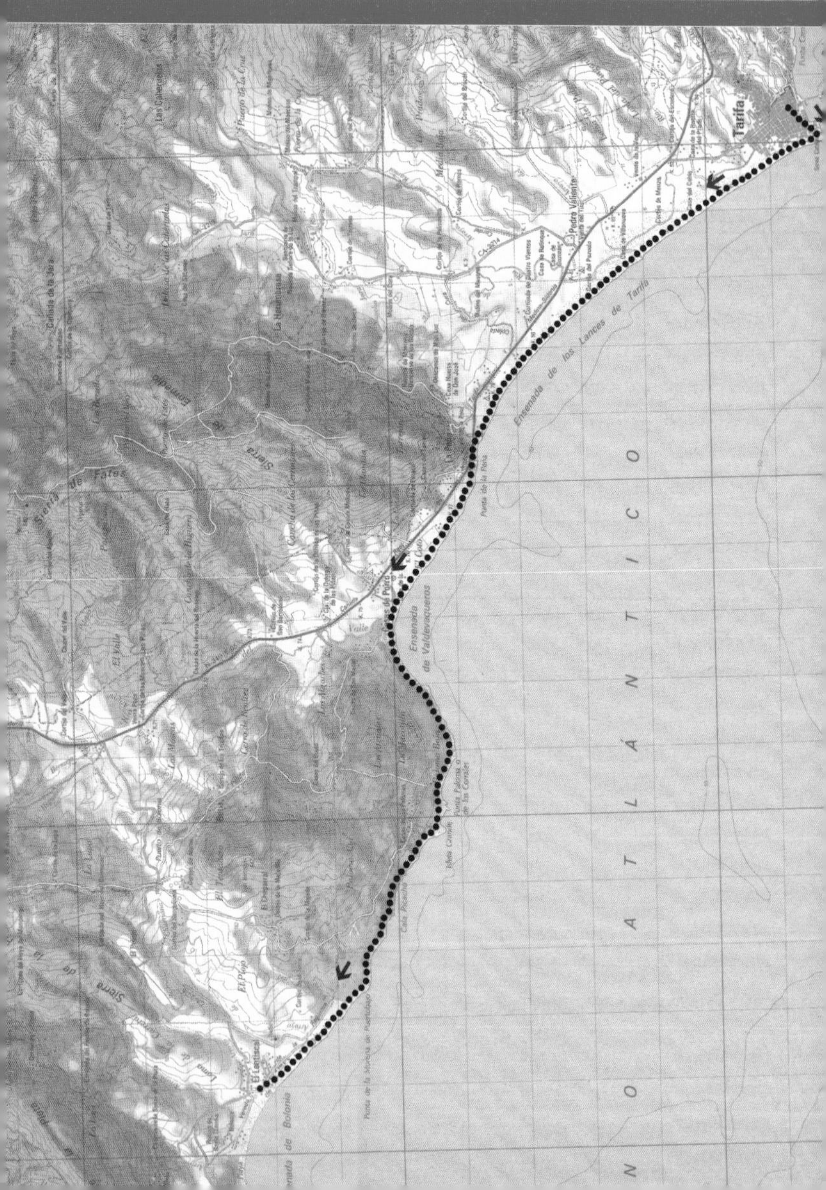

2 Tarifa to Bolonia via Los Lances & Valdevaqueros

Overview

This wonderful day walk follows the ocean's edge all the way from Tarifa to Bolonia. Leaving Tarifa along a causeway linking the old fortified town with El Castillo de Santa Catarina you angle down to the Atlantic Ocean. You next walk the length of the Los Lances beach which numbers amongst the finest stretches of sand on Spain's Atlantic Coast: when the wind is blowing you can expect to see hundreds of kite surfers cutting through the waves. After rounding Punta de la Peña you head on across the bay of Valdevaqueros, still close to the water's edge. Leaving the bay the path winds between rocks then loops up to easier ground just above the ocean as you pass round the second, smaller headland of Punta Paloma. From here the path runs past a series of small coves before reaching Bolonia's stunning arc of sandy beach. The walk ends at the western edge of the village. Just 500m to your left are the extraordinary Roman ruins of Baelo Claudio, one of the most beautiful Roman sites in Spain. No visit to Bolonia would be complete without visiting the site but bear in mind that it is only open on Sundays in the morning.

The Walk

The walk begins in front of the San Mateo church (1) at the centre of Tarifa's old town, to one side of the Plaza de Oviedo. With your back to the church head along Calle Sancho IV. The street bears left then right past the Banesto bank and then once more left along Calle Luz Nuñoz. Following the road to the right you pass El Castillo de Gúzman el Bueno and a statue of Sancho IV. Heading past the entrance to the *Estación Marítima* you reach the causeway linking the town and the fort of Santa

Catarina and a *No Entry* sign ❷. Here cut right down to the beach and head across to the ocean's edge where the harder sand makes for easier walking.

Leaving the town's sprawling western suburb behind, which is over to your right, you pass by a lifeguard's hut ❸. In the distance, to your right, you'll see one of the largest wind farms in Europe. Continuing along the beach you reach the (dry) riverbed of the Río de la Jara ❹ **(45 mins)** at which point you may need to remove your boots and socks. *If after very heavy rain the river looks impassable head further inland to cross the river by a bridge.*

Continuing along the beach you pass by the sienna-coloured buildings of Hotel Dos Mares then the cobalt blue buildings of Hotel Arte y Vida. At the end of the beach you pass a pill box ❺ then a flight of wooden steps and a G.R. sign. Ignore this sign and continue parallel to the sea. At the far end of the beach you pass a flight of stone steps ❻ then a concrete ramp and finally a small bar at the edge of the ocean. Pass beneath the bar by clambering over the rocks then angle up right to find a better path. Soon you drop down to the sea once more and cross a small beach accessed via a flight of wooden steps ❼.

30m beyond the steps cut right up a sandy path. After 10m, angling left, you descend to the next cove. At its far end continue along an indistinct path which passes another pill box ❽ **(1 hr 45 mins)** beyond which you reach Valdevaqueros beach. Walking northwest along the sand you pass another pill box ❾ then the small lagoon formed where the Río del Valle meets with the sea. Reaching the far end of the beach ❿ pick your way across the rocks. Heading along another stretch of sand you again need to pick your way across rocks: a small spring at the far end of this beach is a popular spot for taking a cleansing mud bath. Beyond the rocks continue along the sand.

At this stage it's easier to angle up right 11 and follow a winding path on through the dunes, sticking as close as possible to the sea. The path crosses a (dry) streambed then angles down towards the beach. After passing another pill box with a ceramic plaque dedicated to Nuestra Señora de la Esperanza 12 the path descends back to the beach where you shortly pass beneath another pill box 13. **(2 hrs 45 mins)**

Continuing along the sand you pass round a rocky headland (where you may need to remove your boots) then head along another stretch of sandy beach to reach another more rocky

area where you may need to use both hands and feet. The path becomes clearer as it runs on, left of a fence, then passes to the right of a large concrete monolith (14). Where the path angles back to the water's edge it's easier to stay high and follow a path which at first runs beside a fence. Threading through the undergrowth it passes above the next (pebbly) beach then continues on, parallel to the sea. After looping right away from the sea the path shortly angles once more left and meets with the sand once more. Continuing along the beach you soon need to clamber across the rocks once more then angle away from the beach (15) to pick up a clear sandy path which runs just above the beach, close to the edge of the low cliff before it angles back down to the sea at a point where long strata of rock run parallel to the ocean's edge.

Heading on towards Bolonia you pass a spring (W) (16) **(3 hrs 45 mins)** that runs out between the rocks. At the far end of this beach pick your way over the rocks then angle up a sandy path which cuts away from the sea. Looking back you'll now see the Tarifa lighthouse on La Isla de las Palomas. After running just above the beach the path cuts once more down to the sand where it passes another pill box (17). **(4 hrs)** Continue to end of this stretch of beach. Threading your way between rocks, then passing two more pill boxes, you reach the beginning of Bolonia's beach. Sticking close to the sea you pass the village's first beach bars then a large fading sign for *Prohibido El Nudismo.* Continue along the water's edge until, over to your right, you spot Apartamentos Miramar and Apartamentos Mateo. Here cut right away from the sea then, passing a shower, head up a narrow footpath to reach a small car park at the entrance to the village (18). **(4 hrs 35 mins)**

Heading directly inland from here, following a line of palm trees, you reach Hostal/Bar Bella Vista. It's an ideal rendez-vous point if you're returning by taxi to Tarifa.

Distance: 23 kms **Time Required:** 5.5/6 hours **Rating:** Difficult
Total Height Gain: 575m **Map:** IGN 1:50000 Tarifa 1077 (13-48) & Algeciras 1078 (14-48) Ⓦ **Water:** spring at waypoint 21 @ 3 hrs 20 mins

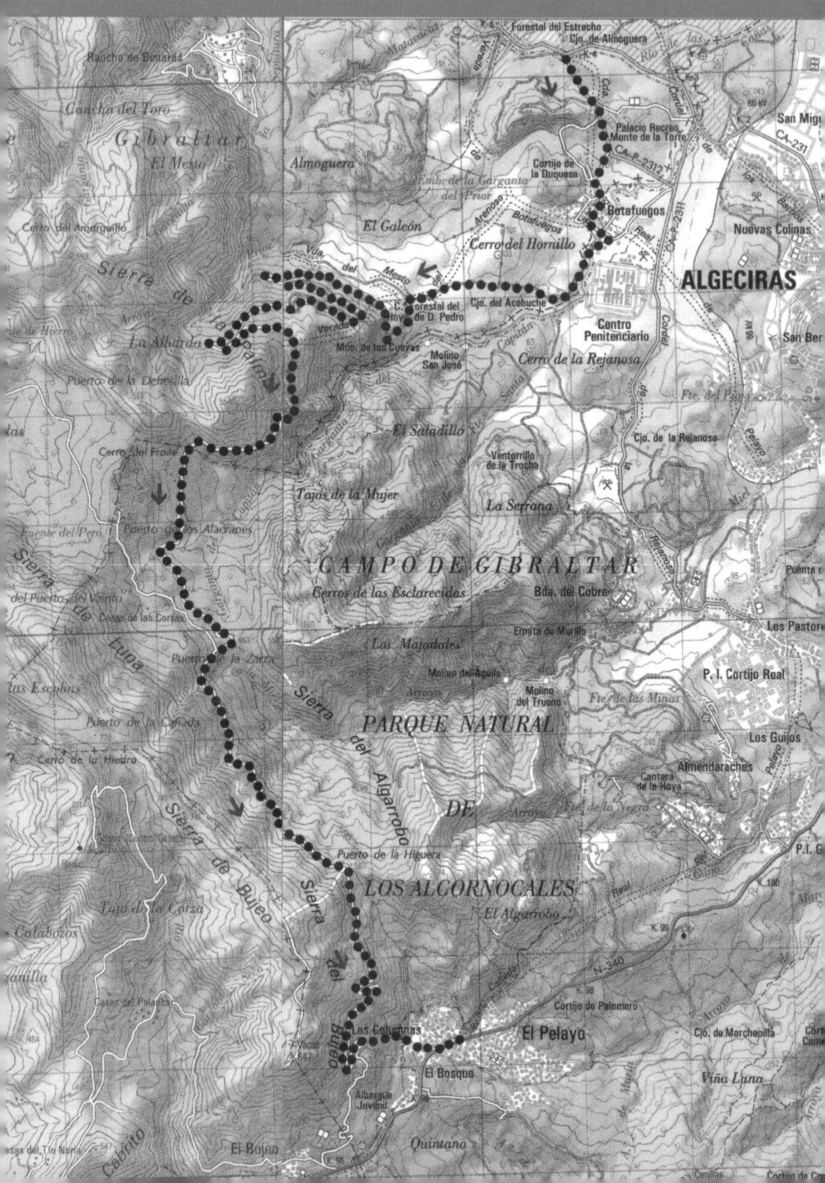

3 Monte de la Torre to El Pelayo via Las Corzas

Overview

This long and challenging walk leads from Monte de la Torre, between Los Barrios and Algeciras, up and over the last high spur of the Los Alcornocales Park. After first following an ancient *cañada* (glossary) you're faced with a long climb via a forestry track up across the wooded hillsides of the Sierra de Ojén. Here vast views open out across the Bay of Algeciras towards Gibraltar. The route then becomes much easier as you climb more gently towards the estate of Las Corzas. This area is home to abundant wildlife and contains pristine tracts of ancient woodland which have recently been declared a zone of special biological interest within the Alcornocales Park: this swathe of the mountains is also home to the diverse flora of the humid *canuto* ecosystem (glossary). After your efforts during the first half of the day the latter section of the walk is plain sailing as you drop down towards the Mediterranean and the roadside settlement of El Pelayo. The wild beauty of the walk belies the fact that the sprawling conurbation of Algeciras lies just a dozen kilometers to your east. *Restaurante Las Piedras, where the walk ends, is an ideal rendez-vous point if you are returning to Los Barrios by taxi.*

Getting to the beginning of the walk

From the wedding cake-like roundabout in Los Barrios, La Fuente de la Constitución, cut south along Avenida III Centenario. Head straight on at a roundabout, pass beneath the A-381 motorway. Follow the CA-9209 round to the left past the Centro de Defensa Forestal, then a car dump where the road bears right. Passing a sign for Parque Natural you reach a junction and sign for Monte de la Torre. Here cut right off the CA-9209 and leave your vehicle to the right or left.

The Walk

From the sign for *Monte de la Torre* 1 head up a cobbled track which shortly passes a cattle shed. After climbing the track arcs right and passes by a gate to Monte de la Torre 2. Here the track levels, bears left then descends to a junction 3. Cut right past a number of ramshackle buildings, cross a bridge, then bear slightly right. Just before the entrance to Cortijo de la Duquesa 4 angling left you reach the outskirts of Botafuegos and a fork 5. Taking the left fork you pass the gates of Casa de la Huerta. Leaving the hamlet the track is less distinct as it runs parallel to a stream then reaches a broader track 6. Cut left and cross the stream via a ford 7. Passing more buildings the track reaches a junction by a galvanised metal gate 8. **(25 mins)**

Turn right along another broad dirt track which passes a ruined farm building. The track narrows, loops right, then crosses the stream 9 you forded earlier, the *Arroyo de Garganta del Capitán*. Bearing left go through a gate marked C.A., the entrance to Cortijo del Acebuche 10. Passing the farm the track runs across open country then cuts through another gate 11. You're now following the *Vereda del Mesto*, an ancient drover's path. Soon you pass through another gate marking the beginning of Finca El Galeón. The track loops steeply up as views open out towards the Bay of Algeciras before passing through another gate and crossing a cattle grid 12. Resuming its upwardly-mobile course the track angles right, passes a white building with a vine-covered terrace 13 then loops up through land where reafforestation has taken place. You reach rockier terrain where cork oaks are more abundant. The track describes a tight hairpin then, climbing still, runs past a *mirador* (glossary) and a sign *Hoyo de Don Pedro* where a ceramic map depicts what lies before you 14. **(1 hrs 40 mins)**

Here the track hairpins right. Continuing its ascent, after a tight double hairpin, it adopts a southwesterly course as it runs high

above the Arroyo del Prior. Looping left ⓯ you pass a section of wire-meshed wall then cut across more open countryside as views open out to the east. Soon you pass another *mirador*, also marked *Mirador Hoyo Don Pedro* from where there's a stunning panoramic view of the bay of Algeciras, Gibraltar and (on clear days) Morocco ⓰. From the *mirador* continue along the track which shortly descends for a short distance then resumes its ascent as it contours round the flank of the Sierra de la Palma: the jagged peaks of the Cerros de los Esclarecidos are to your left. The track runs past another mirador ⓱ then passes through a green gate and crosses a cattle grid ⓲. **(2 hrs 35 mins)**

Beyond the gate the track climbs gently. Over to your left the Casas de Las Corzas come into view amidst a sea of green. Soon the track bears left on a more southerly course then runs past a gate with a sign *Finca Privada: Prohibido El Paso*. The fence of Las Corzas now runs to your right. Passing a metal gate the track angles right ⓳ as it passes an enclosure with a ramp for loading cattle. Soon you pass a second gate that leads to Las Corzas ⓴. The Mediterranean to the east of Tarifa soon comes into view. Passing another cattle grid the track crosses a pretty *canuto* (glossary) and a sign for *Zona de Alta Protección* beyond which you reach a spring (W) to the right of the track (21). **(3 hrs 20 mins)**

The track runs past a water tank then crosses another *canuto* as it snakes lazily on, passing a picnic area and an information board. Beyond the sign the track runs past another *mirador* with a sign *Cabecera del Río de la Miel.* As you lose sight of Gibraltar the track crosses another cattle grid (22) then, looping right, descends. Soon the Strait comes into view and beyond it the massif of Jebel Musa. Passing a clearing where an oak has been surrounded by a stone base (23) the track arcs right, hairpins left then right again, before adopting a more level course. After passing a water deposit the track loops one final time sharply left. Just beyond low marker post marking km20 the track arcs hard right (24). **(4 hrs 25 mins)**

Here cut left down an indistinct path to a wire-and-post gate next to a sign *Monte Repoblado.* Beyond the gate head along an indistinct path following a line of cairns. The path angles left, descends, then loops left before angling once more right as it drops down through the pines. Crossing a plastic water pipe it angles left, clearer now, as you reach a flat swathe of rock (25). Here cut left. Looping right then once more left the path crosses a (dry) stream then runs just left of a fence. Follow the fence for 50m, climb down a low wall then cut right through a wire-and-post gate (26). Turning right down a concrete track you reach the first houses of El Pelayo where, angling left, the track runs up to a junction by La Alquería (27). Cutting right down Calle Sierra de Lucena you reach the N-340. Turn left along the road for 250m and just beyond Restaurante Las Piedras you reach a pedestrian bridge spanning the N-340 (28). **(4 hrs 45 mins)**

Distance: 20 kms **Time Required:** 5.5 hours **Rating:** Medium
Total Height Gain: 100m **Map:** IGN 1:50000 Algeciras 1078 (14-48) & Tarifa 1077 (13-48) Ⓦ **Water:** no springs so take plenty

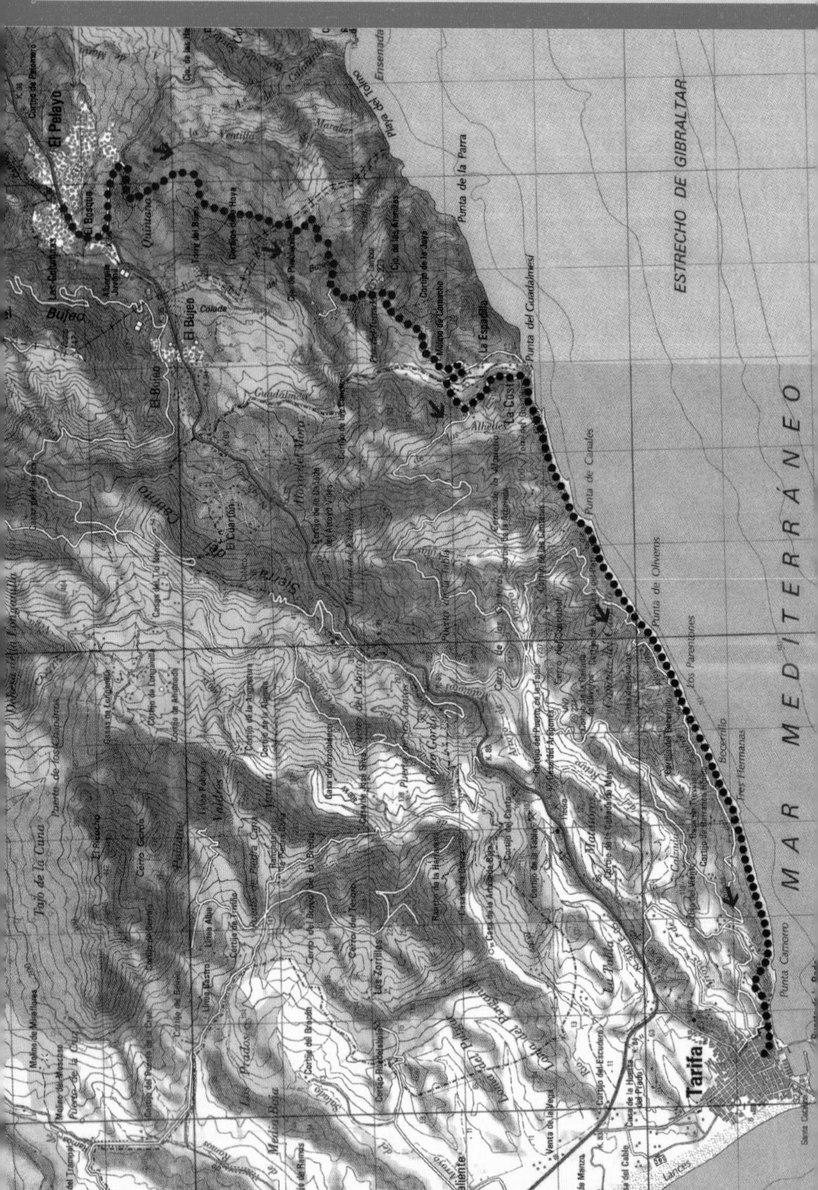

4 El Pelayo to Tarifa via Guadalmesí

Overview

This long and beautiful ocean-side walk leads you from the sleepy roadside hamlet of El Pelayo to Tarifa, the windy city whose fort and isthmus straddle two of the world's greatest seas. The day begins with a gentle downhill section of track across open countryside with fine views west across the Strait and its passing tankers, ships and yachts. Beyond the tiny hamlet of Guadalmesí, whose ancient watchtower protected the coastline from raids from North African corsairs, the second half of the walk runs close to the ocean's edge passing several small coves which you may well have to yourself should you choose to swim or break for a picnic. A stunning final section of narrow footpath leads you into Tarifa and to the square at the heart of this ancient walled town, now home to a colourful multi-ethnic community with great bars, restaurants and places to stay.
Be aware that the walk leads you along the western edge of military land where casual visitors are unwelcome. But the public footpath has recently been clearly marked with green metal posts. If you plan to return to your car by taxi from Tarifa, just a €15 ride, you'll find the rank just outside of the gateway at the north side of the old town, La Puerta de Jerez.

Getting to the beginning of the walk

From Algeciras take the N340 in the direction of Cádiz. After approximately 5kms you reach the hamlet of El Pelayo. Here park just beyond a pedestrian bridge over the N340 next to Restauranta Las Piedras.

The Walk

The walk begins next to the pedestrian bridge spanning the N-340 just south of Restaurante Las Piedras ❶. Cross to the west side of the bridge, turn right past Hostal El Jardín then head up the left side of the N-340. Ignore a sign pointing left to Huerta Grande but rather continue parallel to the road past a sign for *Sendero Cerro del Tambor, 5.5kms*. Keeping to the left side of the road, now following a dirt track, you reach a sign for *Parque Natural*. Follow the track as it loops left ❷ and passes a second sign for *Sendero Cerro del Tambor* and another for *Cortijo La Hoya*. The track descends past a farm with twin palm trees. Crossing a cattle grid the it arcs right as it passes by another palm. Shortly before reaching a pylon with a blue sign for *Calle Algamasilla* you come to a junction ❸. Here bear right along the main track which angles right as it crosses an open tract of land: on a clear day Morocco is now visible. Soon the track angles once more left, now running towards the ocean then loops through a more wooded area. Crossing a cattle grid, then angling left, the track passes a barrel-roofed cowshed ❹. **(45 mins)**

Soon you pass by the track cutting up to Cortijo La Hoya then another sign *Sendero Cerro del Tambor, 2.2 kms*. The track, whose cobbling is visible in parts, crosses another cattle grid. Heading straight on past a stony track which cuts down to the left ❺ the track climbs towards a line of turbines which fan out along the top of a ridge. Crossing a cattle grid you pass a farm entrance where two somewhat surreal model dogs stand vigil. Having passed beneath the line of turbines you reach a second group of turbines and a junction ❻. **(1 hr 15 mins)**

Here branch right past a sign for *Prohibido El Paso: Carril en Mal Estado* and continue down past a building with a sign detailing the specs of the turbines. The track, rougher underfoot, descends through a swathe of pines. Bearing right through denser vegetation it crosses a cattle grid then passes a house with railway sleepers as verandah supports ⑦. The track loops right past more farm buildings then passes a large shed-like building before reaching a junction at the northern edge of Guadalmesí ⑧. **(1 hr 45 mins)**

Cut left towards the ocean. Passing Finca Los Tres Pinos the track loops left then right to reach the Mediterranean ⑨ **(1 hr 55 mins)**. Bear right, cross a (dry) river bed via a ford then

follow the track up past Torre de Guadalmesí. Passing the tower (it's worth a diversion) and continuing parallel to the sea the lighthouse of Tarifa comes into view. You now see green posts marked V.P. (*Vía Pecuaria* or Drover's Track) which indicate the path's left and right edges: a sign soon informs you that this is the *Collado de la Costa/Camino de Algeciras*. The track angles closer to the sea before bearing once more away from it and passing a barrel-roofed building ⑩. Stick to the main track which heads parallel to the sea then crosses a bridge spanning a stream ⑪.

Shortly past the bridge, cutting left ⑫ you pass another sign *Collado de la Costa* then pass some 30m above a stone building with a grey door at one end ⑬. The indistinct path becomes more clearly defined: green V.P. posts mark your way. The path occasionally braids: sticking to the clearest path you reach a wire-and-post gate ⑭. Beyond the gate the path cuts through a rocky defile then runs parallel to the fence of military land, its boundary marked by white pyramids. Soon the path cuts away from the fence then improves as it reaches a pole fence which you pass through via a V-shaped gap ⑮. **(2 hrs 45 mins)** Shortly you reach a ruined military building whose turret provides a superb view of the Strait: an information board tells of the mythology of the creation of the channel between Europe and Africa and the origins of Jebel Musa ⑯.

Heading past this building the lighthouse of Tarifa comes into view once again and, beyond it, the Atlantic. V.P. posts still mark your way, leading on round the upper reaches of a gully as you pass beneath a swish villa, still just left of the rickety-posted fence. The path runs on to a second wooden railing where you pass through another a V-shaped gap ⑰. Beyond the gate follow the most obvious path across more shaley ground. Passing a ramshackle fence made of pallets cross a more rocky area then head on past a farm building ⑱. Soon the path angles left and drops back down to the beach where it crosses a (dry) stream bed before angling right, away from the sea, as it passes a sentry box, a subterranean military structure 19 before passing 50m to the right of an ugly, monolithic building where there are a pair of benches. The path now becomes clearer, occasionally running just outside the V.P. marker posts. Angling right it reaches another wooden railing which you again pass through via a V-shaped gap 20.

Heading inland for 10m then angling left you reach another wooden railing where you pass through a V-shaped gap for a fourth time 21. Continue along the footpath past two military pill boxes then angle away from the beach, cross a wooden bridge 22 **(3 hrs 50 mins)** then climb three flights of wooden steps. At the top of the third flight continue straight along the footpath which passes through another wooden railing via a V-shaped gap. Angling through denser undergrowth you meet with a track next to a sign *Parque Natural* 23.

Head straight on along the narrow path which drops down through a stand of bamboo then crosses a wooden bridge before reaching more open terrain. Here stick to the higher footpath which runs past a small white building then descends to merge with a cobbled track. Tarifa's harbour comes into view. Reaching a junction 24 bear right and continue along the cobbled track just to the right of the sea. You soon pass a marker post *Tarifa-Guadalmesí 11.3 kms*. Bearing right the track reaches a junction 25. Cut left for 20m then bear right along the ramparts following a sign for *Ayuntamiento* then angle once again right to reach La Plazuela del Viento. Exit the square along Calle Aljaranda then take the second street to the right, Calle Coronel Moscardó. After passing *Correos* you reach the neural centre of the old town, La Plaza de Oviedo, where the walk ends in front of the San Mateo church 26. **(4 hrs 15 mins)**

Distance: 15 kms **Time Required:** 6 hours **Rating:** Medium/Difficult
Total Height Gain: 475m **Map:** IGN 1:50000 Algeciras 1078 (14-48) & Tarifa 1077 (13-48) Ⓦ **Water:** at WP 12 @ 2 hrs 15 mins & WP 23 @ 3 hrs 45 mins

5 Los Barrios: The Prisioneros & Río de la Miel Circuit

Overview

This constantly changing itinerary offers a superb introduction to the varied topography of the Alcornocales Park. The *Ruta de las Prisioneros*, which you follow early in the walk, was built by Republican Prisoners in the years following the Civil War: Franco wanted to guarantee rapid movement of troops in the case of a threat to Spain's southern coast. Where the *Ruta* ends you continue on up along a narrow path which winds up through the ferns and cork oaks to a high forestry track. At this stage you can concentrate on the big views out to the south and east as the track contours lazily round the mountain passing a series of *canutos (glossary)*. Branching onto another narrow path you then drop down to the upper reaches of the Río de la Miel. Water runs here all year round, feeding a series of idyllic rock pools where a few in-the-know locals come to bathe in summer: the longish walk from the nearest parking ensures that it's rarely crowded. Parts of the paths leading up and down are a little overgrown so pack long trousers.

Getting to the beginning of the walk

From the A7 motorway take exit 105 for Algeciras Oeste/ Avenida Agua Marina. Turn right at the first roundabout towards Barriada del Cobre. After 200m bear left then continue along a winding road to a roundabout surrounded by palm trees. Take the 3rd exit along Calle Escritora Mariana Carvajal. The road bears right running parallel to an aqueduct. Turn right at a sign Sendero Rio de la Miel passing beneath the aqueduct along Calle Maestra Luisa. After 350m turn left at a second sign Sendero Rio de la Miel. Park on the left after 50m.

The Walk

The walk begins at a signboard for *Sendero Rio de la Miel* in front of a metal gate ❶. From here head west along a broad track. Passing a set of metal gates to your right you reach a fork ❷. Here bear left and climb past another farm. Crossing a (dry) stream the track winds on, levels, then climbs to a fork with an oak in its middle ❸. Angle left (ignoring a marker post) following a line of pylons up a stony track. Reaching a junction ❹ branch right. Crossing an area more denuded of trees the rutted track arcs left then right towards a metal fence in front of a farm ❺. **(35 mins)**

Here angle right along a less distinct track, parallel to the fence. Passing through a metal gate you pass a signboard *Prisioneros de la Posguerra*. Just beyond it the track divides ❻. Keep right and continue your ascent. As you loop right then left, views open out towards Gibraltar. You pass a second signboard explaining how these tracks were part of Franco's geopolitical strategy for controlling the Strait. Reaching more open ground the track passes through a wire-and-post gate then levels as it runs west, past a cattle loading pen then a fading signboard before cutting through a gate ❼ then narrowing to become a path. Passing another faded signboard and crossing a bridge you reach a sign *Fin de Sendero de los Prisioneros* ❽. **(1 hr 15 mins)**

Continue past the sign along a narrow sandy path which laces it way between the trees, gradually bearing left. After a downhill section across an area which has seen a fire in the not-so-distant past the path enters a dense swathe of oak forest as it crosses over two (dry) streambeds then passes a water trough marked *0*. Here the path angles right and climbs more steeply: it occasionally braids but your way up is clear enough. Broadening to become a track it climbs past a ruined building by two huge eucalyptus trees ❾. Angling left, narrower once more, the path

cuts through denser undergrowth to a huge rock topped by a cairn. Here angle right and continue on up. Passing through a wire-and-post gate and bearing right you reach a broad track by a cattle grid at Puerto de la Higuera ⑩. **(1 hr 50 mins)**

Turn right along the track. Things become much easier: you can concentrate less on your feet and more on the views out east across the Bay of Algeciras. You'll be following this level track now for some 3.25 kms. Passing a *mirador* and a signboard *Cabecera del Río de la Miel* ⑪ you shortly pass by a second signboard beside a picnic area before crossing a bridge over a broad *canuto* (glossary). Some 700m beyond the bridge you reach a spring to the left of the track Ⓦ ⑫. **(2 hrs 15 mins)** Passing a cattle grid you pass a sign on a wall for *Las Corzas*. The track now angles right and passes by a track cutting in to the entrance gates of Casa de las Corzas. Continue along the main track for 200m then, 30m before the track angles left past a galvanised metal gate, cut right ⑬ along an overgrown path. Bearing left the path passes through a gate then runs on through the ferns with a fence to your right. Reaching a wire-and-post gate in this fence ⑭ pass through it and continue on through the thick undergrowth. The path becomes less distinct: look for cairns.

Crossing a (dry) streambed the path angles right then descends parallel to its left bank. Angling away from the stream the Bay of Algeciras comes into sight. Crossing another (dry) streambed ⑮ you come to a clearing in the trees. **(2 hrs 45 mins)** Dropping down the right side of the clearing, some 30m before a pylon and just as you reach a solitary oak, the path angles right. After a more tricky 100m section down through thick undergrowth the path improves: cairns again mark your way. Angling left the path crosses a (dry) streambed ⑯ then passes beneath overhead cables. You shortly pass just right of an old stone corral ⑰ built against a huge rock, then head straight on.

The path becomes clearer as it crosses another rocky streambed. Reaching clearer ground and an indistinct junction keep right. The path is now cobbled in sections, running high above the Arroyo de la Miel whose waters you'll hear down to your right. Careful! A few metres before the path crosses a boulder-strewn streambed you reach an enormous solitary oak, clad in ferns at the top of its trunk (believe me, it really is a clear landmark!) where the path divides 18. Cut right down an indistinct path through the ferns which descends into the streambed where you clamber down over rocks to reach the Arroyo de la Miel 19.

Bear left along the stream's left bank for a few metres then cross to its right bank where you pick up a narrow path that descends parallel to the water course as you pass above a series of idyllic rock pools. Heading on down the river's right bank the path follows the course of a metal water pipe which cuts down – you do the same – to cross the river at a point where, to your left, there's a great rock pool with a shingly beach 20. **(3 hrs 40 mins)**

Head on down the river's left bank, still following the metal water pipe. Reaching another rock pool pass along its left edge and hop over a low wall that blocks the path 21. The path shortly passes a wooden barrier and a sign marking *Fin de Sendero Rio de la Miel*. Heading on past the ruined mill of El Molino del Águila 22 you pass by a spring W 23 before crossing a beautiful stone-built bridge 24. Bearing left past a white building the path merges with a track 25 which you should follow back to waypoint 3 3 then retrace your steps back to the beginning of the walk 1. **(4 hrs 10 mins)**

Distance: 10 kms **Time Required:** 3.5/4 hours **Rating:** Medium
Total Height Gain: 525m **Map:** IGN 1:50000 Algeciras 1078 (14-48) & Tarifa 1077 (13-48) Ⓦ **Water:** no springs so take plenty

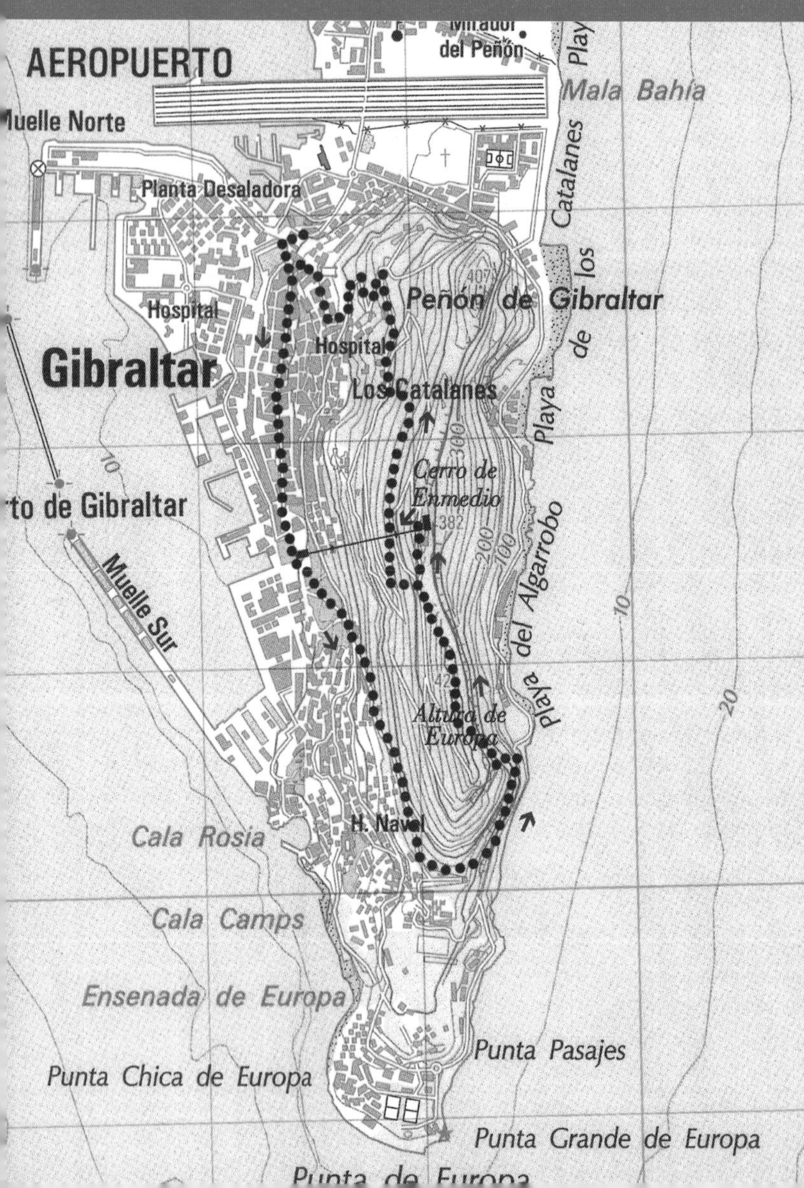

6 Gibraltar Circuit via the Mediterranean Steps & Ingliss Way

Overview

It may come as a surprise to discover this mesmerising trail on Gibraltar which numbers amongst the most spectacular on the Mediterranean Coast. The highlight of the walk – so long as you have a head for heights - is the extraordinary footpath that leads up the sheer, southern face of the Rock, popularly known as Mediterranean Steps. This giddy path has recently been restored by the Bonito Trust and you'll be marvelling at the ingenuity and derring-do of those who built it. But there are many more treats in store. After negotatiating the Steps next comes Douglas' path which cuts along the top of Gibraltar's rugged spine with huge views both east and west. The next challenge comes in the forms of Charles V's Wall which you descend via a series of steep flights of steps. And to end an already magnificent circuit up pops Ingliss Way leading back towards the start point of the walk through a thick stand of Mediterranean scrub: it's beggars belief to think that the cut and thrust of Main Street is just a few hundred metres away.

Getting to the beginning of the walk

From the border cross the runway following signs for City Centre. The walk begins in front of Landport Gate and the tunnel leading to Casement Square.

The Walk

The walk begins in front of Landport Gate ❶ just beyond a drawbridge. From here cut through two tunnels to reach Casemate Square. Head along the square's left side then continue to the far end of Main Street passing John Macintosh Square then The Convent. At the far end of the street pass

beneath an arch ② then cut right across a pedestrian crossing. Bear left, traverse a second crossing and head on past Queen's Hotel. Angling left you reach the hotel's main entrance. Here cross the road, pass right of a restaurant to the lower station of the cable car then angle left across a car park to the gateway to the Gibraltar Botanic Gardens ③. **(20 mins)**

Beyond the gate climb two flights of steps, pass a statue of Elliott (commander of the Rock during the Siege of 1179-83) then after 15m bear left up a narrow path. Climb another flight of steps then continue up Olive Tree Climb which merges with a broader path which leads up to a red post box ④. Here cut left at a sign *Exit Upper Rock* and climb past The Rock Hotel's swimming pool. Passing through the gate to the gardens continue parallel to Europa Road to reach a footbridge. Here cross the road and head up Engineer Road ⑤. The road climbs steeply to the gates of the Nature Reserve of The Upper Rock ⑥. Continuing to climb the road leads to another set of gates and a ticket box ⑦ **(40 mins)** *(it's worth 50 pence and*

a short detour to visit one of the hypothetical sites of the The Pillars of Hercules, Mons Carpe).

Angling left beyond the ticket box to a barrier you reach the beginning of Mediterranean Steps. Passing a metal gate you follow the steps along the near sheer face of Gibraltar's southern flank. Passing a signboard detailing the fauna of the Upper Rock 8 the path cuts left and climbs steeply: ropes help your upwardly mobile course. Reaching a bricked up building 9 **(1 hr)** angle right through a tunnel beyond which you pass two bunkers: the views from the platform just beyond the second one are breathtaking. Angling left the path zigzags up to a signboard describing the Rock's unique flora 10. Passing a group of antennae you reach the highest point of the walk 11 as vistas open out to the west. Angling left and descending you reach the entrance gate to the World War II Tunnels 12. Here cut right down a narrow road for 400m to a junction and sign *1789-1897* 13. **(1 hr 25 mins)** Here cut right past a barrier: you're now on Douglas' Path which angles up to the ridgetop through thick Mediterranean scrub where it reaches *O'Hara's Battery* 14.

Continue along the spine of the Rock, now descending, to St Michael's Road. Angling right here you pass a signboard telling of a Spanish attack on the Rock in 1704 15. Continue along the road then pass beneath an arch where Gib's resident apes often gather to look at tourists. Beyond the arch you reach the top of Charles V's wall 16. Continue up St Michael's Road, angle right at the first fork then climb to the top station of the cable car 17 where there's a café and a viewing platform up to the right: close encounters of the ape kind are guaranteed as well as mesmerising views of Africa and the western end of the Costa del Sol 18. **(1 hr 40 mins)**

Retrace your footsteps to the top of Charles V's Wall 19 then cut right and make your way down the first section of wall. Cutting right then left, drop down its second section. Cut right at a brick building then left through a gate and continue down the third section of wall to a picnic area. Exit onto Queen's Road where, just opposite, you'll see a sign *Ingliss Way* 20. Follow the path up past an old bunker. 15m before reaching a tarmac road the path cuts left 21 and threads its way through thick Mediterranean scrub. Crossing a plastic pipe you reach a fence 22. Cutting right the path climbs then arcs left, parallel to a low wall. Angling left and descending across two metal pipes you come to a road 23. **(2 hrs 15 mins)**

Cut left for 50m then angle right along Queen's Road. Reaching a *Give Way* sign continue straight on towards the entrance to The Great Seige Tunnels 24, angle left down Willis road for 200m then loop hard right. After150m angling once more left past The Moorish Castle you reach twin *Give Way* signs 25. Here angle right and drop down to a crenellated tower then follow the road as it angles left. Just as it arcs once more right past two huge palms 26 cut left along a One Way street.

Reaching a sign for *Castle Steps* 27 turn right down a flight of steps which angle right then left to a junction. Turning right along Engineer's Lane you return to Main Street. From here retrace your steps to the start point of the walk 1 . **(2 hrs 50 mins)**

Costa del Sol: Paraje Natural de Sierra Bermeja & Sierra Crestellina

Walks close to Estepona, Casares & Manilva

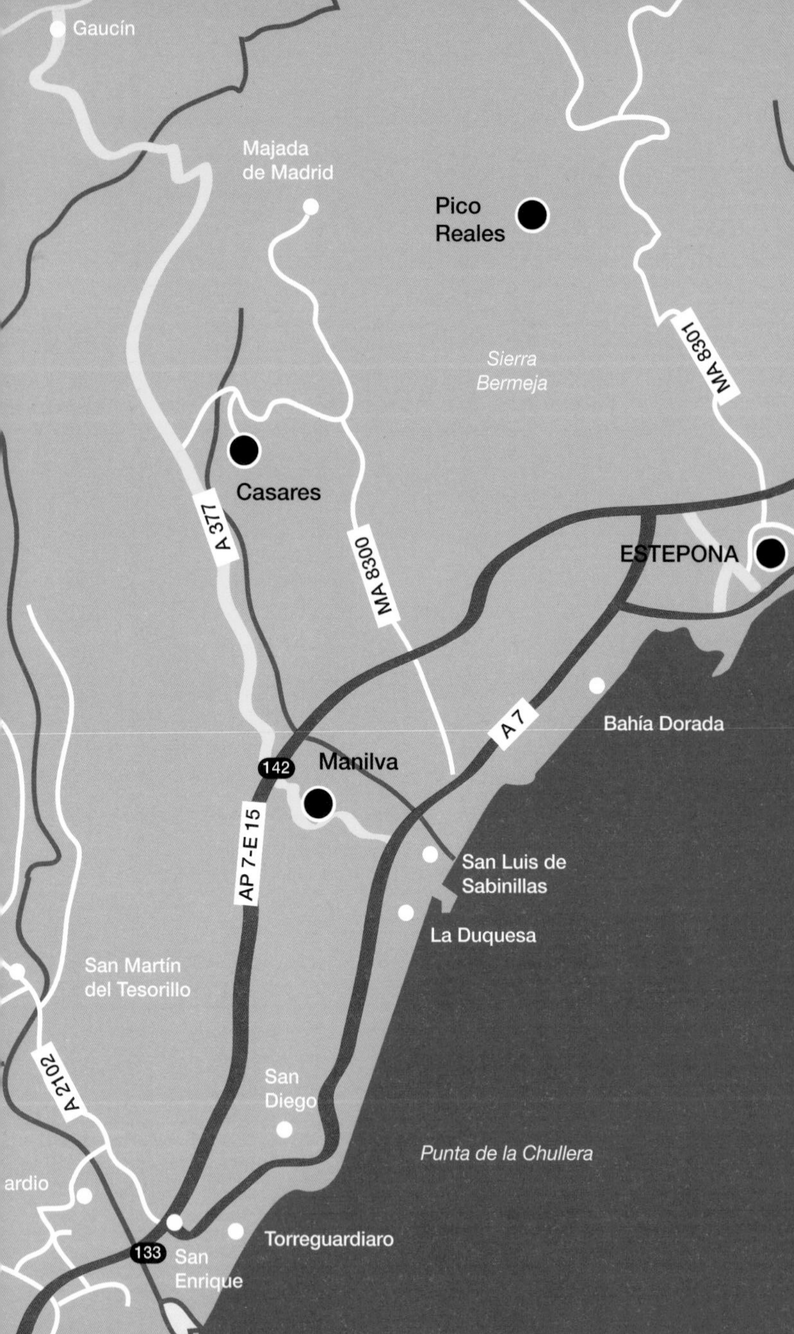

Gaucín
Majada de Madrid
Pico Reales
Sierra Bermeja
MA 8301
Casares
A 377
MA 8300
ESTEPONA
A 7
Bahía Dorada
142
Manilva
AP 7-E 15
San Luis de Sabinillas
La Duquesa
San Martín del Tesorillo
A 2102
San Diego
Punta de la Chullera
ardio
Torreguardiaro
133
San Enrique

Costa del Sol: Paraje Natural de Sierra Bermeja & Sierra Crestellina

The deep red mountainside of Sierra Bermeja - it literally means *Vermilion Massif* - is as unmistakable a landmark of the western Costa del Sol as the shell-like form of La Concha is further to the east. The high magnesium and iron content of its peridotite rocks account for its colour and strangely lunaresque aspect: seen at dawn or dusk the mountain seems to glow like a lantern above the sea. Over the millenia what once were volcanic cones and craters have been gradually rounded off to give the mountains their present aspect even though the peak of Los Reales, a mere 7.5 kilometres back from the sea, still towers up to almost 1500m.

The region's unusual geology, coupled with it being subject to weather systems coming from both the Atlantic and Mediterranean, have given rise to an extremely diverse fauna and flora with a number of endemic species. The botanical jewel of the *sierra* is its stand of *pinsapos*, an arboreal relic from the Ice Age which was first documented by the Swiss botanist de Boissier from whom the full latin name, *Abies Pinsapo Bois*, derives. The Pico Reales circuit described in this section leads you through the beautiful forest of *pinsapos* before it passes to the southern, sea-facing flank of the mountain.

The fauna of Sierra Bermeja is similarly rich in species and this is amongst the best spots in southern Spain for the observation of raptors. The jagged ridge of the Sierra Crestellina, just west of Los Reales, is home to a large colony of griffon vultures. Since the birds became a protected species a number of feeding sites have been established and the Muladar Circuit takes you past one of these avian fast-food outlets. Bonelli's, Golden and Booted eagles are all present in the area along with eagle owls, Egyptian vultures, peregrine falcons and kestrels. The *sierra* is also home to a large number of Egyption mongooses - it was here that they were first recorded outside of Africa – as well as the rare *corzo morisco (Capreolus capreolus)*, a sub-species of roe deer which has adapted to the warmer conditions of this southernmost part of Europe and whose coat is quite different to that of its Spanish cousins.

At the edge of this huge swathe of volcanic magma the extraordinary rock formations of the Sierra de Utrera are very different in feel. The deeply weathered fissures and fantastic forms of its karst limestone are a match for those of the better-known Torcal de Antequera and the path that cuts through its Canuto gorge is among the most spectacular geological excursions in southen Spain. Towards the end of the Utrera Gorge Circuit you pass by Los Baños de Hedionda where you can still take a dip in the hot sulphurous baths which have been known since Roman times for their curative properties.

On all walks described in this section you can expect big ocean views across the Bay of Algeciras, to Gibraltar and on clear days across the Strait to the mountains and villages of the northenmost swathe of Morocco. Casares should be your first choice if you're overnighting in the area: it's a quintessentially *andaluz* creation, wrapped round a jagged peak complete with Moorish castle and an organic cluster of white houses. The village has a cheap-and-cheerful hotel whilst hidden away in the cork forest just east of the village is the enchanting rural retreat *The Hermitage* where in low season you can strike some great deals: it's a perfect base for a walking holiday in this area. Manilva is also pretty untainted by tourism but its one hostal might be a touch too basic for most tastes which is why I've listed a reliable *Costa* alternative in nearby Sabanillas, as well as a great hotel hidden in the woods beneath Gaucín.

BEST SLEEPS

Casares

Hotel Hermitage €€
Tel: 952 895 639 Email: hh@hotelhermitage.es
www.hotelhermitage.es
Hideaway hotel in the forest east of Casares with low season deals.

Hotel Rural Casares €–€€
Tel: 952 895 211 Email: hotelruralcasaresemail.com
www.hotelcasares.com
Inexpensive hotel at the heart of the village with quiet rooms.

Sabanillas

Hotel Don Agustín €
Tel: 952 883 139 Email: reservas@hoteldonagustin.com
www.hoteldonagustin.com
Exceptionally friendly small hotel next to the beach and close to all walks.

Near Gaucín

Hacienda La Herriza €€–€€€
Tel: 951 068 200 Email: info@laherriza.com
www.laherriza.com
Beautiful sylvan retreat close to walks 2,3 & 4.

Taxis: Manilva 952 802 900, Casares 670 884 394, Estepona 952 802 900, Sabanillas 952 802 900.

Distance: 10 kms **Time Required:** 3.5 hours **Rating:** Easy/Medium

Total Height Gain: 275m **Map:** IGN 1:50000 Jimena de la Frontera 1071 (14-46)

Ⓦ **Water:** no springs along the way so take plenty

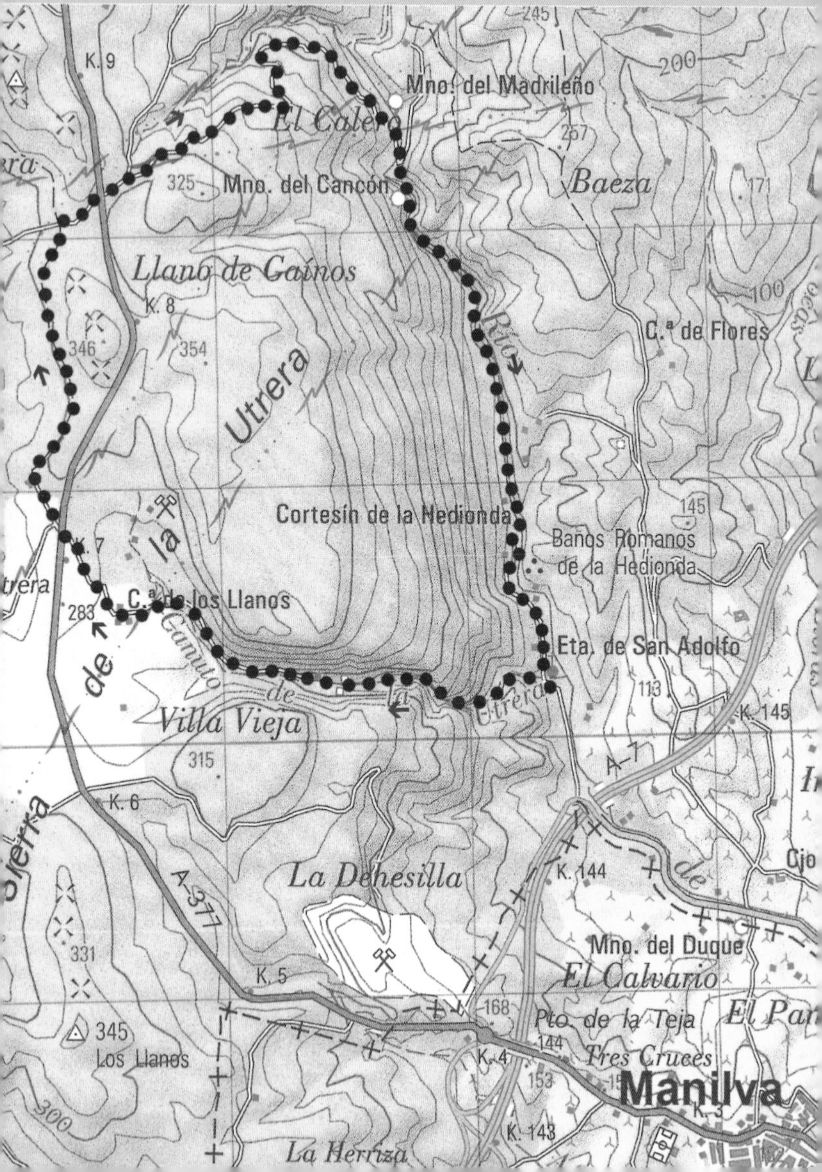

1 Manilva: The Utrera Gorge & Río Manilva Circuit

Overview

The deeply weathered karst formations of the Utrera Gorge, the southernmost of their kind in Europe, number amongst western Málaga's most remarkable natural features. Home to Bonelli's eagles as well as Egyptian vultures the gorge is a fine example of the *canuto* (glossary) ecosystem which is unique to this part of Andalucía. There are more treats in store: a beautiful path leading down the River Manilva past a series of ancient millhouses, soaring views out to Casares and down to the Mediterranean as well as the fascinating Hedionda baths which since Roman times have attracted visitors to their hot, sulphurous waters (see photo on page 115). This walk makes for a wonderfully varied half day excursion and could be combined with a leisurely *al fresco* meal at the Los Alamos restaurant at the end of the walk. Parts of the path along the Rio Manilva are quite overgrown so I'd recommend packing long trousers even if you're undertaking this walk during the hotter months as well as your bathing costume and towel for a dip in the Hedionda baths.

Getting to the beginning of the walk

From Sabanillas follow the A377 to Manilva. Here follow signs for Centro Urbano then turn right at a sign for AP7 Málaga/ Algeciras/Cádiz. Head round the east side of the village to a point where the road doglegs left then right. Here cut right down Calle Padre Mariano. Follow this road to the bottom of the hill then turn left. Pass the Roman Oasis restaurant then just before you reach the motorway bridge cut right at a sign Zona Verde Pública Charca La Mina. You soon reach Restaurante Los Álamos where there's space to park to the left of the track. From here head north along the track for 300m until it bears left to reach a sign Ruta no. 11 El Canuto de la Utrera.

The Walk

At the signboard *Ruta 11 El Canuto de la Utrera* 1 cut left on a narrow footpath which leads into the mouth of the Utrera gorge through thick stands of oleander, at first following the left hand bank of the *canuto*. Crosssing to the northern bank the path leads you to the area known as *El Torcal de Utrera*, a remarkable swathe of karst limestone which rises to both sides of the stream. In parts the path is made up of huge slabs of limestone. Green and white waymarking leads you through the gorge past stands of oleander, wild olive, carob, lentiscus and fan palm. You occasionally need to use hands as well as feet as you clamber between the rocks. The gorge widens as it reaches twin concrete water deposits 2. **(25 mins)**

From here there are fine views back along the gorge to the Med'. The floor of the gorge becomes broader and flatter as the path climbs before widening to become a track where you reach

an information board about *La Sierra de la Utrera* 3. **(1 hr 5 mins)** The track runs on towards a line of wind turbines, passing through a rickety wire-and-post gate (sometimes left open). Reaching the top of the rise the track passes between two white buildings of Cortijo Los Llanos 4 then bears sharply right, then once more left, crosses a cattle grid before running up to meet a tarmac road, the A377 5.

Head straight across the road, cross another cattle grid then angle right through a set of white gates. A fence runs to your left. Reaching a second white gate 6 cut left through a wire-and-post gate, angle right and after 5m go through a second metal gate. Beyond the gate continue along the track which leads through another metal gate before passing just right of a small farm building. Follow the track across the open hillside, roughly parallel to the line of turbines up to your right. The track eventually runs up to a broader track 7. Here cut right. Passing just left of a turbine the track loops left then right, crosses a cattle grid, then reaches the A377 ⑧.

Cross the road and head along a dirt track which at first runs towards the Sierra Crestellina. After 125m you reach a fork ⑨. Take the right option. Passing an area of quarried sandstone Casares comes into view and, to the northwest, the reddish slopes of the Sierra Bermeja. The track begins to loop downwards as the Med' again comes into view. Reaching a junction ⑩ ignore a track which angles hard left: stick to your course and follow a line of telegraph poles down towards the valley floor. Passing between two white gate pillars the track runs towards a concrete ford across Río de Manilva. 30m before the ford cut right along a less distinct track then after 50m cut left then cross the river via a footbridge ⑪. Beyond the bridge the path angles right, passes a ruined mill, then climbs and cuts through a gate. **(1 hr 30 mins)**

The path, overgrown on this section, runs on parallel to river's left bank: look for P.R. waymarking. To your right more spectacular karst formations are visible as Manilva comes into view to the south. Looping round a landslide the path drops down to the river which you cross via stepping stones ⑫. Beyond the river, angling right, the path passes just right of a huge fig tree then arcs left and resumes its course parallel to the river's right bank. Passing a stand of eucalyptus it crosses the river again before looping back to the right bank. Reaching a fence around a mill and a sign *Prohibido el Paso* the path cuts once again to the left bank then, passing beneath a rocky overhang where an an enormous bolder spans the river bed, cuts back to the opposite bank ⑬. Here it angles up to merge with a broader path which, after some 50m, cuts right through the undergrowth to a wide track ⑭. **(2 hrs 5 mins)**

Bearing left along the track Manilva again comes into view as you pass another mill house then a recreational area with a large

swimming pool before you descend to reach a track leading to the complex of *Hermanos Ocaña* 15. Passing a set of gates bear right along this track. Shortly you'll spot a number of steep paths which cut down left to the Roman baths of La Hedionda where you could take a dip in their hot, sulphurous waters 16.
Passing by a line of bins continue down the valley on a path which runs parallel to the river's right bank then angle back up to the track you left earlier. Here you pass the buildings of the old spa then a chapel dedicated to San Adolfo. Crossing the bed of the Canuto de Utrera the track leads back to your point of departure 1. **(2 hrs 25 mins)**

Distance: 10 kms **Time Required:** 3/3.5 hours **Rating:** Easy/Medium
Total Height Gain: 375m **Map:** IGN 1:50000 Jimena de la Frontera 1071 (14-46)
Ⓦ **Water:** spring at waypoint 2 @ 10 mins

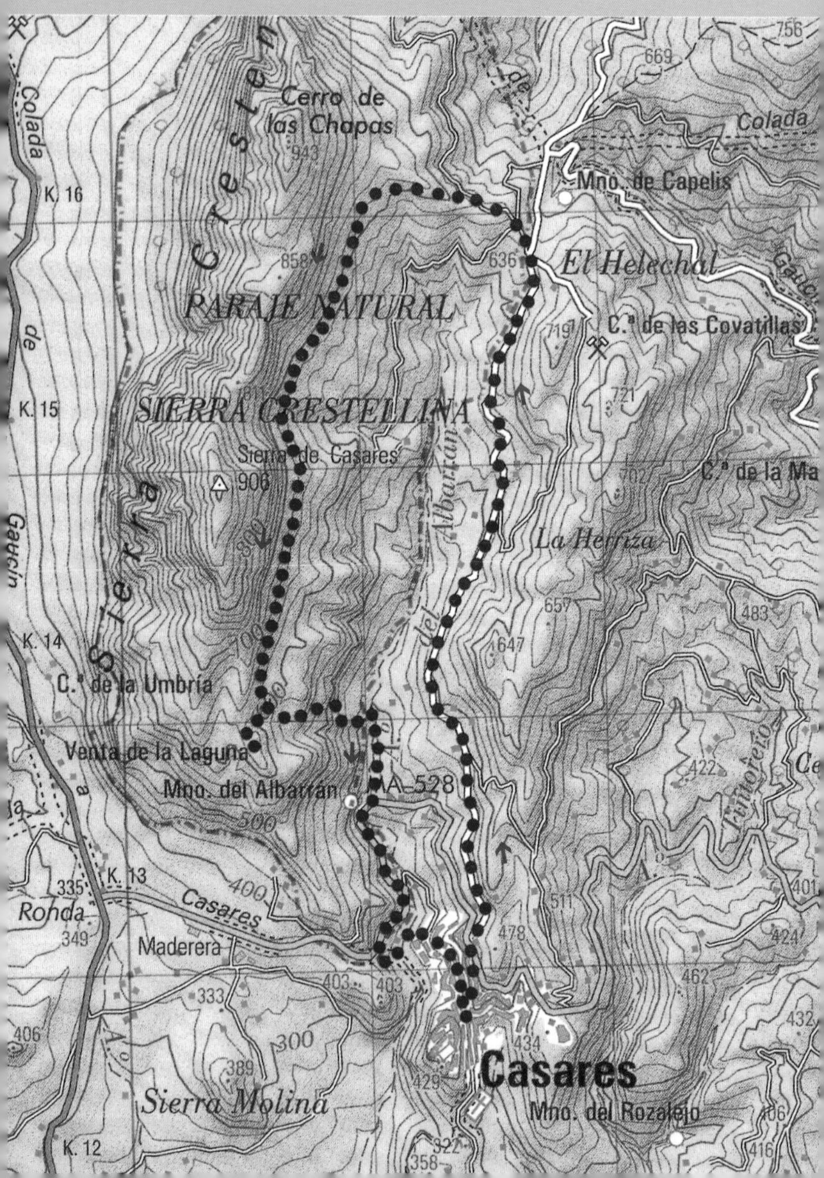

2 Casares: The Crestellina Circuit

Overview

The hilltop village of Casares, just a few kilometres inland from the Mediterranean, numbers amongst the most dramatically situated villages in Andalucía and is well worth an excursion in its own right. To the south of the village there are vast views out towards Gibraltar and Morocco whilst to the north the jagged spine of the Crestellina sierra - it's recently been given protected *Paraje Natural* status - provides a stunning backdrop to Casares' organic cluster of whitewashed buildings. There's a steep section early in the walk up to the Puerto de la Viñas but once you loop west towards the Cerro de las Chapas the going gets much easier. If you're looking for a more challenging walk, take the footpath that leads off to the right at waypoint 5. After a short section of footpath then some hands-on scrambling it leads you to the summit of the Cerro de las Chapas. On the return leg you may spot ibex on the eastern flanks of the Crestellina and will certainly see plenty of vultures riding the thermals high above you.

The Walk

The walk begins in the Plaza de España, the main square of the village, next to a line of benches (1). With your back to the benches bear left across the square then, passing right of bar La Bodeguilla de Enmedio, head up past a *No Entry* sign to the road which runs round the top of the village. Bearing left after 40m you reach a sign *Sendero Crestellina Natural.* Here cut right up a steep concrete road whose surface soon changes to tarmac. Soon you pass a spring opposite a huge eucalyptus, *La Fuente de la Arquita* (W) (2). Soaring views open out to the West

and the to the eastern flank of the Crestellina as you climb on up past a number of houses and villas. After 15 minutes the tarmac ends. Carry on along the main track which cuts through thick stands of oak and pine forest with dense undergrowth, evidence of the high rainfall to which the area is subject. Soon you pass an area where quarrying has taken place.

Reaching Finca Cueva Aranda cork oaks begin to give way to pines. The track runs on past Finca Puerto de las Viñas then, after 200m, reaches a fork 3. Here, ignoring a concreted track which cuts up to the right, stick to your same course. After 50m you reach another fork. Here again take the left hand option. After 200m you reach another fork and a second sign *Sendero Crestellina Natural*. Here, bearing left, you pass a green metal barrier 4. **(45 mins)**

The narrow forestry track climbs steeply as views open out towards the East. Reaching the top of a rise and another

marker post you come to another fork 5. Here keep left once more. **The right hand option leads to the highest point of the Crestellina, El Cerro de las Chapas. Be aware that part of the way up demands a hands-on scramble should you decide to divert.* The track begins to gently descend as it loops round the bowl of the valley as views open out south to Casares and on clear days to Gibraltar and North Africa. The rocky crest of the Crestellina is now to your right and the vegetation much sparser, evidence of a fire in the not-so-distant past. Eventually, reaching a point where the forestry track arcs left, you come to a sign for *Mirador 300m* 6. **(1 hr 20 mins)**

Here cut right on rocky path which leads to an information board about Griffon Vultures: the chances are that several will be riding the thermals up above you. Beyond the sign the path angles hard left then climbs steeply to the end of a bluff and the Mirador de Castillón 7. From here there are soaring views across the valley and, beyond, to the Sierra de Bermeja.

Retrace your footsteps back to point where you cut up to the *mirador*, turn right and continue your descent. After approx 200m you reach the back wall of a mountain refuge 8. Passing right of the refuge you'll spot a marker post which marks the continuation of the path which now loops steeply down between pines and fan palms to the valley floor. Care should be taken: the path is loose in parts. Reaching a fence the path angles right before dropping down to a dirt track. Here cut left. After 25m you reach a junction 9 where cutting right you cross the concreted bed of Arroyo del Albarrán beyond which track descends to meet the A7150. Here turn right along a balustraded path lined with solar lamps. At a point where the road bears sharply right you reach an information board 10.
(2 hrs 5 mins)

Here cut left off the road then angle hard left along a concrete road which passes just left of a white building. The track reverts to dirt as it drops steeply down to the fertile valley floor where it crosses a pretty bridge 11 then bears right and climbs towards the village. Reaching a junction bear right and continue up to the first of the village's houses beyond which you pass a map of the village. Heading straight along Calle Carrera you pass La Casa Natal de Blas Infante which doubles as a tourist office. Reaching a square, open to its right side, head straight on to return to the main square of Casares, La Plaza de España 1.
(2 hrs 25 mins)

Distance: 12.5 kms **Time Required:** 4/4.5 hours **Rating:** Medium
Total Height Gain: 400m **Map:** IGN 1:50000 Jimena de la Frontera 1071 (14-46)
Water: no springs along the way so take plenty

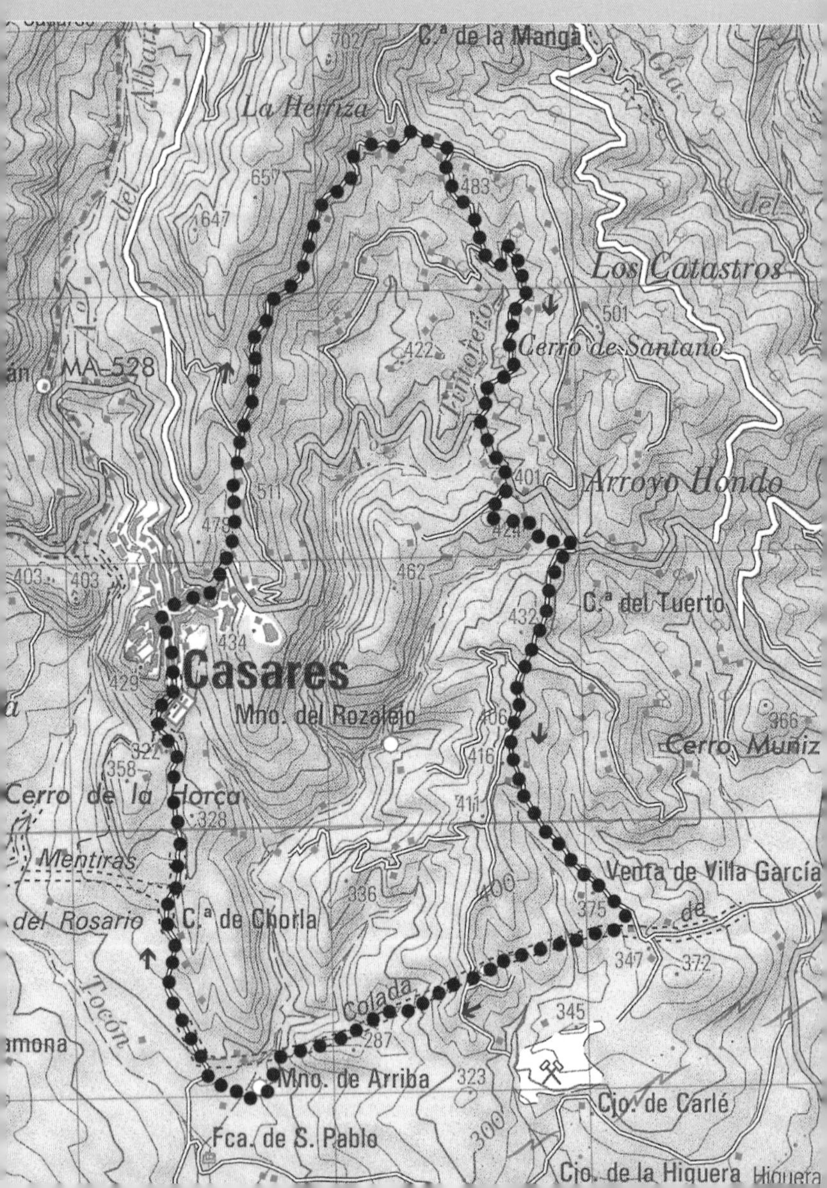

3 Casares Eastern Circuit via Manga Celima & Arroyo del Tocón

Overview

This second Casares circuit combines two of the walking routes which have been marked out by the Casares town hall. I've linked them together to make a more interesting half day excursion and so as to avoid their long sections of walking on tarmac. The route takes in the forested hillsides to the northeast of the village and the open farmland to its south whilst for most of the walk you're treated to fine panoramic views of the Campo de Gibraltar, east to the Sierra Bermeja and when the weather is clear all the way to the mountains of Moroccan Rif . You should steel yourself for a steep final climb up to the village from the point where you cross the Tocón stream: its waters once powered the millhouses which you pass by as you head back towards the village. The final stage of the walk leads you past Casares' unfinished cemetery which has lain abandoned for many years. It's a grim monument to the profligacy that has marked local municipal government in Andalucía for the past couple of decades.

The Walk

The walk begins in the Plaza de España, the main square of the village, next to a line of benches (1). With your back to the benches angle left and pass just right of bar La Bodeguilla de Enmedio. Head up the hill then take the first right into Calle Copera which leads up past Hotel Rural de Casares. At the next fork keep left, climb a flight of steps then cut right then left along a narrow stepped street which climbs to meet the MA8300. Cutting right past Casa Curro after 125m you reach a sign *Ruta Circular 3: La Manga Celima/Arroyo Hondo* next to the municipal

rubbish bins ②. Here cut left up a narrow path which climbs steeply parallel to the right bank of a stream. Passing through a flimsy wire-and-post gate the path merges with a wider track. After 75m, at a point where the track arcs left, cut right up a narrow path whose ancient cobbling is visible in parts. You should see faded green and white waymarking. The path meets with a tarmac road where, angling left and climbing for 40m, you reach a fork ③.

Take the right fork and continue climbing along a broad track following a line of pylons. Reaching another fork keep left and continue along the main track which becomes concreted for a short section. Reaching a second fork again keep left: marker posts indicate the way. Soon the track abruptly narrows to become a path ④ which runs on through a stand of deciduous oaks. Views open out towards Estepona and the sea. Reaching more open ground the path shortly angles right then meets with

a broad track 5. **(35 mins)**

Bear right along the track which shortly begins to descend through a swathe of cork oaks. After some 150m you reach a junction 6. Turn right following a signpost *SL-3 Celima*. The track, now concreted, loops past a water deposit then arcs once more right. At the next junction keep left, ignoring a sign to the right for *Hotel Hermitage*. Looping right you soon pass by Cortijo Los Castaños. The concreted road loops lazily down past several villas then meets with the MA8300 (marked on some maps as the MA546) 7. **(1 hr)**

Turn left along the road. A few metres past Restaurante Arroyo Hondo cut right away the MA8300. Follow a short section of steep track, concreted in parts, up and over a rise to a reach a 4 way junction 8. Here cut left (unless you wish to shorten the route, in which case take the right hand option to return to Casares in 30 mins). You pass immediately above a house which is down to your right. At the next fork keep left along a sandy track which descends through the oaks before it narrows then loops past a house with a pool, Finca El Tejar. Widening once more it climbs back to the MA8300 where, to your right, is a layby. Here angle right past a line of bins then cut right up a track following signs *Cortijo El Robledal/Cerro de los Higos* 9. **(1 hr 20 mins)**

The concrete ends as the track runs on between cork oaks. Reaching a 3 way junction 10 head straight on following a sign *Cerro de los Higos*. After 325m you reach a fork. Again, branch left, following a second sign for *Cerro de los Higos*. The panorama is somewhat marred by pylons but shortly these cut away to the left and, following a high ridge towards the sea, the vistas improve as Gibraltar comes into view.

Reaching a fork 11 **(1 hr 45 mins)** cut right following a sign for *SL2-Los Molinos*. The track cuts across open fields, passes a group of farm buildings, then becomes prettier, if rougher underfoot, as it descends between hedgerows then crosses a (dry) stream bed. Passing a wooden-posted corral the track once more descends as spectacular views open up towards Casares. The track passes between the twin gates of the Semental El Robledal horse stud. The path, more overgrown, continues its descent then crosses a (dry) stream, El Arroyo del Tocón 12. **(2 hrs 15 mins)**

Bear left until you reach a track that leads down to the stream bed 13. Here bear right and follow this track, whose ancient cobbles are visible, up towards the village. Passing through a wire-and-post gate you reach another junction with a broader track 14. Here cut right following signs *PRA 162 Casares* and *SL2 Casares* and steel yourself for a hard climb. The track leads past an old mill, El Molino de Arriba, whose race is still visible at its right side 15. The concreted track eventually climbs past the unfinished cemetery then on past the village rubbish tip. Both of are bound to make you ask, 'Why?'. After a steep final pull, after passing a signboard depicting *El Camino de Jimena*, you reach a fork. Here take the left option and head straight on up into the village along Calle de Juan Cerón which leads you back to the main square 1 and your point of departure. **(2 hrs 50 mins)**

Distance: 12.5 kms **Time Required:** 3.5 hours **Rating:** Medium
Total Height Gain: 325m **Map:** IGN 1:50000 Jimena de la Frontera 1071 (14-46)
Ⓦ **Water:** no springs along the way so take plenty

4 Casares Circuit via La Acedía & El Muladar

Overview

The Sierra Bermeja has a stark beauty all of its own and this longish walk, leading to a beautiful rock pool in the upper reaches of the Garganta de las Acedias, could be a great introduction to its lunaresque landscapes and the vermilion rock formations after which it is named. The walk leads you past El Muladar, one of several sites in the southern *sierras* where carcasses are laid out for the resident colonies of griffon vultures. These enormous, carrion-eating birds are a protected species and numbers have increased enormously since the sites were set up. If this sounds too macabre for your liking there's no denying that the sight of these enormous raptors, winging in to feed, is truly magnificent, and by quickening your pace you can be past the site in seconds. The early and later parts of the walk, which lead past a number of grand rural retreats hidden away in leafy stands of oak, stand in marked contrast to the harsher landscapes of the middle section of the walk.

Getting to the beginning of the walk

From the coastal road take the MA546 towards Casares. Some 50m past the km8 post look for a sign to the right for La Acedía and a signboard for Pasada del Pino/La Acedía. Turning in right from the road the track is plenty wide enough to leave your vehicle a few metres along on the right.

The Walk

From the signboard for *Pasada del Pino-La Acedía* (1) head away from the MA546. After 30m concrete gives way to dirt track and you shortly pass a sign with a map of the route you'll follow: it suggests allowing 5 hours but you'll need far less.

Ingoring three tracks which cut off to the right (the second with a sign *Hacienda*) follow the main track as it loops down through a swathe of cork oaks to a stand of eucalyptus trees where it crosses the (dry) stream bed of the Garganta del Palo 2. The track winds on past the entrance to *La Serena* then crosses another (dry) watercourse. Bearing left the track continues to ascend as it passes the oleander-lined boundary of Casa Isabel then reaches a triple fork 3. **(30 mins)**

Here take the left option. The track arcs hard left and enters an area of sparser vegetation. The jagged ridge of La Crestellina comes into view to the northwest as the track leads you through a galvanised metal gate 4. After a few metres it arcs back right and you're now are treated to views of Estepona and the sea. You pass a sign for *Red Andaluza de Comederos de Aves Caronñeras* 5 and a fenced enclosure, El Muladar, where carcasses are laid out for the resident griffon vultures. As you

climb higher Gibraltar and (on clear days) Morocco come into sight. Shortly after bearing hard left the track divides next to a concreted storm drain 6. Take the right fork, following green and white waymarking. The track runs in a northeasterly direction towards the head of the valley, high above the Garganta de las Acedias whose rushing waters you'll hear down beneath you. Angling right the track crosses a first (dry) watercourse then after 150m reaches the Garganta de las Acedias 7. **(1 hr 20 mins)**

20m before reaching the stream it's worth making a short diversion by taking the rough track which cuts off to the left. Following it for some 150m, as it arcs left then back right, you reach a waterfall and a rock pool 8 reached by scrambling down the steep bank of the Acedias. It's a beautiful place to break for a picnic and a dip in the stream. After visiting the rock pool retrace your steps to the point where you left the track. A few metres after crossing the Garganta you reach the highest

point of the walk (approximately 550m) as the track arcs back towards the sea. *At this stage, high above the track over to your right, the crumpled fuselage of a light aircraft is visible which crashed on the mountainside in December 1998.*

The track abruptly narrows to become a path [9] which runs along the top of a ridge then descends: care should be taken because sections are loose underfoot. The path occasionally braids but waymarking guides you down through a swathe of pines before you reach a broad dirt track [10]. **(2 hrs)**

Here bear right and continue your descent through the pines passing the entrance gates of Villa Bermeja. Continue down the main track which is shaded in parts by ancient cork oaks. Passing an open-fronted shed you reach a junction [11]. Here turn right. The track runs past more gated villas then arcs left, passes a paddock, then angles back to the right and crosses the Acedía via a concrete bridge. Climbing steeply the track eventually angles right to reach the track you followed earlier in the walk and the ceramic sign for *Hacienda* [12]. Here cut left and retrace your footsteps back to the start point of the walk [1]. **(2 hrs 30 mins)**

Distance: 8 kms **Time Required:** 2.5 hours **Rating:** Easy/Medium
Total Height Gain: 300m **Map:** IGN 1:50000 Jimena de la Frontera 1071 (14-46)
Ⓦ **Water:** tap with unchlorinated water at waypoint 8 @ 1 hr 15 mins

5 Pico Reales Circuit via the Pinsapo Path & Mirador de Salvador Guerrero

Overview

This circular walk leads you to the highest point of the Sierra Bermeja Paraje Natural, the Pico Reales. Although just 8km inland from the Mediterranean this mighty vermilion massif rises to 1450m and from its antennae-topped peak there's an extraordinary panoramic vista of a huge slice of Andalucía: north to the Genalguacíl valley and the Sierra de las Nieves, east to the Sierra de Ojén and La Concha, west to La Crestellina and the last reaches of the Alcornocales and south to Gibraltar, the Strait and Africa. An added bonus is that the first part of the route leads you through the *Pinsapar de los Reales*, home to one of the few existing stands of this unique pine tree. The second great viewing point on the walk, the Mirador de Salvador Guerrero, entails a short diversion but it's well worth the extra effort. The drive up to the start point of the walk, which lies within the Pico Reales protected area, is an adventure in it own right.

Getting to the beginning of the walk

From Estepona take the MA8301 towards Jubrique (it begins next to the Mercadona supermarket on the north side of the town) for 15kms to the top of the pass, Puerto de Peñas Blancas. Here turn left past a sign for Los Reales, pass a green barrier then continue for 2.75 kms to a signboard to the right of the road marking the beginning of the Pinsapo walk, Paseo de Los Pinsapos.

The Walk

From the signboard *Paseo de los Pinsapos* (1) head down a narrow, rocky path which drops away from the road into the *pinsapo* forest. 75m after crossing a small concrete bridge you reach a junction 2. Cut left following a sign *Los Realillos/Los Reales 2.2kms*. The path leads past a signboard about pinsapo pines then on past a ceramic sign of a poem by Lorca inspired by trees. The path climbs steeply through dense undergrowth: as you climb higher Mediterranean pines begin to take the place of the *pinsapos*.

Careful! Some 5 minutes beyond the ceramic sign of Lorca's poem you reach a junction marked by twin cairns 3. Here cut hard left and continue your ascent, zigzagging up through the pines and the reddish rocks. Passing a small breach in the rocks the path runs up to the top of the ridge where views open out to the southwest and the Bay of Algeciras 4. **(30 mins)**

Here the path bears left towards the transmitter antennae atop the Reales peak, through another swathe of *pinsapo* pines. Marker posts help guide you up. Passing across another jagged ridge the path bears right and continues to climb. Reaching a flatter area and bearing left it runs on up to the antennae. Here, reaching a white hut, cut right right, pass a second hut then follow a narrow path up to the trig point marking the top of Los Reales (1450m) 5. **(50 mins)**

This is a great spot to take a break and gulp in the incredible panorama that lies before you. Leaving the peak retrace your footsteps back towards the first white hut which you passed earlier. 5m before the hut cut right on a narrow path which drops down to the track leading to the transmitter masts where you'll see a signboard for *Sendero de los Realillos* 6. Here angle right down a stony track which loops down the eastern flank of Los Reales, shortly passing by another transmitter mast. Looping on down past a group of forestry buildings you reach a junction with another track and a plaque dedicated to Edmond Boissier 7 who first cataologued the unique *pinsapo* pine. **(1 hr 10 mins)**

Here cutting right for 100m you reach a picinc area, *Área Recreativa*, where there are picnic tables and, just beneath, the Mirador de la Costa del Sol. There's a tap with water W to the right: a sign warns that it isn't chlorinated but the taste is all the better for that 8. Continuing on along the track you reach a turning circle and a sign *Mirador de Salvador Guerrero* 9. From here continue along a narrow path to reach one of the Costa del Sol's most spectacular viewing points 10. After visting the *mirador* trace your steps back to the Boissier plaque 7 then follow the track on for approximately 1.6 kms to return to your point of departure 1. **(1 hr 55 mins)**

Costa del Sol: Parque Natural de Sierra Blanca de Ojén

Walks close to Marbella, Ojén & Istán

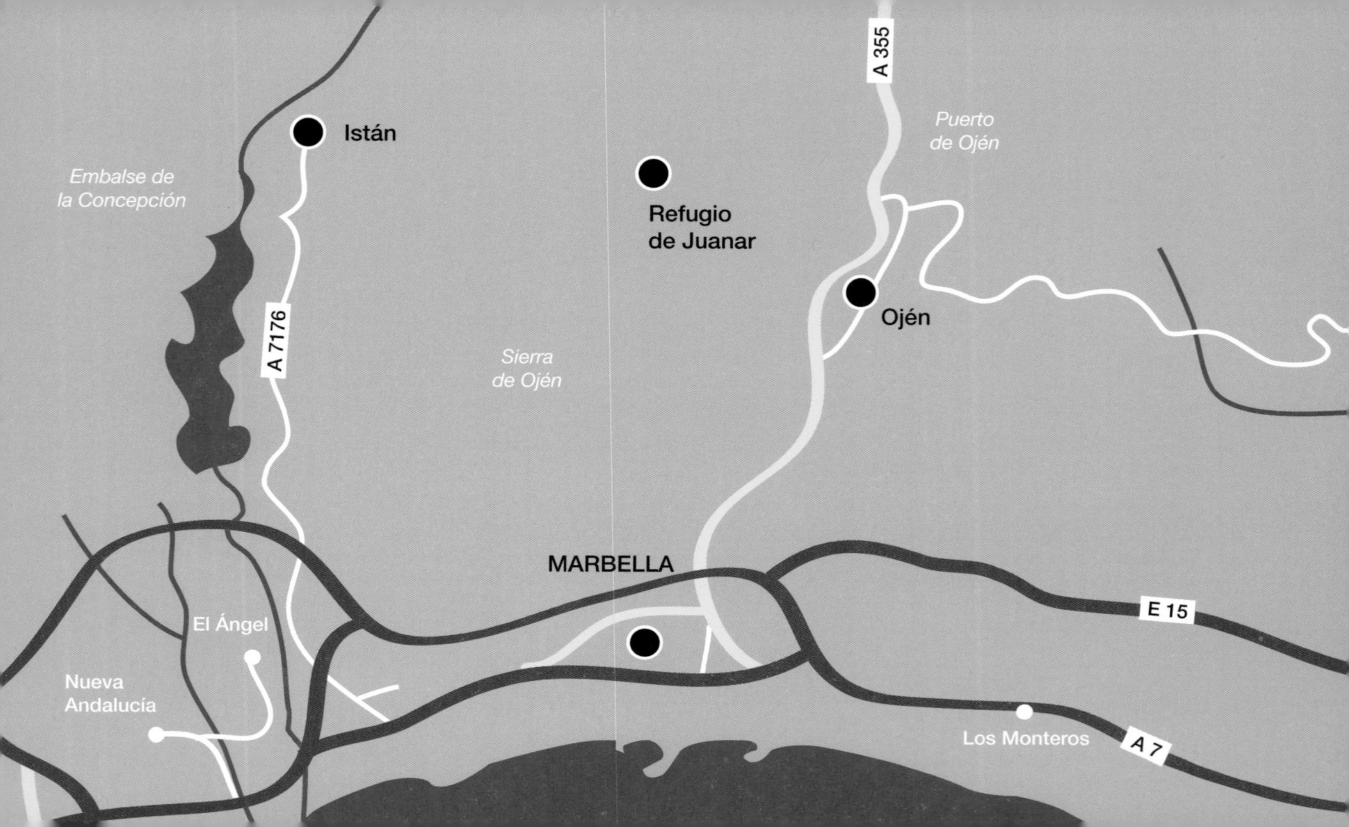
Istán
Embalse de
la Concepción
A 7176
Sierra
de Ojén
Refugio
de Juanar
A 355
Puerto
de Ojén
Ojén
MARBELLA
E 15
El Ángel
Nueva
Andalucía
Los Monteros
A 7

Costa del Sol: Parque Natural de Sierra Blanca de Ojén

At the southern tip of the Parque Natural de la Sierra de las Nieves, the Sierra Blanca is associated in most people's mind with one emblematic mountain: La Concha. Wherever you are on the stretch of coast between San Pedro and Marbella its gracious, shell-like southern face rises up like a multi-layered cake, providing a stunning backdrop to the villas that dot its lower slopes. Like the rest of the Cordillera Penibética of which it forms a part, the mountain is predominantly composed of limestone which has been metamorphosised into alternate strata of grey and white marble, conferring its banded aspect when seen from the south.

Behind La Concha's denuded, sea-facing slope a more verdant swathe of *sierra* stretches between Istán and Ojén and north and south from the Refugio de Juanar. Extensive stands of repopulated pines, ancient groves of olives, cherry trees and chestnuts are interspersed with stands of holm and cork oaks along with two small expanses of *pinsapo* pines. The arboreal diversity and the abundance of game makes walking in the Park all the more special and explains why the area was once a National Hunting Reserve. And it's easy to see why as late as 1947 groups of *maquis* resistance fighters were able to fight on against Franco, retreating from the Nationalist troops to the refuge of Sierra Blanca's dense forests and deep gorges.

Since the advent of tourism to the area many of the traditional resources of the Sierra have ceased to be exploited: charcoal from its oak trees, talcum powder, marble, iron and magnesium from its mines and quarries, esparto grass and fan palm for basket manufacture, whilst the groves of olives that were once worked around the Cortijo de Juanar lie abandoned. The Cortijo has been reborn as a centre for research into the *Cabra*

Hispánica whose numbers have greatly increased since they were declared a protected species: on any of the walks that pass close to Juanar you'll have a good chance of spotting them on the higher rock faces. Other mammals you may see in the Park include roe deer, foxes, badgers, genets and Egyptian mongooses. Raptors are easy to spot, the *sierra* being home to several types of eagle, griffon vultures as well as to hawks, kestrels and a variety of owls.

The two villages which lie to the east and west of the Sierra Blanca feel surprisingly remote from the nearby Costa del Sol, especially Istán, even though this pretty white village is the starting point for some of the region's most exciting trails and a gateway to the Sierra de las Nieves. The village has an excellent small hotel just to its south and is linked to Marbella by bus or an inexpensive taxi ride. Ojén is more easily reached from the coast since the completion of the new road from Marbella to Coín. The village has a charming main square and a pretty small hotel at its centre.

No visit to this region would be complete without a stay or at least a meal at the *Refugio de Juanar*. This former hunting lodge is now part of the state-run *Parador* chain even though it's managed as a co-operative venture. The *Refugio* is plum at the centre of the park and accessed by way of a serpentine mountain road. The hotel showcases game on its menu and retains the cosy-rustic feel of the original lodge, complete with open fires in winter and numerous hunting trophies in its sitting and dining rooms. *Juanar* is an incredibly peaceful place and you'll understand why Charles de Gualle chose to hide away here when penning his memoirs in the early 70s. The lodge is the starting point for the walk that leads to the summit of La Concha as well as the Cuchillos Circuit.

BEST SLEEPS

In the Park

Refugio de Juanar €€–€€€
Tel: 952 881 000 Email: juanar@juanar.com
www.juanar.com
A perfect base for your sorties with trad' Andalusian cuisine.

Istán

Hotel Los Jarales €–€€
Tel: 952 869 942 Email: info@losjarales.com
www.losjarales.com
Inexpensive and friendly family-run hotel just south of Istán.

Ojén

La Posada del Angel €€
Tel: 952 881 808 Email: info@laposadadelangel.nl
www.laposadadelangel.net
Charming small hotel with 17 pretty bedrooms decorated in an angelic theme.

Marbella

Hotel Finlandia €
Tel: 952 770 700 Email: info@hotelfinlandiamarbella.com
www.hotelfinlandia.es
Pristine, simple hotel run by a friendly Anglo-Spanish couple.

Taxis: Marbella 952 774 488, Ojén 952 881 280,
Istán 686 262 481

Distance: 13.5 kms **Time Required:** 4.5 hours **Rating:** Medium/Difficult
Total Height Gain: 350m **Map:** IGN 1:50000 Marbella 1065 (15-45)
Ⓦ **Water:** springs at 15 mins @ waypoint 5 & 1 hr 45 mins @ waypoint 9

1 Istán: the Infierno Valley Circuit

Overview

Even if there isn't anything that I'd refer to as 'hellish' about this itinerary which includes a rocky ascent along the *La Cañada del Infierno* ('Hell's Footpath') this is a more demanding footpath to follow than most in this book. The first section of the walk is the easiest as you cut out of the village along a restored footpath that follows the course of a Moorish *acequía* (glossary) before swinging north past the Río Molinos spring along a broad forestry track. After a couple of kilometres of walking the track's tarmac surface turns to dirt as you angle east towards Monda. The return leg is quite different in flavour as you first climb the boulder-strewn course of the Infierno before heading back to Istán via a narrow footpath that countours round the lower, western flank of the Sierra Blanca. At this stage the path is a little overgrown and you'll be glad to have a long pair of trousers in your day pack. Be sure to stop for a break at the *Nacimiento del Río Molinos* and put time aside to visit the village's pretty central *plaza* which is just 200m beyond the starting point of the walk.

The Walk

The walk begins in front of the Istán *Ayuntamiento* in the Plaza de Andalucía ①. From here head back towards Marbella then after 50m cut left up Camino del Nacimiento. At the next junction turn right ② then after 100m ③ angle left beneath a wooden arch at a sign *PRA-136 Cañada del Infierno*. Head along a recently restored footpath which follows an ancient water channel with a wooden barrier to its left. Passing an aviary, then the spring of *El Fuente del Pobre* and then a second aviary angle right to meet once more with the road 4. Here bear left and follow the road as it arcs left past a sign *Parque Natural Sierra de las Nieves*. Continue on past *El Nacimiento del Río Molinos* W 5. **(15 mins)** Prepare yourself for a 2km section of walking on tarmac as you head on north, high above the Rio Verde. The tarmac eventually turns to a dirt as the track runs up to a fork 6. **(50 mins)** Here angle right following a sign for *Monda*.

The track loops lazily round the mountain, gradually angling east before it passes beneath a black plastic water pipe. Looping hard back to the left you cross the course of the Arroyo Castaño 7. Having angled once more east and then round to the north you pass beneath overhead power lines. After some 100m the track again swings round to the east. Passing twice beneath the overhead lines the track descends towards a (dry) stream bed. A few metres before you reach it, where the track becomes concreted 8, cut right up a rocky streambed: you're now following what locals refer to as La Cañada del Infierno or 'Hell's footpath'. Cairns now mark your way. At a point where a huge boulder blocks the stream bear right and climb (hands are required) and continue up the streambed. The path cuts past a spring-fed water tank: it's a tempting spot for a dip in hot weather. From here follow a black plastic pipe up the stream bed past a spring which rises between a cleft in the rocks above a metal manhole cover W 9. **(1 hr 45 mins)**

Here cut right out of the stream bed on a narrow path which climbs steeply past an ancient carob tree to reach a terraced olive grove. Keep to its higher, left hand edge. Reaching a group of three carob trees angle slightly left to pick up the continuation of the path, marked by a faded yellow arrow on one of the trees. 75m beyond the carobs angle up left to a metal post with yellow waymarking 10. Here the path widens into a rough dirt track: the next 250m are rough underfoot. Reaching a junction 11

(2 hrs 5 mins) cut left and upwards then reaching another junction 12 cut right: you'll now be pushing past gorse bushes so will be more comfortable in long trousers. Crossing an oleander-lined (dry) streambed 13 the path passes through a swathe of pines. Just beyond the trees look for an indistinct path that angles left 14 and passes between a cleft in the rocks where P.R. waymarking reappears. The path shortly merges with the one you were following earlier. Things become much easier as the path improves and runs on fairly level. Angling left its descends, crosses a (dry) streambed 15 **(2 hrs 20 mins)** then climbs as it arcs back to the right.

Passing through an area where olives have recently been planted the path angles steeply left then right to a higher course. Running on just beneath a track it descends to merge with another dirt track 16 by a marker post. Here turn left then after 20m cut left at fork to reach a metal gate 17. Passing through a gap to the left of the gate maintain your course across an olive grove then after 30m drop down to a lower terrace to pick up the continuation of the path which exits the grove past a metal post marked with a splash of yellow paint. The path angles gradually left as Istán comes into view. Passing beneath a rock face then traversing a scree 18 the path drops steeply down as a weird villa comes into sight down beneath you.

Crossing another (dry) streambed you pass a sign prohibiting the hunting of rabbits. Descending steeply once again the path cuts behind La Casa de Diego Rosa then drops down to meet with a broad dirt track 19. Angle left along the track through the olive groves towards Istán. At a point where the track loops hard right be ready to cut left 20 on a narrow path which zigzags down to the road 21. Here cut left and retrace your footsteps back to the Plaza de Andalucía 1.
(3 hrs 35 mins)

Distance: 15 kms **Time Required:** 4 hours **Rating:** Medium
Total Height Gain: 350m **Map:** IGN 1:50000 Marbella 1065 (15-45)
Ⓦ **Water:** no springs along the way so take plenty

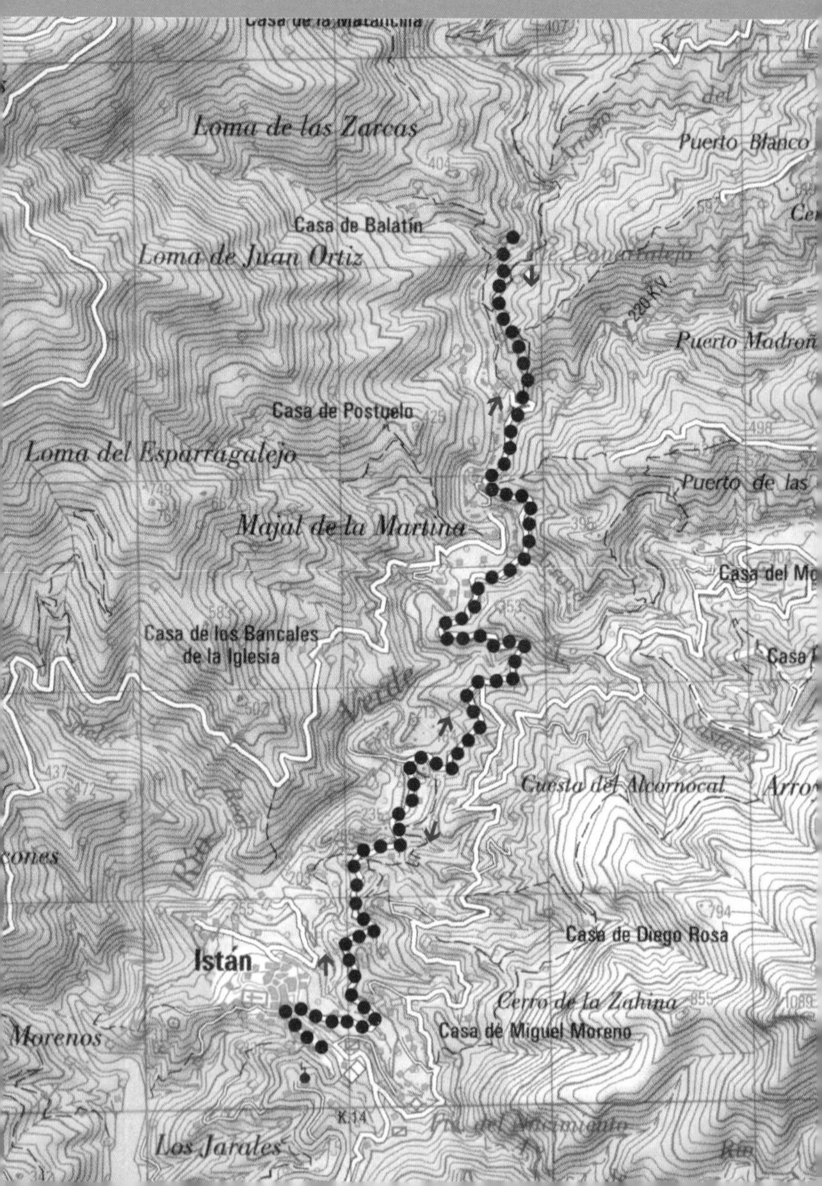

2 Istán to the Río Verde & the Charco del Canalón rock pool

Overview

This easy there-and-back walk leads north from the pretty village of Istán to the beautiful river pool El Charco del Canalón, a great spot for a dip during the summer months. The walk first leads you through the irrigated terraces that lie just beyond the village: since Moorish times they have been irrigated by an intricate series of water channels or *acequias* fed by the waters of the Río Molinos. Angling north you cut through a swathe of avocado plantations before descending to the valley floor of the Río Verde. Here you follow a track along its eastern side before crossing to the west bank via stepping stones to reach the Charco del Canalón. From here you can head further up the river (see end of walk) but you'll need to wade along a water channel for a few hundred metres so this option is really only enjoyable in summer. Set time aside at the beginning of the walk to visit Istán's diminuitive main square where there are a couple of cheap-and-cheerful bars for a *café con leche*. It feels a thousand miles from the fast-and-frantic *Costa* which is just a dozen kilometres down the road.

The Walk

The walk begins in the Plaza de Andalucía next to the Istán *Ayuntamiento* which you'll see on your left as you arrive from the coast ①. From here cut left and head in towards the village centre passing by an esplanade with benches looking out to the valley to the village's west. Cutting right past a ceramic plaque marked *Istán* you reach a three way junction. Here pass right of Bar Rincón de Curro and drop down a flight of steps to the Unicaja bank ② then cut right and drop down to a junction.

Here, turning right, you leave the last village houses behind as you head east along a track with fences to either side. After 350m the track angles left and crosses a ford: you can cross via the concrete footbridge to one side 3. Climbing in a northerly direction you pass a high breeze block wall as the track cuts past thick stands of prickly pears, running more or less parallel to the Río Verde which is down to your left.

Passing the green gates of Casa Los Abuelos the track descends then crosses a (dry) watercourse 4 where it angles left then climbs past a white building with twin porthole windows. Gently descending, with great views out into the valley to your left, the track runs on through avocado groves before passing above a small white building with a statue of Saint Anthony 5. Looping across the course of a (dry) streambed the track angles left before climbing up to meet with a broader track 6. **(40 mins)**

Angle left and head down the track to the floor of the valley then follow the track on north parallel to the river. After passing by an area where cars can park then crossing the Arroyo Bohornoque you reach a junction 7. Here cut right at a sign *Charco Canalón* up a steep concrete track. Reaching a metal gate angle left then climb a narrow path to meet again with the track. Turn left. Climbing gently, sticking to the main track, Istán comes into view back to the south. As the track begins to descend back towards the river a sandy-coloured house comes into sight to the north. Crossing a (dry) streambed via a concrete section 8 the track bears right and climbs before angling back left and passing above the sandy-coloured house beyond which you reach a fork 9. **(1 hr 15 mins)**

Cut right following a sign *Ruta 5 Casa El Balatín*. As the track arcs left you reach another fork 10. Take the lower branch which descends through pines and cork oaks to the Río Verde which

you cross via stepping stones or by slipping off your boots and wading through ⑪. Beyond the river continue up the track for 75m then cut right ⑫ along a narrow path signposted *Charco del Canalón*. Reaching a first fork take the left hand option which crosses a (dry) streambed. Cutting right at this point you come to the Charco del Canalón which has been dammed up with rocks and fed by a tumbling 5m cascade of water ⑬. It's a perfect place for a dip. **(1 hr 30 mins)** From here retrace your footsteps to Istán and the starting point of the walk ①.
(3 hrs 5 mins)

If you're looking for a more adventurous walk which involves a wade along a water channel, continue up the left side of the Río Verde. You shortly find yourself following a narrow water channel. Where the channel angles right towards the edge of the rock face above the river cut left up a narrow path which climbs steeply before dropping back down to the water channel ⑭. From here you can wade along the channel for about 350m to reach a point where the river has been dammed. Shortly beyond is another beautiful river pool ⑮ where you're certain not to encounter another soul. Add half an hour up and down if you intend to wade the channel!

Distance: 4 kms **Time Required:** 2.5 hours **Rating:** Easy/Medium
Total Height Gain: 275m **Map:** IGN 1:50000 Marbella 1065 (15-45)
Ⓦ **Water:** no springs along the way so take plenty

3 Istán: Reservoir Circuit via El Camino de la Cuesta & San Miguel Chapel

Overview

The *Camino de la Cuesta* would once have led down to the Río Verde but since the building of a dam some 5kms south of Istán it now leads you down to the edge of the Pantano de la Concepción reservoir. The descent is by way of a steep, stony track which picks up the old footpath just before you reach the water's edge. The next part of the walk is the highlight of the circuit as you follow an old *cañada* (glossary) parallel to the water's edge before climbing steeply up to the A7176. Another steep ascent leads you past the mountain chapel of San Miguel to reach a higher track which you follow back northwards to the village. This is a well marked route (yellow and white P.R. stripes and posts) and were you to read through these notes before setting out you could slip this book back in your pack and concentrate more on the lovely views out across the reservoir. I've graded this very short circuit as *Easy/Medium* because of the steep pull up from the reservoir to the road.

The Walk

The walk begins in the Plaza de Andalucía next to the Istán *Ayuntamiento* (town hall) which you'll see on your left as you arrive from the coast ①. From here cut left and head in towards the village centre passing by an esplanade with benches looking out to the valley to the village's west. After passing a ceramic sign for *Istán* you reach a 3 way junction in front of Bar Rincón de Curro. Here turn left ② to reach a square then exit via Calle Río. Angling right you reach a junction where there's a map of the walk you'll be following ③.

Turn left following a sign I*stán/Camino de la Cuesta/Ermita*

PRA–137 along a steep concrete road which loops steeply down towards the reservoir. At the point where the track ends 4 continue on down a path whose original cobbing is visible in parts. Reaching a junction close to the water's edge 5 cut hard left along a more overgrown path which arcs round the edge of a gully then crosses a streambed 6 **(25 mins)** before running on parallel to the edge of the reservoir. Climbing slightly away from the water the path enters a stand of pines then crosses a concrete bridge 7. Still climbing steadily the path widens to become a track which descends and crosses a second (dry) streambed via another concrete bridge 8. Shortly you reach a track that leads down to a house next to the reservoir 9. **(50 mins)**

Here turn left and follow the track up towards the Marbella to Istán road. Views now open out towards the western flank of La Concha. Looping hard left you reach the road 10. **(1 hr 5 mins)** Turn left towards Istán then after 30m cut right at a sign

PRA –137 Istán and a second one *Ermita de San Miguel* 11. 25m in from the road you reach a fork. Here cut right (that's after angling left to visit the Ermita) and climb a steep track which soon reaches a junction with a broader track 12. Turn left then at the next junction bear right following a sign for *Istán* and head on past several rural properties. Looping past a white building 13 the track becomes concreted as it loops to the left and passes Hotel Los Altos de Istán. 20m past the hotel cut right down a loose, stony path to a lower road. Cut left along the road towards the village for 60m then branch right 14 along a broad footpath. Passing a water deposit, an aviary, the *Fuente del Pobre* spring then another aviary the path angles back to the road. Here bear right and continue down past the municipal football pitch and pool to a *Stop* sign. Cut left then at the next junction right to return to the start point of the walk, the Plaza de Andalucía 1. **(1 hr 40 mins)**

Distance: 15.5 kms **Time Required:** 6 hours **Rating:** Difficult
Total Height Gain: 925m **Map:** IGN 1:50000 Marbella 1065 (15-45)
Ⓦ **Water:** no springs along the way so take plenty

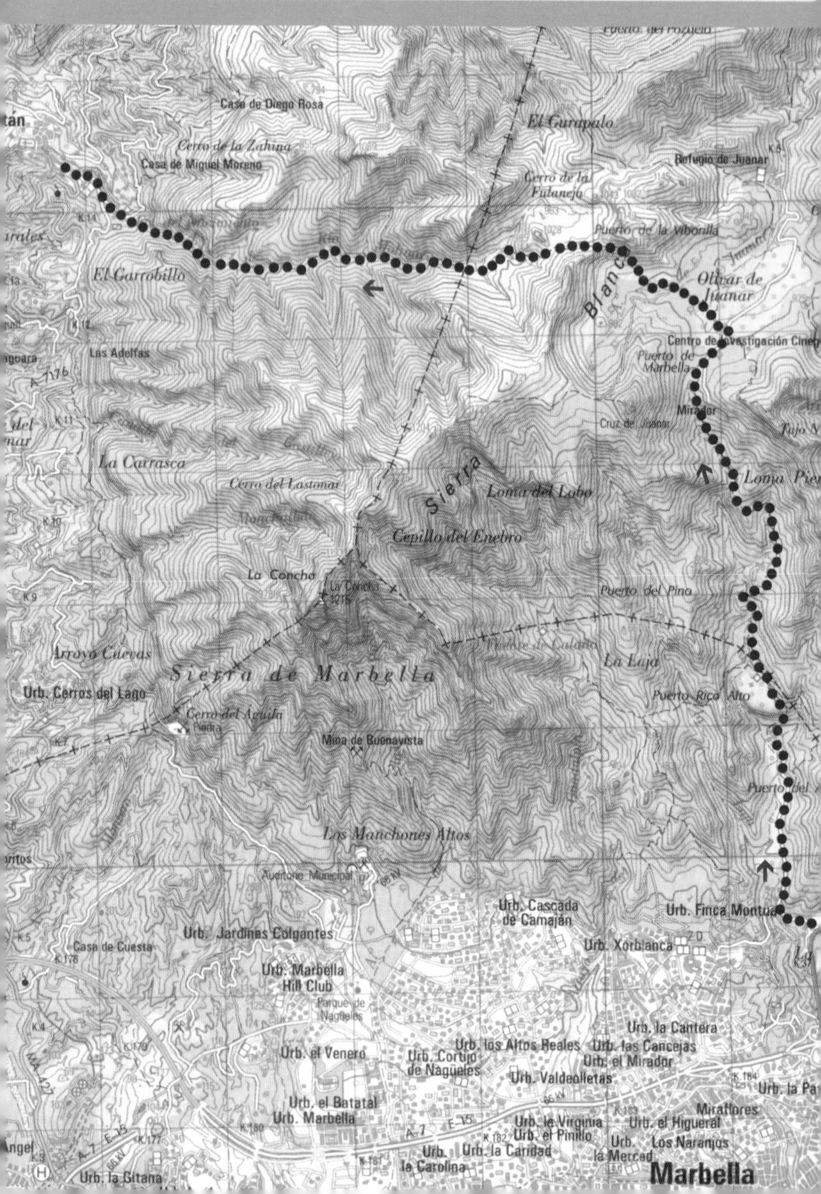

4 Marbella to Istán via the Mirador del Macho Montés & Río Molinos

Overview

Although this walk begins at the northern reaches of Marbella and close to the coastal motorway within minutes you'll find yourself in wild mountain scenery. After a few kilometres of fairly level walking there's a long, steady climb towards the towering peak of the Cruz de Juanar. Reaching a forestry track a short diversion takes you to the viewpoint of the *Macho Montés* from where you're treated to a giddy view down to the Mediteranean coastline. From here you cut back past the east flank of Cruz de Juanar then climb a stony path to the walk's highest point, *Puerto de la Viborilla,* where vast views open out towards the peaks of the Sierra de las Nieves. From here you have a long descent down the Río Molinos valley to Istán, much of it along the riverbed itself. At first it's fairly hard going but the path becomes clearer as you reach a spectacular section of the Molino gorge. Parts of the path are a little overgrown so pack long trousers and don't attempt the route if heavy rain is predicted. The *Difficult* grading is not so much for the distance but rather takes into account the fairly demanding descent down the Molinos valley.

Getting to the beginning of the walk

From the A7 motorway exit for Marbella/Ojén in A355. Continue on towards Ojén via two roundabouts then turn left at a sign for Cementerio where there's parking space to your right.

Returning to the beginning of the walk

Taxi approx €20. Tel: 649 149 005 or 686 262 481
Buses depart from the stop in front of the Town Hall at 16h and 19.45h.

The Walk

With your back to the cemetery car park turn right along a tarmac road following a sign for *La Cascada* 1. Just before you reach La Nueva Kaskada restaurant 2 cut right and climb northwards passing the ramshackle building of Casa Marqués de Guaro then the forlorn-looking entrance to Finca Minza Manzah al Kamd where a signboard details the route you'll be following. The tarmac surface turns to dirt as you pass a metal barrier: you'll see P.R. waymarking. Up ahead the nipple-like peak of El Juanar comes into sight as the track runs on between the pine, carob and eucalyptus parallel to the bed of El Vertiente de la Laja. Reaching a fork 3 and branching right you pass a concrete drain chamber then climb a very steep bulldozed track. Swinging hard left it reaches a small white hut 4 fed by a water pipe. **(30 mins)**

Here cut right up a narrow stony path which zigzags steeply upwards, cobbled in parts. To your left you'll now see a

spectacular overhang, a popular destination for rock climbers. Zigzagging on past a hollow in the rock face, at times close to the water pipe, the path levels as it bears left through low-growing vegetation to reach the back wall of the ruined Cortijo Rico Alto 5. Passing right of the ruin after 100m you reach a signpost *Puerto Rico Alto* 6. **(45 mins)** Continue straight ahead, following signs for *Juanar* and *Casa del Pino*. The path threads its way through thicker vegetation: a (dry) stream runs to your left. Angling left then right the path passes by two paths cutting down left. Keep right at both junctions and continue ascending across more open terrain: cairns mark the way. There's no missing the path as it loops up through the pines on the right side of the valley. After a long, steady climb you reach a more open area where angling slightly right you come to a broad forestry track 7. **(1 hr 50 mins)**

Here cut right following a sign *Mirador*. After 200m you reach a first mirador. Here angle left to reach the *Mirador del Macho*

Montés 8 from where there are stunning views. Up above you is a statue of the eponymous *Macho Montés*. Retrace your steps to waypoint 7 7 then continue straight on. Passing by the mesh fence surrounding Cortijo de Juanar (a research centre for the *Cabra Hispánica*) after 100m you reach a junction 9. Here cut left away from the track, back towards the Cortijo, then angle hard right down through an olive grove for 100m to a 4 way junction 10. Here cutting left into a stand of pines you come to a 3 way junction 11. **(2 hrs 15 mins)**

Turn right following a sign *PRA-167 Istán*. A broad path leads through the pines before breaking out into open terrain. Passing right of a concrete water installation the path zigzags steeply upwards, looser underfoot. Crossing the saddle of *Puerto de la Viborilla* 12 its levels as you cross into the next valley as views open out towards the Sierra de las Nieves. Careful! Descending for some 100m you reach an indistinct junction. Ignoring a path angling hard down to the right, head straight on. Crossing a swathe of denuded rock you pick up cairns which guide you on towards Istán. Passing left of a rocky pinncale you gradually descend into the upper reaches of the Molinos valley. The path at first cuts down the valley's left side before descending to cross a tributary of the Molinos 13. It now becomes more overgrown but cairns guide you down to the river where you cross to its northern bank 14. **(3 hrs)**

Head on down the riverbed, threading your way through the rocks and occasionally cutting left or right to an easier, higher course: you'll see P.R. waymarking. Angling left away from the Río Molinos you cross one of its tributaries 15. The path now runs above the river's left bank then crosses a low bluff where a big vista opens out to the West. Crossing another oleander-lined tributary of the Molinos after 150m the path drops back down to the river 16. From here a spectacular descent begins as the gorge narrows and you clamber down over the rocks:

you'll need to use your hands once or twice. Passing through an incongrous metal gate 17 **(4 hrs 10 mins)** continue down the river then angle up its left bank and pass left of a dam spanning the riverbed. The path merges with a broad, stony track which passes an open-fronted white building as Istán comes into view. Angling right you pass a sign pointing back towards Ojén then reach a junction with a concrete road 18.

Here bear right, pass Hotel Los Altos de Istán, then continue down past the municipal football pitch and pool until you reach a *Stop* sign 19. Cut left then at the next junction right to reach the Plaza de Andalucía and the Istán *Ayuntamiento* 20.
(4 hrs 30 mins) The bus stop is on the left just before you reach the square.

Distance: 12.5 kms (up & down) **Time Required:** 5/6 hours **Rating:** Medium/ Difficult **Total Height Gain:** 600m **Map:** IGN 1:50000 Marbella 1065 (15-45)
Ⓦ **Water:** no springs along the way so take plenty

5 Ascent of La Concha from the Refugio de Juanar

Overview

Marbella without La Concha would be like Cape Town without Table Mountain. Wherever you are in the town you catch sight of it's seductively symmetrical form rising volcano-like above the coast, its appearance constantly changing as the sun slips round the horizon. The views from its summit are mesmerising: east and west along the coast, south to Morocco and all the way to the Sierra Nevada on a clear day. This classic route up the mountain numbers amongst Andalucía's most special walking adventures. You approach the peak from its northern side, setting out from Refugio de Juanar (it's a wonderful place to overnight: see *Best Sleeps* in the general section). From here the walk leads you past a hidden, flat-bottomed valley before you climb steeply up through pine forest towards the Cruz de Juanar. After crossing a first col you follow a ridge for most of the way to La Concha: on this section you'll occasionally feel safer using your hands as well as your feet. That said, so long as you have a reasonable head for heights you shouldn't find the walk intimidating: a friend regularly takes her teenage kids up and down this route and even sleeps out on the summit.

Getting to the beginning of the walk

From the A7 motorway exit for Marbella/Ojén on the A355. Continue on towards Ojén via two roundabouts. Passing by two turnings off right towards the village cut left from the A355 at a sign Refugio de Juanar along the MA5300 which you follow all the way to the Refugio.

The Walk

The walk begins at the entrance of the car park of El Refugio de Juanar ①. From here descend 100m to a junction ② then turn right at a sign *Mirador*. Looping up through the pines you reach a parking area ③ then pass a green metal gate. Passing by a sign pointing left towards Ojén continue along the track following a sign *GR243.1 Istán*. Head on along the eastern edge of a flat-bottomed valley where an abandoned olive grove is bordered to both sides by thick stand of pines. After passing a ruined stone hut you reach a sign *PR-A 168 La Concha* pointing right off the track ④. **(20 mins)**

Here cut right away from the track towards the green mesh fence of Cortijo de Juanar then angle hard right down through an olive grove for 100m to a 4 way junction ⑤. Cutting left into a stand of pines you come to a 3 way junction ⑥. Here angle left following another sign *PR-A 168 La Concha*. The pines thin out as the path becomes sandier and climbs more steeply: you'll soon see a fence running to your left. To your left the Cruz de Juanar is visible as you climb on up the left side of the valley. Reaching the top of the ridge head straight on for a few metres ⑦ then angle right and continue along the ridge, now heading almost due west between low-growing ilex oaks. Big views now open out to the south and to the Mediterranean. Having run just left of the ridge the path cuts up right to its highest point and passes a large cairn ⑧ **(1 hr 10 mins)** before descending for a short distance, now just north of the ridge. Cairns mark the way as well as P.R. waymarking.

Angling slightly left the path passes beneath a steep cliff face, El Salto del Lobo, where there are steep drops to the right: care should be taken on this section. Zigzagging steeply up left (a hands-on approach at this point will be useful) it then drops steeply back down to a more level path which runs on towards La Concha. Climbing back to the top of the ridge ⑧ the sea and

Marbella again come into view as the path angles right, adopting a southwesterly course. Cairns and P.R. waymarking still mark your path as you head on just south of the ridge before angling back up to the top of the ridge (once again you may feel safer taking an occasional hand hold) as you head on round the south side of the Cerro del Lastonar. A massive panorama opens out to the south as as you reach a cairn where you'll see blue and red stripes on a rock (10). *At this point you're actually a few metres higher than the official summit of La Concha.*

From here angle down left following cairns and red and blue waymarking, sticking close to the ridgetop. The Istán reservoir comes into view to the west. The path runs a few metres beneath the ridge, on its southern side, before cutting up to a 3 way marker post (11). **(1 hr 45 mins)** Here carry straight on following a sign *La Concha 15 mins* along the ridge to a large cairn (12). Here the path angles right, descends, then picks up the continuation of the ridge before climbing steeply once more (where you may again feel safer using your hands from time to time: there are steep drops to your left). Red and blue flashes still mark the way and lead you up to the summit of La Concha (1215m) (13). **(1 hr 55 mins)** It's worth continuing on along the ridge for 60m to the southern edge of the Concha from where the views down to Marbella are even better. A trig point here marks 1203m (14). After gulping in the amazing panorama retrace your footsteps back to the Refugio (1).
(3 hrs 45 mins)

Distance: 8 kms **Time Required:** 3/3.5 hours **Rating:** Easy/Medium
Total Height Gain: 525m **Map:** IGN 1:50000 Marbella 1065 (15-45)
Ⓦ **Water:** El Pozuelo spring @ 50 mins though it can run dry in summer

6 Los Cuchillos Circuit out from the Refugio de Juanar

Overview

This shortish circular route takes you round the rocky massif that lies just to the north of the Refugio de Juanar with an optional 45 minute diversion to the top of the jagged ridge of Los Cuchillos, El Picacho de Castillejos (1238m). Even though I've graded the walk as *Easy/Medium* don't imagine that this is in any way a dull route. At different stages of the walk you'll be treated to massive views towards all four points of the compass and the terrain through which you'll be passing feels wild and untamed: the chances of seeing ibex here are very good. The path up to the top of Los Cuchillos isn't that clear but it's a relatively short, easy climb with just a bit of hands on: provided you keep your wits about you it's easy enough to plot a course. An added bonus is that the walk leads you through a stand of *pinsapo* pines (glossary), one of the Sierra de Ojén's botanical jewels. I haven't marked the Pozuelo spring with a water symbol because in summer it can slow to little more than a trickle. The path is slightly overgrown in parts so this is another walk where you'd be best to slip a pair of long trousers or gaiters into your day pack.

Getting to the beginning of the walk

From the A7 motorway exit for Marbella/Ojén on the A355. Continue on towards Ojén via two roundabouts. Passing by two turnings off right towards the village cut left from the A355 at a sign Refugio de Juanar along the MA5300 which you follow all the way to the Refugio.

The Walk

The walk begins at the entrance of the car park of El Refugio de Juanar ①. From here descend 100m to a junction ② then turn left along the MA5300. Descending gently, at a point where the metal barrier to your left has been clad with wood, you reach a signboard for *Ruta del Pozuelo* and a second ceramic sign *Senda de José Lima* ③. **(10 mins)** Here cut left and follow a path which zigzags down and crosses the Arroyo de Juanar ④ then climbs through low-growing Mediterranean scrub. Views open out towards the east and the north, and you shortly get your first sight of the Mediterranean before crossing a low col ⑤. **(30 mins)**

Beyond this breach the path angles hard left, now adopting a more westerly course: you now have a ravine to your right. Descending the path cuts across a (dry) streambed ⑥ then begins to climb more steeply before crossing back to the stream's left bank. Heading on up towards the jagged ridge of Los Cuchillos you reach the spring of El Pozuelo, marked by a rusting metal sign ⑦. Here the path swings left and resumes its ascent through a swathe of more mature pines and evergreen oaks. Reaching the top of the pass, El Puerto del Pozuelo, you arrive at a junction ⑧. **(1 hr)**

Here cut right (unless you don't intend to climb the Cuchillos) and follow a narrow path up through low-growing scrub. Views open out to the west towards the Sierra Bermeja. Reaching a rock field on the western side of the Cuchillos the path bears slightly left, running more or less along the top of the treeline, more overgrown and loose in parts, heading straight towards a steep rock face. Some 70m before you reach this west-facing face angle right at a cairn (please add to it) ⑨ and continue up a steep, loose path: you'll occasionally need to use your hands. The path zigzags indistinctly up: it's a question of following your nose at this stage. Big vistas begin to open out towards the

north and northeast. Angling slightly right head up to a solitary evergreen oak 10 beyond which is stand of *pinsapos*. Here swing hard right then, heading almost due east, pick your way across the rocks - there's no clear path but there are cairns - to reach the highest point of Los Cuchillos, El Picacho de Castillejos (1238m) 11. **(1 hr 20 mins)**

From here retrace your footsteps back to waypoint 8 8 **(1 hr 40 mins)** where you should bear right in a southwesterly direction. Descending gently the path then runs once more uphill and cuts through a stand of mature *pinsapo* pines. Shortly a fence runs over to your left. As you round a bluff the fence cuts up left 12. Here angle right then arc hard round to the left. Descending through the last of the pinsapos you come to a flatter area. Here the path angles left 13 as the northern flank of La Concha comes into view. You pass through a more denuded area, evidence of a recent forest fire. Passing through a breach in the rocky hillside 14 the path becomes sandier as it zigzags steeply down before climbing to meet with a track 15 and a junction. Maintaining your course take the lower fork and follow the stony track as it loops back down towards El Refugio de Juanar. Cutting into the thick swathe of trees that surround the Refugio you pass a chain blocking vehicle access (sometimes left open) then angle right to reach the road. Angling left you return to the start point of the walk 1. **(2 hrs 30 mins)**

Distance: 13.5 kms **Time Required:** 5 hours **Rating:** Medium/Difficult
Total Height Gain: 950m **Map:** IGN 1:50000 Marbella 1065 (15-45)
Ⓦ **Water:** no springs along the way so take plenty

7 Ojén to the Cruz de Juanar via El Puerto de Marbella

Overview

The Cruz de Juanar's pyramidal peak is one of the most distinctive landmarks as you look north from the Costa del Sol. The peak is topped by a cross and a shrine to the Virgin to which an annual pilgrimage takes place. Legend tells that a fishing boat was lost in heavy seas and dense fog when part of the sky miraculously opened to reveal the Juanar, allowing the sailors to plot a safe course back to port. The first part of the walk is the most challenging as you climb away from Ojén up the old footpath that leads across the *sierra* to Istán. Reaching a broad forestry track you cut south past the Cortijo de Juanar before climbing steeply up to Juanar's summit (1184m) and to its cross and shrine. The views on a clear day are magnificent, encompassing a vast sweep of the coast, north Africa as well as the high peaks of the Sierra Blanca. You might prefer to shorten the walk by an hour and a half by setting out from El Refugio de Juanar. In this case follow the first part of the route which describes the ascent of La Concha as far as the Cortijo de Juanar then instead of cutting right towards La Concha pick up these instructions at waypoint 9.

The Walk

The walk begins from the pretty main square of Ojén next to a fountain in front of the church of La Encarnación (1). With your back to the church turn right and leave the square along Calle Cruz then angle left along Calle Almona and climb several flights of steps. Angling right the steps meet a road next to a pedestrian crossing (2). Cross the road, bear right, then cut left up Calle Fuengirola. At the end of this street climb a steep

flight of granite steps to reach a tarmac road. Here angle left up Paseo del Castillo. Following the road where it angles right you reach a *No Entry* sign. Here head straight up Calle Azahar for 40m, cut right up a steep flight of steps, then turn left and head on past Edificio Sierrasol. Reaching the end of the street (3) continue straight ahead along a path that runs just to the left of an irrigation channel. You shortly pass a ceramic plate set in the concrete depicting…Montreal!

The path runs on between a number of irrigated *huertas* (glossary). Passing a small house with a yellow chimney and a green gate cross to the right side of the water channel. 60m after passing above a ruined building cut right (4) up a narrow path which zigzags steeply up then angles right, parallel to a streambed which you shortly cross via a bridge made of metal scaffolding. Bearing left follow a concreted track up to a junction with a broader track (5). Here turn right then at the next junction

cut left up a track by a sign *Reserva Andaluza de Caza* 6. After 75m pass through a black gate to the left of a larger one blocking vehicle access to reach *El Parque Botánico El Cerezal*. You now pick up P.R. waymarking. Following the track parallel to a stream you pass a series of signboards about the park's flora then a picnic area. Passing left of a white building you reach a junction. Here bear left down a track to a gate 7 **(20 mins)** beyond which you cut through a tunnel beneath the A355 then pick up a pretty path which climbs up the course of a stream, looping from one side to the other.

You're now on the old path that linked Ojén to Istán across the middle of the Sierra Blanca. Climbing steadily upwards the jagged flank of Cerro Nicolás rises steeply up ahead of you. Reaching a marker post set in a large cairn 8 the footpath, sandier now, angles right. You may spot ibex on this section. Levelling then descending for a few metres the track resumes its

ascent up through the forest. Levelling a second time the path then runs down to meet with a broad forestry track ⑨.
(1 hr 10 mins)

Here turn left following a sign *GR243.1 Istán* along the eastern edge of a flat-bottomed valley where an abandoned olive grove is bordered to both sides by thick stands of pines. Up ahead of you the peak of the Cruz de Juanar is now visible. After passing a ruined stone hut the broad track reaches a sign for *Marbella*. Here head straight on past El Cortijo de Juanar: it's now an investigative centre for the study of the park's resident population of ibex. The track begins to climb and passes a wooden post topped with a white arrow. Reaching a point 10m beyond a rubbish bin where the track bears hard left (you've reached what is marked on some maps as El Puerto de Marbella) cut right along an indistinct path ⑩. Maintaining your course across a flat sandy area for some 50m you come to a fork. Here angle right (ignoring P.R. waymarking which marks the path down to Marbella) along a narrow path that cuts through the pines. Bearing left it soon begins to loop up the eastern side of the Cruz de Juanar through thick clumps of rosemary, gorse, cistus and lavendar. Climbing higher the vegetation becomes more sparse as the path runs across sections of bare rock and scree. Angling left you reach the Cruz de Juanar and, just behind it, a shrine to the Virgin ⑪. **(1 hr 50 mins)**

With your back to the cross angle slightly right along the ridge top then after some 25m cut left through the rocks ⑫ to pick up the beginning of the path that leads down the western flank of the Cruz de Juanar. Zigzagging steeply down through scrubby vegetation the path levels as you reach a three way junction and a col ⑬. Here cut right (heading straight on along the ridge would lead you up towards the Concha) and continue your descent through low-growing oaks, gorse and cistus. Soon you'll see a fence running to your right. Levelling, the path widens, then runs on through a stand of towering pine trees. Reaching a three way junction 14 cut right. The path breaks out of the pines then runs across a grove of olives to reach a 4 way junction 15. Here cut right up to Cortijo de Juanar's green mesh fence then angle hard back left along a broader path which leads you back to the dirt track you followed earlier in the walk 16. Here cut left and retrace your steps back down to Ojén 1. **(3 hrs 35 mins)**

Costa del Sol: Sierra de Mijas

Walks close to Mijas, Benalmádena & Alhaurín

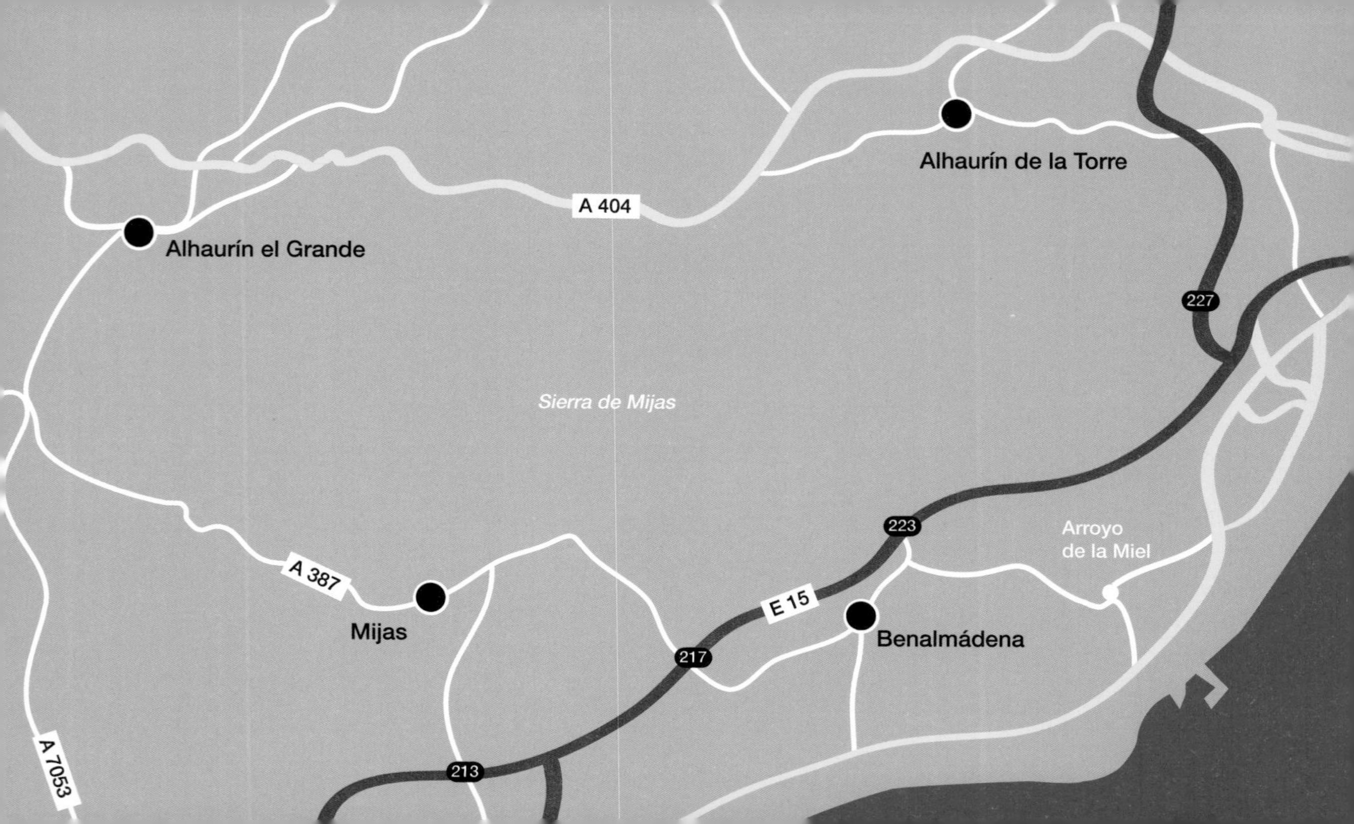

Alhaurín de la Torre
A 404
Alhaurín el Grande
227
Sierra de Mijas
223
Arroyo
de la Miel
A 387
Mijas
E 15
Benalmádena
217
213
A 7053

Costa del Sol: Sierra de Mijas

At the southernmost tip of the Cordillera Bética the compact massif of the Sierra de Mijas rises like a defiant buttress above the burgeoning villages, golf courses and motorways of the central Costa del Sol, a green lung between the Mediterranean and the Guadalhorce valley. At present it has the purely honorific title of *Complejo Serrano de Interés Ambiental* but within the next few years will become a *Paraje Natural* with the corresponding kudos and additional funding the title confers. The mild temperatures of this part of the coast, with an average of some 3000 hours of sunshine per annum, ensure that you can walk comfortably here all year round with the possible exception of July and August.

If proximity to the coast has meant that the *sierra* has long been exploited for its mineral resources there are still wild tracts of forest and mountain to be explored, especially on its northern face. On all four sides the massif rises steeply up to 1000 metres or more and all walks described in this section involve steep sections of climbing. The network of footpaths is generally well maintained, waymarking has recently been added and the vegetation is surpisingly varied given its reduced surface area. If the fauna is less abundant than in other parts of the coastal mountains - you may be lucky enough to spot a genet, fox or roe deer - there are many resident raptors including imperial and booted eagles as well as the enormous eagle owl.

Since Roman times the mountainsides of the Sierra de Mijas have been quarried for dolomitic white marble. The material was highly sought after by the Patricians of Rome and the proximity of the mines to the sea meant that it could easily be shipped back to the Empire's capital. Lead, silver, iron and zinc were also all once mined whilst nowadays, on the north-facing slopes, the enormous quarry above Alhaurín still works the *sierra's* limestone outcrops for the production of cement and plaster. The quarry has been at the centre of a long-running dispute between local environmental groups and the owners and workers at the plant and its associated industries. There's no denying that the quarry has left a deep scar on the hillside above the village: the walks described in this guide give the quarried area a wide berth.

The region's vegetation is predominantly composed of reafforested swathes of Mediterranean pine with pockets of oak, carob and wild olive beneath which the predominant species are thyme, rosemary, fan palm and gorse. In the past the forests suffered greatly due to the charcoal production whilst proximity to the capital meant that it was exploited as a source of wood for construction. The dangers of the reafforestation of the middle part of the last century with fast-growing pine rather than indigenous species have recently been made manifest with two major forest fires on its southern flank. The land affected by the fire that swept through the *sierra* above Mijas in 2001 has made a fast recovery and walking here is once more enjoyable even though you do see many fallen trees.

At the southern fringe of the mountains are two of Málaga's prettiest villages, Benalmádena Pueblo and Mijas Pueblo, which should not be confused with the coastal settlements of the same name. The former has won accolades and prizes thanks to its recent prettification and the village should be first choice if you plan to stay in the area, especially now that a delightful sister hotel to La Fonda has been opened (see listings that follow).

BEST SLEEPS

Benalmádena Pueblo

La Posada €–€€
Tel: 952 448 273 Email: info@laposadabenalmadena.es
www.laposadabenalmadena.es
A fabulous small hotel in a quiet backstreet. Excellent value for money.

La Fonda €€–€€€
Tel: 952 569 047 Email: info@lafondabenalmadena.es
www.lafondabenalmadena.es
Great location at edge of village with views down to the Mediterranean.

Mijas Pueblo

El Escudo de Mijas €–€€
Tel: 952 591 100 Email: reservas@ el-escudo.com
www.el-escudo.com
Plum in the village centre, pretty rooms and good deals in low season.

Close to Cala de Mijas

El Águila €€
Tel: 611 607 543 Email: info@bedandbreakfastinandalucia.com
www.bedandbreakfastinandalucia.com
Great rooms, food and welcome. Overlooking La Cala Golf @ 20 mins from Mijas.

Taxis: Mijas 952 476 593, 952 478 288, Benamádena 952 441 545, Alhaurín de la Torre 952 410 444, Alhaurín El Grande 952 491 010

Distance: 12.5 kms **Time Required:** 5.5 hours **Rating:** Medium/Difficult
Total Height Gain: 775m **Map:** IGN 1:50000 Fuengirola 1066 (16-45)
Ⓦ **Water:** no springs along the way so take plenty

1 Mijas: Pico de Mijas Circuit via the Ermita del Calvario

Overview

This averagely challenging walk links in three of the local network of footpaths to make a more interesting circular route. Climbing steeply up from the village by way of a *Via Crucis* you pass the mountain chapel of the Ermita del Calvario. From here you have a steep climb of some 700m to the Pico de Mijas (1150m) which is easily recognised on the approach thanks to its spherical astronomical observatory, know to locals simply as *La Bola* ('The Ball'). If you plan to break for a picnic I recommend diverting a few hundred metres to the east to the top of a slightly lower peak which has a much wilder feel and the same panoramic views. On a clear day you'll see the eastern and western *Costa*, Gibraltar, Málaga, the Sierra de las Nieves and all the way to the distant Sierra Nevada. The return leg down from the Pico de Mijas is rather longer given that you're walking two sides of a triangle. A steep descent takes you back to the track which was created after the forest fire of a decade or so back. From here the path runs southwest before gradually angling round towards Mijas before leading you back to the Ermita del Calvario. On a few sections of the path you push past prickly gorse so slip a pair of long trousers or gaiters into your day pack.

Getting to the beginning of the walk

From the A7/E15 exit for Fuengirola/Mijas. Arriving in Mijas at a roundabout with three palm trees turn left and at the next roundabout take the A387 towards Coín/Alhaurín. After 1km you reach a parking area to your left, El Mirador de Mijas.

The Walk

The walk begins at the Mirador de Mijas ①. With your back to the village turn right along the road. After 150m cut left ② up a cobbled path passing a sign board depicting local footpaths. Following a *Via Crucis* upwards you reach a junction ③. Cut left following a sign *Ermita del Calvario*. 20m before the chapel turn right ④ and continue up a sandy path. Fallen trees are evidence of a forest fire that swept through about a decade ago. Looping up you reach another junction ⑤. Angle right following a sign *Ruta Puerto Málaga*. At the next junction ⑥ angle left, still following *Ruta Puerto Málaga*. The path zigzags steeply on up to reach a track ⑦. **(35 mins)**

Turn right along the track for 40m then cut left up the continuation of the path. Climbing on a northerly course you reach a junction ⑧. Here angle hard left following a sign *Pico de Mijas*. Crossing a low ridge the path angles left then right then descends. The Pico de Mijas and its observatory come into sight. Angling right to another junction ⑨ **(1 hr 15 mins)** bear right following another sign *Pico de Mijas*. After running due north the path crosses a (dry) streambed then adopts a more westerly course before crossing a second (dry) streambed. Red dots now mark the path which runs up towards the col just east of the Pico de Mijas. Reaching the ridge top by a small hut ⑩ angle left along a track for 100m to a 4 way junction. Here ⑪ cut left by a cairn up a steep path. Reaching a track angle left then right to reach the Pico de Mijas (1150m) and the observatory ⑫. **(2 hrs)** After taking in the extraordinary views retrace your footsteps back to the concrete hut at waypoint 10 ⑩. **15m beneath the hut you can cut along an indistinct path that after 225m leads up to another peak just to the east. It's wilder in feel than the Pico de Mijas and is great spot for a picnic ⑬.*

From the hut head back down the path you followed earlier to the junction at waypoint 9 9. **(2 hrs 35 mins)** Here cut right following a sign *Ruta de las Cañadas*. The path runs in a southwesterly direction before reaching another sign for *Ruta de las Cañadas* pointing back the way you've come 14. Angling left follow the path down to the track you crossed earlier in the walk 15.

Cut right along the track for 275m to a sign for *Ruta de las Cañadas* 16. Here cut left down a path which loops down across more denuded terrain. Adopting a westerly course it crosses a rocky ridge then swings right into the next ravine where, angling left, it crosses a (dry) streambed 17. After climbing for a short 19 distance the path angles left and adopts a southeasterly course before looping across another (dry) steambed. Soon you reach a fork and a sign pointing back the way you've come 18. **(3 hrs 20 mins)** Head straight on. Reaching another 3 way junction again carry straight on following a sign *Cruz de la Misión*. Reaching a stand of eucalyptus the path begins to climb. Levelling you pass a signboard about *caleras* (glossary) beyond which you cross a ridge as views open out to the sea. After climbing once more the path descends before crossing another (dry) streambed 20. **(3 hrs 50 mins)**

Angling right runs towards a rocky outcrop then zigzags steeply down to a sign post 21. Cut left along a broad track following a sign *Ruta Cruz de la Monte*. Reaching an abandoned quarry you come to fork. Here take the right option, passing just beneath a pylon then the quarry's graffiti-daubed buildings. The track, concreted now, climbs then angles right before narrowing to become a path. Passing beneath a beehive-shaped hut you shortly reach a 3 way junction 22. Keep straight ahead following a sign *Ermita del Calvario*. Reaching the chapel retrace your path to the start of the walk 1. **(4 hrs 30 mins)**

Distance: 12 kms **Time Required:** 4 hours **Rating:** Medium/Difficult
Total Height Gain: 550m **Map:** IGN 1:50000 Fuengirola 1066 (16-45)
Ⓦ **Water:** no springs along the way so take plenty

2 Mijas: Puerto de Málaga & Los Arenales Circuit

Overview

This circular walk out from Mijas could be a great introduction to the stunning mountain trails of the Sierra de Mijas. You're faced with a fairly tough climb during the first third of the walk as you follow the Cañada Gertrudis up the south-facing flank of the *sierra*. Reaching Puerto Málaga (it's not marked on the ING 1:50000 map) you cross to the northern side of the range. Here you encounter a radical change in vegetation as you descend through a thick stand of oaks interspersed with pines to reach a broad forestry track which you follow on towards the east. At this stage of the walk there are soaring vistas out across the Guadalhorce valley. After angling back south towards the Puerto de las Canteras you begin your descent back towards the sea. Passing by the Los Arenales quarry, now disused, you pick up a beautiful narrow path that leads down to the A368. From here you're faced with a section of road walking but within half an hour you'll be back at the start point of the walk.

Getting to the beginning of the walk

From the A7/E15 exit for Fuengirola/Mijas. Arriving in Mijas at a roundabout with three palm trees turn left and at the next roundabout take the A387 towards Coín/Alhaurín. After 1km you reach a parking area to the left, El Mirador de Mijas.

The Walk

The walk begins at the Mirador de Mijas (1). With your back to the village turn right along the road. After 150m cut left (2) up a cobbled path passing a sign board depicting local footpaths and a sign post for the route you'll be at first following, *PRA-171*. Following a *Via Crucis* upwards you reach a junction (3).

Continue straight ahead following a sign *Ruta Cañada Gertrudis*. Soon you cross a (dry) streambed. The path climbs on in a northerly direction. Levelling it swings hard left ④ then climbs to reach a junction ⑤. Cutting right and climbing for 75m you come to a broad forestry track ⑥. Here turn right at a sign *Ruta Puerto Málaga* then after 20m cut left up a path by a blue marker post ⑦. **(50 mins)**

Climbing steeply towards the north you come to another junction ⑧. Head straight ahead following a sign *Puerto Málaga* and a second P.R. sign for *Puerto de las Ovejas*. Angling east you reach the Puerto Málaga pass ⑨ and a damaged information board about the *Cabra Montés*. Views open out towards the north. Passing a trig point the path descends through a stand of low-growing holly oaks and pines to a broad forestry track ⑩. Here turn right and follow the track on in a northeasterly direction. Angling hard right after 350m you reach a fork ⑪. Here angle left along the main track which runs on through the pines. After 1250m the track bears right, adopting a southerly course, before it hairpins back to the left ⑫. **(1 hr 45 mins)**

20m beyond a steel wire stretching between two posts (sometimes down) you reach a junction ⑬. Cut right along a broad track for 35m to reach another junction. Taking the left fork you descend to the quarry of Los Arenales, marked on the ING map as *Áridos* ⑭. Fuengirola and the sea come into view as a wall runs to your left. Reaching a gap in the wall ⑮ cut left down a narrow path. Descending for some 200m you pass right of an old mine shaft ⑯. Cairns mark your way. Angling left the path drops down to the quarry access track ⑰. **(2 hrs 20 mins)**

Here cut left. The track soon bears hard left. After some 200m, just as the track angles right, cut right ⑱ at a small cairn and continue down a narrow path which drops down to a (dry)

streambed. Following it down for 50m you reach a low wall spanning its course 19. Cut right and continue on down parallel to the stream's right bank, following an old terracotta water pipe. Passing a rocky outcrop your path merges with a broader one which drops down to the right of the stream. Angling left it runs towards an old *calera* (glossary). 10m before you reach the *calera* cutting right you meet again with the track 20. Cutting right down the track you reach the A368 road 21. **(2 hrs 45 mins)**

Turn right and prepare yourself for a spell of road walking. Passing by *Urbanización La Noria* you reach a roundabout 22 and Mijas. Bear right to a second roundabout then angle left at a sign *Centro Urbano.* Passing a line of restaurants you reach a fork in the road next to a small fountain. Here angle right. When you reach the village *Consultorio* cut right up Cañada Gertrudis. Follow the street round to the left then at house no. 71 angle right. At the end of the street, reaching Villa Juan Antonio, cut right up a flight of steps. At the first junction cut left then once more right to return to the Mirador de Mijas 1. **(3 hrs 15 mins)**

Distance: 9.5 kms **Time Required:** 3/3.5 hours **Rating:** Medium/Difficult
Total Height Gain: 675m **Map:** IGN 1:50000 Fuengirola 1066 (16-45)
Ⓦ **Water:** spring at waypoint 8 @ 50 mins

3 Alhaurín El Grande: Puerto de la Encina Circuit via La Cañada de las Palomas

Overview

Of all the walks in the Mijas Sierra this stunning half day figure-of-eight walk numbers amongst the most memorable. The first section of the walk follows the beautiful Cañada de las Palomas, an ancient thoroughfare which climbs up towards the steep northern face of the Sierra de Mijas via the stream of the same name. Reaching a *Casa Forestal* (glossary) the walk takes on a different tempo as you follow a spectacular mountain footpath that contours round the southern and eastern flanks of the towering massif of the Tajo del Caballo. Reaching the high pass of Puerto de la Encina you have a choice. My preferred option, which adds 3 kms to the route and 40 minutes to the timings, is to continue to the summit of the Pico de Mijas. From here, on a clear day, you're treated to a heartstopping panorama that encompasses the mountains of North Africa, a vast swathe of the Mediterranean coast and range after range of the Subbaetic system. From the Encina pass another beautiful footpath leads you back down to the Casa Forestal from where the remainder of the walk is by way of forestry tracks.

Getting to the beginning of the walk

Arriving in Alhaurín El Grande from the coast follow the ringroad to the east side of town to a roundabout with a large cross in the middle. Here cut right along Camino de Málaga. Head straight across a roundabout next to a BP petrol station for 75m to a ceramic sign to the left of the road marked Alhaurín El Grande, El Pueblo que yo soñé. There's parking space to either side of the sign.

The Walk

The walk begins next to a ceramic sign for *Alhaurín El Grande, El Pueblo que yo soñé* ❶. Cross the road and head along a narrow road that cuts in towards the mountains following a sign Cañada de las Palomas. The tarmac road climbs steadily. Reaching a fork ❷ angle left, continuing along the old *cañada* (glossary) which runs parallel to the road you've just left as it follows the course of streambed upwards. As you climb higher the valley narrows down to become a gorge. Passing a cave the path cuts up to a higher level before dropping back down to the streambed where it winds on through the rocks. Passing an old *calera* (glossary) ❸ the path meets with a broad dirt track ❹. **(25 mins)**

Head straight across the track and continue up the (dry) streambed, passing from one bank to the other. A path runs down from the left to join yours. Soon the path climbs up to another broad track ❺. Angle left across the track and climb a

steep bank to pick up the footpath once more. Reaching a wider path 6 bear right and climb past a stand of cypress trees to reach a *Casa Forestal* (glossary) 7. Head round to the eastern side of the building then drop down a footpath which leads down to the Fuente del Acebuchal W 8. **(50 mins)**

Retracing your steps for 20m from the spring you reach a point where the path divides by a carob tree. Take the higher path that leads up into the pines. Crossing three scree slopes you pass beneath the steep, north-facing flank of the Tajo del Caballo. Big panoramic vistas open out to the south and to the east. Angling hard right the path runs due south, still climbing, as you cross the more denuded terrain of the Caballo's eastern side. Angling right you cross a scree slope then cutting back left cross it once more: there are chains to help your upwardly mobile course. Some 50m beyond the chains the path crosses a rocky ridge then angles right and descends for a short distance: it's indistinct but white and green waymarking and cairns mark your way. The path becomes clearer as it continues to climb, eventually running up to meet a broad track at a flat sandy area, the Puerto de la Encina 9. **(1 hr 30 mins)**

If you wish to climb the Pico de Mijas (3.2 kms up and down requiring about 40 minutes and an additional height gain of 225m) head straight across this sandy clearing to pick up a footpath which angles left, fairly level at first, before climbing more steeply. Reaching a cairn the path divides. Here take the left fork. The sandy path soon angles right, left, then right again before running up to a junction with a broader path 10 at a flatter area. Continue straight on past a cairn to reach a track where, bearing left then right, you reach the Pico de Mijas, topped by an astronomical observatory 11. Retrace your steps back down to the Puerto de la Encina and waypoint 9 9.

If you don't intend to climb up to the Pico de Mijas angle right across this flat, sandy area for 15m to a sign post 12 beyond which you drop down a beautiful footpath through the stand of evergreen oaks from which the Encina pass takes its name. Levelling the path cuts through the remains of an old stone wall 14 before leading you back to the *Casa Forestal* 7.
(1 hr 50 mins)

Angling left retrace your footsteps back to the forestry track 5. Here (unless you wish to return by the same route you followed earlier) cut right down the track. Soon it bears hard left and adopts a course running back towards Alhaurín. Reaching a fork where a sign post points back the way you've come 14 continue down the main track. Passing an abandoned olive grove the Bay of Málaga comes into view out to the east. Continue straight past two tracks which cut in to the left towards a forestry building. Bearing left you reach a junction 15. Here take the right option and descend for a little over 200m. Here, as the track loops right, cut left 16 along an indistinct footpath which threads

its way down through the pines then angles down into the streambed to reach the *Cañada de las Palomas* 17. From here retrace your footsteps back to the beginning of the walk 1.
(2 hrs 30 mins)

Distance: 11 kms **Time Required:** 3.5 hours **Rating:** Medium
Total Height Gain: 375m **Map:** IGN 1:50000 Fuengirola 1066 (16-45)
Ⓦ **Water:** springs at 1 hr 5 mins @ waypoint 5 & 2 hrs 5 mins @ waypoint 10

4 Alhaurín de la Torre: Cortijo de Jarapalos Circuit

Overview

This shortish circular walk leads you across the wooded hillsides of the northern flank of the Sierra de Mijas up to the solitary farmstead of Cortijo Jarapalos. It's an easy trail to follow, sticking mostly to broad forestry tracks. The early part of the walk leads you steeply up through a thick swathe of pine forest. As you climb higher a vast panorama opens before you, first to the east and the Mediterranean coastline beyond Málaga then north to the villages along the lower reaches of the Guadalhorce valley. After climbing in a series of lazy loops you reach the highlight of the walk, the abandoned terraces next to the ruins of Cortijo de Jarapalos. This is a perfect place to break for a picnic, having replenished your water bottle from the spring that lies just to its east, in the knowledge that the second half of the walk is nearly all downhill. After another section of track you pick up a narrow path which leads down to the beautiful spring-fed water deposit of Cortijo de la Mezquita. From here it's an easy ramble back to the start point of the walk.

Getting to the beginning of the walk

From Alhaurín de la Torre follow signs towards Coín along the A404 (marked on some maps as the A366). Passing Venta Vázquez continue to the km17 marker post then cut left at a sign Real Sociedad de Tiro de Pichón Jarapalo. Reaching a large sliding gate angle right along a track until you reach a fork where two tracks are cut off by metal chains.

The Walk

At the junction where chains block access to two tracks 1 take the left fork past a sign prohibiting vehicle access then a shrine dedicated to Juan López Pérez. The track climbs through pine forest past a fenced area used for clay pigeon shooting then passes a small white hut 2. As you climb higher views open out to the north across the Guadalhorce valley. Ignoring a track that cuts hard left 3 stick to the main track which angles right as it passes beneath a white hut. Soon the track begins to arc back to the left and adopts a southerly course towards the northern slopes of the Sierra de Mijas. Breaking out of the pines the track bears hard right then crosses the (dry) steambed of Arroyo Hondo 4. **(40 mins)**

Running back to the northwest for some 700m, at which stage the sea beyond Málaga comes into sight, the track arcs once more left. Running on towards the south it then angles right

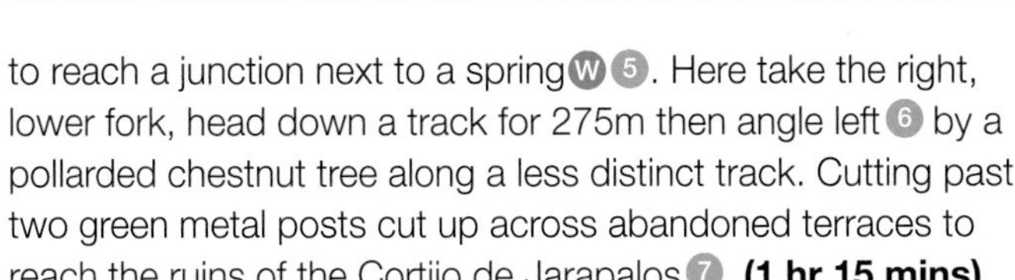

to reach a junction next to a spring W 5. Here take the right, lower fork, head down a track for 275m then angle left 6 by a pollarded chestnut tree along a less distinct track. Cutting past two green metal posts cut up across abandoned terraces to reach the ruins of the Cortijo de Jarapalos 7. **(1 hr 15 mins)**

After breaking journey at the ruin retrace your steps to waypoint 6 6 then angle left along the track you left earlier. Reaching a divide next to round drain cover you reach a fork 8. Angle left, sticking to the main track. Looping right you pass beneath a building that was used for loading gravel. The track bears gently right, adopting a course along the western flank of the Tajo de las Grajas. Views again open out to the north across the Guadalhorce valley. Careful! Descending past a storm drainage channel with faint red lettering continue on for 45m to a point where the track begins to bear left 9. **(1 hr 35 mins)** Here cut right up a steep path.

The path becomes better defined as it arcs right through pines and low-growing holly oaks before cutting down the spine of a ridge. Bearing right the path descends through a rocky area then arcs once more left, now less distinct, and passes above a rusting black and white *Coto* sign. Angling slightly left the path runs indistinctly on along the ridge to a swathe of open land where bulldozing has taken place. Here, bearing right, it widens to become a track which loops sharply right then left as it 9 passes through an abandoned olive grove. A streambed runs to your right: things become much more verdant. Still descending you pass a spring-fed water tank: it's a perfect place to cool off in hot weather or to replenish your water bottle W 10.
(2 hrs 5 mins)

Descending for a little over 100m and passing through a set of white metal gates 11 you reach a broad track. Here, cutting right for 125m, you reach a fork 12. Take the right branch which leads through a second set of white gates. The track runs on fairly level: the forest provides welcome shade in summer. Crossing a (dry) steambed 13 **(2 hrs 20 mins)** the track hairpins left. Angling once more round to the east after 250m a track runs down to dissect the one you're following 14. Carry straight on along the main track, still heading almost due east. After describing two lazy loops you return to the start point of the walk 1.
(2 hrs 40 mins)

Distance: 13.5 kms **Time Required:** 4/4.5 hours **Rating:** Medium/Difficult
Total Height Gain: 500m **Map:** IGN 1:50000 Fuengirola 1066 (16-45)
W **Water:** no springs along the way so take plenty

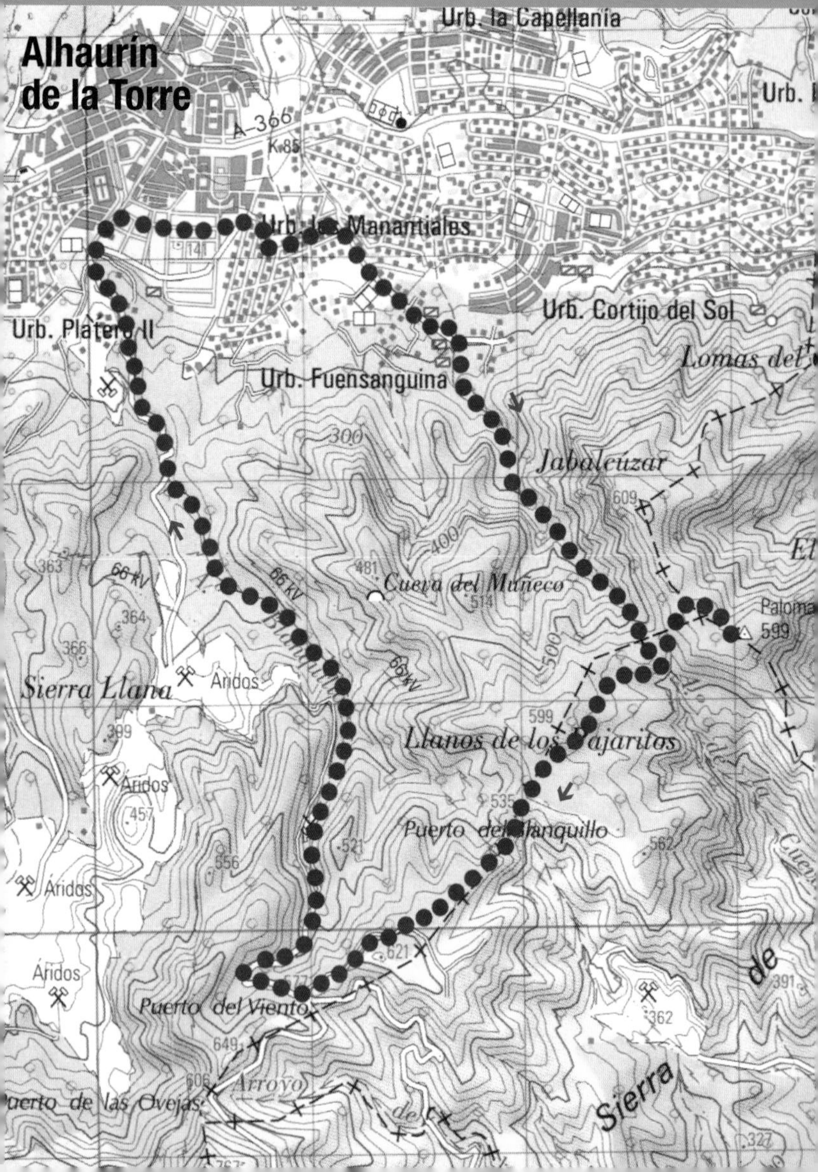

5 Alhaurín de la Torre: Puerto del Viento Circuit via the Palomas peak

Overview

The first section of this circular walk follows one of the most beautiful footpaths in the Sierra de Mijas, an ancient thoroughfare that connected the village of Alhaurín with those on the southern slopes of the Sierra de Mijas. The walk gathers in tempo as you climb up the Arroyo de Zambrano towards the jagged crest of the Jabalcúzar. Reaching the first pass a short diversion to the east leads you to the top of the Palomas peak from where you're treated to a dizzy view out across Málaga to the mountains of the Sierra de Almijara. The next section of the walk leads gradually up to a second high pass, El Puerto del Viento, from where you have a few kilometres of forestry track to negotiate before picking up another lovely path leading down the Blanquillo stream. The final section as you traverse Alhaurín from the bridge at waypoint 15 is a bit of a schlepp, especially the last 750m as you climb steeply back to your car. You could avoid this section by leaving a car close to the Juan Pablo II park then taking a taxi to the start point of the walk. *See general section for taxi numbers.*

Getting to the beginning of the walk

Approaching Alhaurín de la Torre from the west head through the town along the A366. Reaching Cervecería Venta El Alemán turn right up Calle Río Grande. Follow the street up past Bar Casa Paca. At a fork where you can turn left or right angle right then head straight over a mini-roundabout. Passing the last of the town's houses the road bears hard left towards a white sign Cañada de Canuto. Here park just right of the road close to a green marker post for SLA-50, next to green post with a chain.

The Walk

From the marker post *SLA-50* head up a broad path in a southerly direction ❶ parallel to a breeze block wall with a (dry) streambed to your right, the *Arroyo de la Cueva de la Higuera*. Angling right cross the (dry) streambed ❷ continue up through the pines parallel to the right bank. After 250m the path cuts back to the streambed and crosses to its left bank ❸. The path climbs on close to the stream: the rocky defiles of the northern side of the *sierra* now tower majestically above you. Reaching a flat area ❹ the path angles left and climbs across an open swathe of land to reach the top of the pass, El Puerto del Canuto, and a junction where you'll see a marker post *SLA-50* and a sign pointing back to *Alhaurín* ❺. Here cut left along a footpath that runs steeply away from the col marked by yellow dots in a northeasterly direction. Reaching a junction ❻ cut right (turning left would lead you to the top of the Jabalcúzar peak) then make your way along a path which threads its way through

the rocks, marked by cairns. Angling left it climbs to the white trig point on top of the Palomas peak (599m) 7. **(50 mins)**

From the peak make your way back down to the col and the wooden marker post for *SLA-50* 5. Head straight on in a westerly direction. Angling slightly left the path passes a group of ruined buildings: a stone wall now runs to your left. Crossing through a gap in the wall the path enters a stand of pines then runs along the top of a ridge. To your right the Alhaurín quarry comes briefly into view. The path begins to descend, becoming looser underfoot. Climbing once more you pass by a path that cuts left as you reach *Puerto Blanquillo*. Keep straight ahead. You shortly pass another path cutting down left: again, head straight on to reach a pylon and tower that were part of an ariel lift for transporting rock from the quarry which is down to your left 8. Continuing along the ridge the path broadens to become a track as you pass the *Refugio Cañada del Lobo* 9.

The track runs on, flanked by incongrous street lights, towards a fire observation tower. Passing by a second building *Albergue Cañada del Lobo* you reach a junction 10. Here cut right following a sign *Sendero. *Cutting left would take you to a mirador just beyond the Albergue from where you're treated to more soaring views of the Costa*. The track runs on parallel to the ridge top before descending to a junction at the pass of Puerto del Viento 11. **(1 hr 45 mins)**

Here cut right for 10m then turn right again past a sign *Prohibido La Circulación de Vehículos a Motor No Autorizados*. After 25m the track divides 12. You can take either fork: the one to the left is a much steeper descent. After looping down the track adopts a northerly course. Reaching a quarried area angle right 13 and continue parallel to the track on a narrow footpath. Leaving the quarry the path drops loosely down to the (dry) bed of the Blanquillo stream. Things now become much prettier as you follow the streambed down towards Alhaurín. Eventually you reach a junction with an asphalted track 14. **(2 hrs 35 mins)** Turn right and continue down towards the village. Running past the graffiti-daubed buildings of an abandoned mine you reach the first houses of the village then come to a bridge 15.

Beyond the bridge cut sharp right then follow the path that dissects the Parque Juan Pablo II. At its far end cut across to the park's northern side to a roundabout with palm trees. Head straight on past Apartamentos Santa Clara then follow the road as it angles right. After 150m you reach a junction. Cut left along Calle Peteñeras which soon becomes Calle Pablo Milanés. At the end of the street cut right and follow the road steeply upwards. Angling left you return to the start point of the walk 1. **(3 hrs 20 mins)**

Distance: 9 kms **Time Required:** 3/3.5 hours **Rating:** Medium
Total Height Gain: 500m **Map:** IGN 1:50000 Fuengirola 1066 (16-45)
Ⓦ **Water:** no springs along the way so take plenty

6 Benalmádena: Puerto Viejo de Mijas Circuit via the Quejigal stream

Overview

Even though this walk begins close to the busy coastal motorway, just to the east of Benalmádena, within just a quarter of an hour you enter a very different world as you climb a beautiful old footpath parallel to the Regajo del Quejigal stream. After a long and steady ascent things get much easier as you head along a high ridge that runs from west to east towards the Calamorro peak. The views at this stage are magnificent: on a clear day you'll see the mountains of North Africa to the southwest as well as the mountain ranges of La Axarquía beyond Málaga to the east. Bear in mind that the path back down via what's known locally as *El Camino de los Leñadores* ('The Woodcutter's Path') is steep and loose underfoot in parts. If you wish to avoid this slightly tricky section you could retrace your footsteps back down from Puerto Viejo de Mijas or from there continue to the summit of the Calamorro (the path is waymarked from the signboard at the top of the pass) then take the cable car down to Arroyo de la Miel. From there you'd have just a short 3km taxi ride back to the walk's start point.

Getting to the beginning of the walk

From the A7/E15 motorway exit 217 for Mijas/Benalmádena. Head through the top end of the village then continue along the A368 towards Arroyo de la Miel. Where the road bears sharply right cut left at a signboard detailing the network of walks in the Sierra de Mijas. There's room to park a couple of cars just in on the right.

The Walk

From the signboard 1 walk north to a fork then angle left along a tarmac road. 50m after passing beneath the A7 motorway you reach an open area where angling slightly left you reach a wooden signboard 2. Here cut left up a narrow footpath which zigzags away from riverbed. Climbing for some 300m you reach a fork 3. Here cut right following a sign on a rock *Ruta 3*. Soon the path loops hard back towards the motorway. You now pick up blue waymarking as the the path arcs back left and climbs to a junction. Cut right following another sign on a rock *R3* 4. The path now runs high up to the left of the Regajo del Quejigal stream. Passing by a sentry box inspection hut the path runs across a swathe of scree, passes a second hut then descends and crosses to the right bank of the Quejigal 5. **(35 mins)**

Beyond the steam you pass a spring (sometimes dry) and a signboard of the route you're following. The path climbs steeply towards the jagged peaks of the Tajo de la Sabia and El Quejigal before bearing right and crossing a (dry) streambed. Reaching a fork 6 branch right: fabulous views now open out towards the Mediterranean. The path soon descends once more to the sandy course of the Quejigal 7. Follow the streambed uphill for 35m then angle right to pick up the continuation of the path. Angling right you reach a junction 8 and a signpost. Here bear right following a sign for *R6*. The path runs eastwards for 400m then angles left and climbs: you'll see blue waymarking. Bearing once more right you readopt an easterly course, more or less parallel to the ridge which is up to your left. Soon you cross the Puerto de la Cruz pass (unmarked on the ING map) where, looking north, you'll see the huge Alhaurín quarry. **(1 hr 5 mins)**

Continue east along the path towards the Cerro Calamorro. After dropping down for a few metres the path runs once more uphill to reach the Puerto Viejo pass 9 **(1 hr 30 mins)** where there's a signboard detailing the local walking routes and twin

signposts. Here cut hard to the right *(unless you wish to extend the walk by climbing the Calamorro)* and begin your descent back towards the sea. You shortly pass a (dry) spring and two stone benches. The path drops steeply down and passes beneath overhead power lines. Looking to the southwest you'll now spot the graceful form of the Buddhist temple just beyond Benalmadena. Bearing round to the southeast the path crosses a (dry) streambed 10 then climbs to wooden signpost. Here cut right 11 down a steep, loose path which soon improves as it runs along a ridgetop above a quarry then reaches another sign warning that the next section of is loose underfoot 12. A final section of steep footpath leads you down to the access track of the quarry 13 where another signboard details the local footpaths. Turn left and follow the road south towards the sea. Crossing the motorway 14 the road arcs hard right and after 225m reaches a *Stop* sign. Here angle hard round to the right along a broad footpath which soon loops back left and descends to the start point of the walk 1. **(2 hrs 20 mins)**

Costa Tropical: Western Sierra de Tejeda, Almijara & Alhama

Walks close to Cómpeta, Canillas, Sedella & Alcaucín

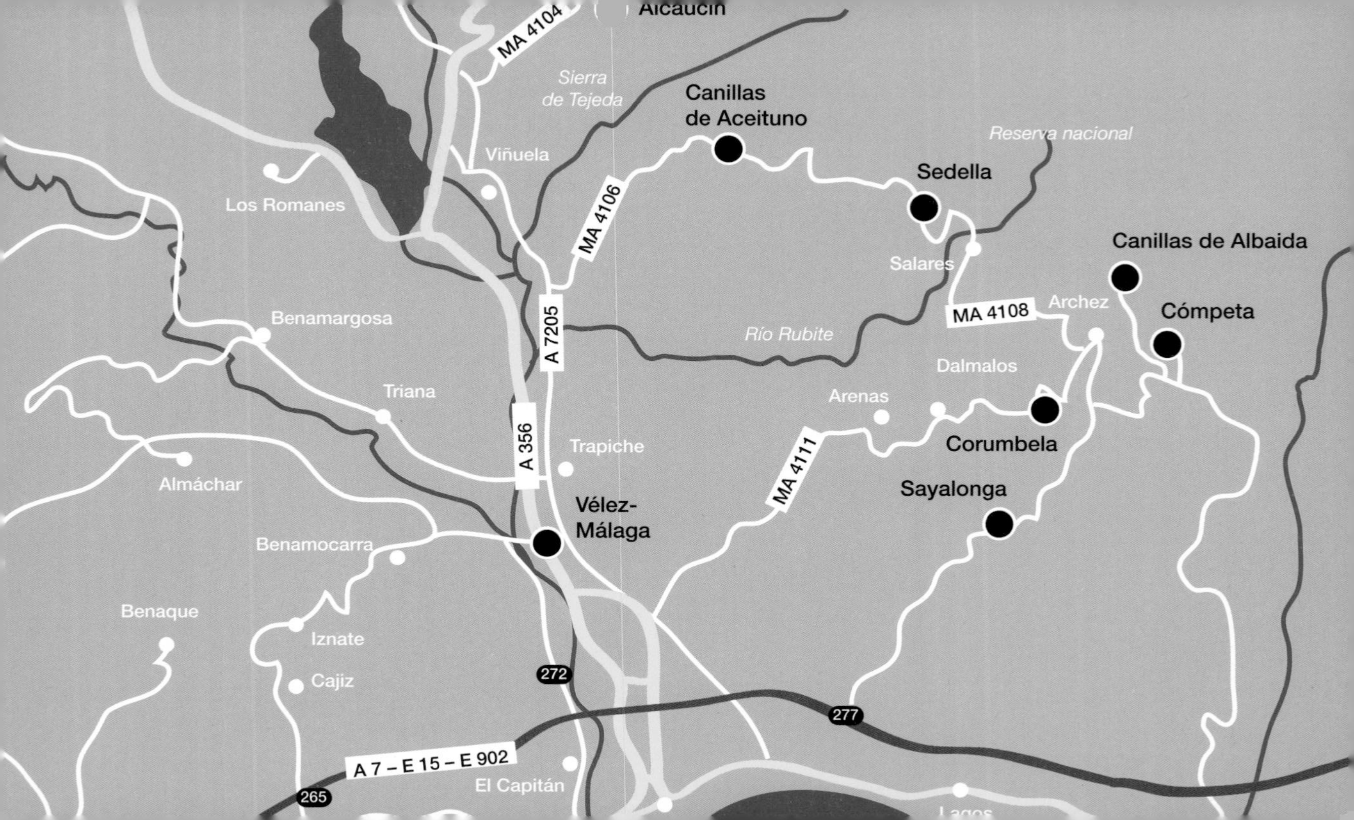
MA 4104
Sierra
de Tejeda
Canillas
de Aceituno
Reserva nacional
Sedella
Viñuela
Los Romanes
MA 4106
Salares
Canillas de Albaida
MA 4108
Archez
Cómpeta
Benamargosa
A 7205
Río Rubite
Dalmalos
Triana
Arenas
Corumbela
A 356
Trapiche
MA 4111
Sayalonga
Almáchar
Vélez-
Málaga
Benamocarra
Benaque
Iznate
Cajiz
272
277
A 7 – E 15 – E 902
El Capitán
265

Costa Tropical: Western Sierra de Tejeda, Almijara & Alhama

The Parque Natural de Sierra de Tejeda, Almijara & Alhama, created in 1999, encompasses a massive 40,663 hectare slice of the Sierra Subbética and forms a natural boundary between the provinces of Granada and Málaga. The landscape is of its southwestern, sea-facing flank is characterised by deep gorges and steep-sided limestone ridges whilst white and grey seams of dolomitic marble give its higher reaches the look of a multi-layered cake. Rising up behind the fertile valleys of the Costa Tropical to over 2000 metres the towering crest of La Maroma provides a stunning backdrop to all walks in this section, especially during winter when there is often snow on its higher reaches. The ascent of La Maroma from Canillas de Aceituno, described in this section, numbers amongst Andalucía's most spectacular on-foot adventures.

The Park is home to the largest group of *Capra Hispánica* of the Iberian peninsula. Since the hunting of the mammals was limited by law in the 1970s numbers have increased ten fold and it's estimated that the resident population now numbers more than 2000. A similarly rapid appearance has recently been made by the red squirrel which in just three years spread from the east to the west of the Park. This is another superb area for raptor spotting with resident breeding pairs of Golden and Bonelli's eagles along with Short-toed and Booted eagles during the migratory season. Small numbers of peregrine falcons are also resident in the *sierra*.

A belt of white villages, nearly all with views down to the Mediterranean, fans out along the southern flank of the mountains and most walks described in this section follow the old muleteer paths, many of Moorish origins, that linked these different villages. My personal favourites are Canillas de Albaida with its diminuitive *plaza* and cluster of white houses and Cómpeta. Both villages have excellent places to stay as well as decent restaurants and tapas bars. Expect to hear a fair amount of English: there's a large ex-pat population and several northern European companies organise walking holidays in the area.

The wild terrain of La Maroma's southern flank is in marked contrast to the swathe of land between the villages and the sea which is extensively cultivated and peppered with small farmsteads. The Sayalonga/Corumbela circuit and the one leading north from Canillas de Albaída are great introductions to this fertile landscape where a huge variety of subtropical species are grown including avocado, mango, pomegranate, custard fruit and lychee. Cultivation is aided by a benign climate and an intricate system of irrigation: many of the water channels or *acequias* date back to the Moorish period. The hillsides, especially round Cómpeta and Canillas, are covered with olive groves and vineyards where the sweet moscatel grape is grown. Nearly all of the region's farms have one or more of the characteristic platforms or *secaderos* (glossary) which are used to sun-dry and fortify the grapes which are then transformed into *vino de moscatel.*

A couple of the walks described - the ascent of La Maroma, the Blanquillo circuit and the Sedella to Alcaucín walk - take you high up the Sierra's southern flank where weather conditions can change rapidly. Be sure to check the forecast, pack appropriate clothing and let somebody know of the route you'll be following.

If you're lucky enough to find a room, Finca El Cerrillo close to Canillas would make an ideal base for a week of walking in the park (it's used by UK walking groups and has a library with maps and route descriptions) whilst Lagabella offers the most imaginative breakfast menu I've come across in Spain (see Best Sleeps listings).

BEST SLEEPS

Cómpeta

Hotel Balcón de Cómpeta €€
Tel: 952 553 535 Email: info@hotel-competa.com
www.hotel-competa.com
Friendly mid range hotel with a pool and views out towards the sea.

Canillas de Albaida

Posada La Plaza €–€€
Tel: 952 030 444 Email: info@hotelfinca.com
www.hotelfinca.com
Comfortable small hotel in the pretty square of Canillas de Albaida.

Finca El Cerrillo €€
Tel: 952 554 807 Email: info@posada-laplaza.eu
www.posada-laplaza.eu
Fabulous small rural hotel with great food and very friendly hosts.

Sedella

Lagabella €€
Tel: 649 035 387 Email: lagabella@lagabella.com
www.lagabella.com
B&B with exceptional food a few kilometres from the village on the Alcaucín road.

Taxis: Cómpeta/Canillas de Albaida 952 516 056, 657 56 133, 952 516 205, Sedella 952 518 041, 658 905 446

Distance: 18 kms **Time Required:** 6.5 hours **Rating:** Difficult

Total Height Gain: 975m **Map:** IGN 1:50000 Zafarraya 1040 (18-43)

Ⓦ **Water:** springs at waypoint 9 @ 1 hr 20 mins & waypoint 16 @ 2 hrs 30 mins

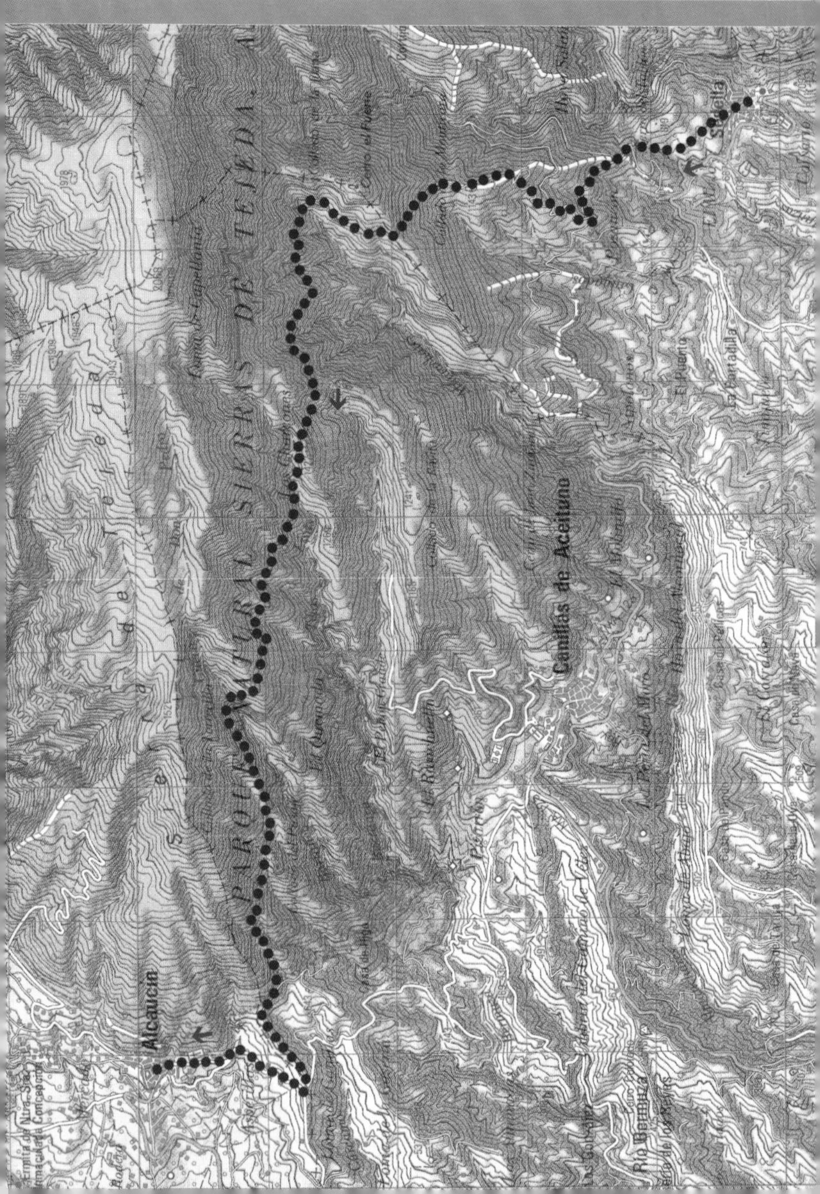

1 Sedella to Alcaucín via El Collado de la Gitana

Overview

The Sedella to Alcaucín route is one of the finest longer walks in the Axarquía, a big traverse that follows a high mountain path round the southern flank of the Maroma massif. You're faced with a challenging climb for the first couple of hours but your effort is amply rewarded by a stunning middle section of hiking which leads past magnificent rock formations and two remote springs, the Pisadico and the Collado de la Gitana (spelled Jitana on the IGN map). Both make great spots to rest or break for a picnic: the views just couldn't be better. The footpath you follow during the latter part of the walk, which leads down to Alcaucín past the Collado del Pasaje, is overgrown in parts but is easy enough to follow. Bear in mind that cloud can descend fast on the Maroma: it's doubly important to pack a mobile and compass on this day and to let people know of your planned movements, especially in winter. Amongst the pines you pass during the latter section of the walk you'll almost certainly see the distinctive cocoons of the processionary caterpillar: it has become a pest in recent years in southern Spain.

The Walk

The walk begins in front of the church in the main square of Sedella, La Plaza de la Constitución (1). With your back to the church cross the square and exit it along a *No Entry* street. A few metres before El Mesón de Frasco turn right and climb a cobbled footpath passing a sign *Molino Los Pozuelos*. The path widens as it becomes concreted. Angling right it reverts to dirt track then narrows to become a path which cuts round the edge of the terraces at the edge of the village before zigzagging more steeply up, cobbled in parts. The path crosses a water channel 2 as it cuts through groves of almonds then runs up to a track in front of El Molino Los Pozuelos: it's easily identified by the high water channel which still feeds its mill stones 3. **(20 mins)**

Turn left along the track then after 100m cut sharp right 4 and follow a track which loops steeply up past a fenced water deposit then a group of white buildings, also water deposits 5. The track climbs gently as it contours round a deep ravine, running through an area of sparse pine plantation. The track runs past a small, pole-roofed stone hut. 75m past the hut 6 cut hard right and head up another broad track. After a steep looping climb, you reach another track. Follow this track as it cuts sharply left and passes through a gap in a wooden post-and-wire fence 7. It soon loops right then climbs steeply as panoramic views open out across the Axarquía. The track cuts once more through the wooden post-and-wire fence then angles left across a fire break.

Adopting a straighter course it soon angles right then crosses the firebreak once again. After climbing steeply the track arcs hard left (ignore the branch which angles right, running downhill) to reach a levelled area where helicopters can land 8. **(1 hr 10 mins)** Here, passing right of a boundary fence, you pick up a narrow path which contours round the mountain. Reaching an area of exposed rock the path loops higher before resuming its previous course. Soon you reach a junction where cutting left for 40m you arrive at the *Fuente del Pisadico del Niño Dios* W 9. After a break at this exquisite spot rejoin the path which loops to a higher level then runs to the left of a wire fence. Climbing more steeply it zigzags to the top of the ridge 10. **(1 hr 30 mins)**

Here the path angles right then bearing left begins to descend as it contours round the bowl of the valley. The path is loose and steep in parts: care should be taken. The path loops across

a (dry) streambed 11, climbs, then looping right traverses a second streambed 12. It climbs once more, passes over a rise then descends to cross a third streambed 13 then a fourth. It then climbs again, waymarked with daubs of red paint. Passing a *calera* (glossary) you reach the top of the next divide and a junction where a marker post points right 14. **(2 hrs 15 mins)**

Cut right and climb: cairns mark the path. Descending you pass another marker post before crossing another ridge 15. Beyond this ridge the path contours round the saddle of another valley, passes above another *calera* then reaches a spring W 16 marked on the IGN map as simply *Fuente*. The path cuts past the spring over rocky, more overgrown terrain: cairns mark the way. Reaching the top of the ridge 17 the path angles right and reaches a breach in the rock marked by twin cairns at the *Collado de la Gitana* pass 18. **(2 hrs 40 mins)**

Beyond the rise, descending for 10m, you reach a junction and another marker post with an arrow pointing right. Ignore this and cut left and down, roughly parallel to the ridge you've just crossed. Reaching the bottom of the valley the path angles right towards the streambed at the upper end of the *Barranco de Tajos Lisos* where you reach a junction 19. **(2 hrs 55 mins)** Cut right here and after 35m cross the (dry) streambed. As you contour gradually up round the *barranco* (glossary) the path becomes more overgrown. This is an area where ibex can often be spotted. The path crosses a ridge 20 then bears left into the next *barranco* where there's evidence of logging. After running fairly level the path begins to descend as views open out to the west. At this stage long trousers will make the descent a more comfortable experience. The path angles right and descends as it contours round another deep gulley. You soon cross a (dry) rocky streambed where there's a small water deposit 21. **(3 hrs 45 mins)**

The path, invaded by rosemary, climbs again through thicker undergrowth. At times it's easier to drop off the path though care should be taken: parts are loose underfoot. After climbing steeply for a few metres the path resumes its descent, running down a ridge between two *barrancos*. Cairns help to guide you down. The path soon crosses another (dry) streambed by a solitary pine 22. Ahead you now see the rocky outcrop next to the Collado del Pasaje. Approximately 100m before reaching the outcrop 23 angle right and continue your descent. The path becomes clearer but is loose in parts as it traverses more denuded terrain which has seen a fire in its recent past. Cairns and red dots mark the way. After following a ridge the path loops right and crosses another (dry) streambed 24 before descending to the boundary fence of the Park. Angle left for 25m then go through a metal gate in the fence 25. **(4 hrs 35 mins)**

Beyond the gate head for a gap between two pylons. Just beyond the second pylon angle right 26 along a narrow path which angles across the hillside back towards the fence. After

looping over a (dry) streambed, then climbing, the path passes above a *calera* (glossary), drops down a few metres then angles slightly left to reach a white building next to a fenced quarry 27. Here cut left along a broad track which soon passes a small cottage. At the next flat-roofed building you reach a fork 28. Keeping left (or see below *) you pass beneath transmitter masts then reach a junction with a broad dirt track 29. Turn right and descend towards the village. The track runs past a number of houses then the quarry entrance. At the next junction 30 head straight on, now climbing gently. Reverting to concrete the track levels then passes beneath the village cemetery. Continue straight ahead then follow Calle Calvario down into the village. At house no.10 turn right to reach the village square, La Plaza de la Constitución 31. **(5 hrs 5 mins)**

** It would be tempting to cut right here, then shortly once more to the right, and drop through an olive grove, cutting off a large section of track walking. But there is no official path.*

Distance: 21 kms **Time Required:** 7 hours **Rating:** Difficult
Total Height Gain: 1625m **Map:** IGN 1:50000 Zafarraya 1040 (18-43)
Water: spring at 4 hrs 50 mins @ waypoint 24

2 Canillas de Aceituno: Ascent of La Maroma returning via La Rávita

Overview

Of the three better-known routes leading to the summit of la Maroma (2068m) the one that departs from Canillas de Aceituno gets my vote. For most of the way up and down you have glorious views back to the Mediterranean and the route leads you past the magnificent south face of the Loma de Capellanía to the spectacular promontory of Proa del Barco *(The Ship's Prow)* where the views out west give a foretaste of those awaiting you at the summit. The vast panoramic vistas on a clear day are hard to better and are particulary memorable when the Sierra Nevada is cloaked in its winter mantle of snow. The great thing about the Canillas ascent is that once you're back down at Los Charcones you follow a different path back to the village, descending parallel to the gorge of Los Almanchares: this was the path that was once used to bring ice down from the summit. This is a walk that merits five star status and one to be savoured so be sure to set out reasonably early. I've included instructions on how to reach the main square because this can be confusing if you arrive from the east. *Note that you can make the initial ascent less abrupt by following the forestry track without deviating from waypoint 2 to waypoint 9.*

Getting to the beginning of the walk

Arriving in the village from the west head towards the village centre. Reaching a playground for children park on the left then continue along Avenida de Andalucía to lower end of the Plaza de la Constitución.

The Walk

The walk begins in the main square of Canillas, the Plaza de la Constitución 1. Facing the town hall exit at its top, left hand corner then cut right past a statue with a bust and guitar following a sign for *La Maroma*. Angling left then right continue up a narrow concreted street, ignoring a sign off right for *La Rábita*. Head straight on at the next junction passing left of an ornamental olive tree. Angling left the road descends to a junction then arcs left 2. Here turn right following a sign for *Campo de Fútbol*.

Climbing a steep concrete road, La Cuesta de los Picachos, you pass the village cemetery then a football pitch where the track angles right. After 300m cut left at a marker post 3 up a narrow path. Reaching the track once again 4 by a bird hide bear left. After following the track in a northwesterly direction look for a cairn to its right 5 where you should again cut a corner, rejoining the track at a concreted section where you reach the *Mirador de Castillejo* 6. Follow the track to the right then as the concrete ends cut left at a cairn 7 up a path which shortly angles back to the track which now levels as it runs on to the east. Passing a forestry building 8 after 600m you reach a sign post pointing left for *La Maroma* 9. **(1 hr)**

Cut left through the pines down a path which shortly crosses two (dry) streambeds then climbs past an old *calera* (glossary). Continuing up the footpath you pass a second *calera* 10. The pines thin out as you climb higher up the right side of the Barranco de las Tejas. Soon the path begins to descend. 25m before reaching the bed of the *barranco* (glossary) 11 cut right at a cairn and marker post. After running directly away from the stream the path arcs left, clearer now, as it climbs parallel to the streambed. Zigzagging steeply up you reach a junction with a clearer path as you come up to the Los Charcones pass. In front

of you is a sign post *Sendero SLA-142* 12. **(1 hr 30 mins)**

Here cut left. Running north the path crosses a tributary of the Arroyo de las Tejas where you pass another sign for *SLA-142*. The path zigzags steeply up past a rocky promontory as it runs west before angling back to the right 13. Zigzagging up to the north the path again arcs to the west and traverses a swathe of scree. Passing green arrows on a rock you reach the promontory known as the Proa del Barco and a marker post with a cairn at its base 14. **(2 hrs 10 mins)**

Here angle right. The path becomes less distinct but cairns guide you across a vast field of rock. The Barranco de la Cueva de Don Pedro is now down to your left. Reaching a jagged outcrop the path angles left. 30m before it reaches the tail end of the *barranco* 15 angle right, away from the path you've been following, to pick up another which leads to the summit, initially on a due easterly course. Angling back down to a (dry) streambed 16 continue along its course, passing just right of a fenced enclosure then angle right. Care should be taken: the path now runs close to the steep southern face of the Loma de Capellanía. *From here on it's a good idea to occasionally look behind you: it will make coming back down easier.* After angling left then crossing a rise you'll see a nipple-like cairn at the left side of the summit ridge. Head up to the cairn 17 from where, passing well to the left of a high metal pole, continue up to the tower-like trig point at the summit 18 (2068m). **(2 hrs 50 mins)**

You may wish to check out the deep pot hole 19 which is some 25m left of the tall metal post cemented into the rock.

Leaving the summit make your way back down to waypoint 12 12. **(4 hrs 10 mins)** Here instead of angling right down the path you followed earlier cut left through a breach in the rock. Running south along the ridge the path angles left then zigzags down and passes a (dry) spring 20. Running more level the path

cuts through a stand of young pines before angling right to the top of the Rávita ridge, marked on the IGN map as *Collado de la Rávita* 21. Here angling right you pass an *SLA-142* marker post. Continuing south for 300m you reach a junction 22. Take the right branch. The path adopts a southwesterly course, descending towards Canillas across an area more denuded of vegetation, high above the ravine of the Arroyo de Almanchares. Just before the path angles hard right you reach the cave of La Rávita and a signboard 23. Angling right a few metres before the cave the path passes a *calera* then reaches a spring, El Fuente de la Rávita W 24. **(4 hrs 50 mins)**

The path now angles slightly left, along a ridge, before adopting a course towards Canillas. Occasionally looping down to a lower level the path eventually drops down past a signboard *Sendero Casa de la Nieve* to a track 25. Cut right for 50m then reaching a pylon cut left 26 between two ramshackle farm buildings to reach the first village houses. Just before reaching a sign *Calle Sierrecilla* cut right down a zigzagging path. Passing a sign for *La Rábita* angle left then cut right down Calle Calleja. Pass beneath an arch then at the next junction cut left to return to the start point of the walk 1. **(5 hrs 35 mins)**

Distance: 14 kms **Time Required:** 4.5 hours **Rating:** Medium/Difficult
Total Height Gain: 500m **Map:** IGN 1:50000 Zafarraya 1040 (18-43)
W **Water:** springs at waypoint 6 @ 35 mins & waypoint 18 @ 2 hrs 40 mins

3 Cómpeta to Sedella via La Cruz del Muerto

Overview

This averagely challenging day walk leads you through another beautiful slice of the Sierra de Almijara. The walk begins with a gentle stroll through the irrigated terraces that stretch west from Cómpeta past avocado, prickly pear, agave, olives and almonds. After passing through the pretty village of Canillas de Albaida and its diminutive main square (where you may be tempted to linger over a coffee) you follow a steep, cobbled path down to the Cájula river which you cross via its Roman bridge. Beyond the river a long climb, mostly by way of forestry track, leads up to the high pass of Cruz del Muerto where stunning vistas open out to the villages of the eastern and western Axarquía, to the towering Maroma massif and south to the Mediterranean. After a longish but gentle descent you angle away from the track and follow a water channel steeply upwards. Cutting down past a ruined farm on a steep, eroded footpath you cross another beautiful Roman bridge just to the north of Sedella from where you climb up to the village's pretty main square. *You could shorten the walk by continuing down the main track at waypoint 19 and ending the walk in Salares. Cómpeta is a short taxi ride from either village.*

The Walk

The walk begins in the main square of Cómpeta, la Plaza de la Almijara. With your back to a church (1) cross the square, climb a flight of steps then cut left along Calle San Antonio. At the end of the street continue past the Hotel Balcón de Cómpeta then a small chapel dedicated to San Antonio. Follow the road as it swings right for 40m then cut left (2) on a newly-renovated path.

The path runs past stands of agave and olive groves, roughly parallel to a water channel which is to your left. After crossing a concrete drive the path meets a tarmac road 3. Bear right here then after 300m cut left off the road 4 at a cairn. You again pick up the narrow path which runs on through groves of avocado and olives. The path merges with a track which passes a pylon with a yellow warning triangle then, bearing right, meets the road you left earlier 5. Turn left and drop down past a water deposit to a four way junction 6. **(35 mins)**

Take the left fork, passing a spring W, and drop down to the left of the Capilla de Santa Ana. After 60m the road bears left. Here head straight ahead past house no. 2 where a sign warns *Cuidado con El Gato*. Take the first sharp turning left into Calle Laberinto then cut right down a flight steps along Calle Sierra Almijara which angles right then left. Head on down Calle Alta which bears left then cuts right to reach the main square of Canillas 7. Leave the square at its western end along Calle Málaga then cut left down Calle Axarquía. At the end of street bear right past house no. 16 then left following a sign *Los Llanos/Fuente Santa*. Passing an electricity hut you drop down to a cobbled path which zigzags down towards the Cájula river. Reaching the road 8 turn right then after 35m cut left and drop down to the river which you cross via a narrow bridge: a sign indicates that you're on a *calzada romana*, a Roman path. Beyond the bridge the path winds up to the road. Head straight across the tarmac and continue up the path which runs up towards a house with a palm tree where you reach a stony track 9. **(1 hr 5 mins)** Here turn right and follow a line of pylons up hill. Reaching a fork 10 cut right and continue along the track which descends through vineyards then crosses a tributary of the Cájula where you pass a farm. The track loops up past a house with a weather vane. Eventually you arrive at a three way junction next to a sign *Parque Natural* 11. **(1 hr 30 mins)**

Here bear hard left. The track levels then begins to climb again as it angles round the side of a gully. At a point where you are opposite a ruin (which is on other side of the gully to you) cut right up a narrow path 12 which climbs steeply through pines then reaches an area of young olives. Carry straight ahead: here the path becomes less distinct. Passing 10m above a *Parque Natural* sign climb steeply past a vineyard towards another *Parque Natural* sign. Angling left you reach a track 13. Turn left along the track which contours round the mountain through an area more denuded of vegetation. Angling right it passes a fenced water deposit 14. The track climbs steeply then looping left passes a grove of almonds and a vineyard before running up to a concrete water tank 15. Here bear right along a broad track: views now open out to the west. Climbing gently you pass a marker post. The track runs up to reach a 3 way junction at the Puerto de la Cruz del Muerto pass where there's another marker post and a *Parque Natural* sign 16. **(2 hrs 5 mins)**

Leave the pass by bearing left: the track is now lined with cypress trees, planted to secure its left side. Soon the track loops right, with a deep gorge down to your left, El Arroyo de Perales. Angling left it crosses the *barranco* (glossary) via a concrete bridge 17 then passes a water deposit. Sticking to the main track you pass by a ruined farm then cut past another water deposit with a tap where you can replenish your water W 18. **(2 hrs 40 mins)**

The track continues its descent, shortly passing above a goat farm 19. 50m beyond the farm cut right at a G.R. marker post along a track which climbs steeply upwards. After 250m you pass a house with a round tower. Sedella comes into view and shortly you reach a fork 20. Bear right then after 150m cut left off the track at a marker post and angle down to pick up a narrow path which climbs parallel to a concrete water channel. The path and channel level as you approach a group of pines. Just before

the pines cut left, cross a streambed then climb to the top of a ridge where you reach another marker post 21. Continue straight ahead. Down to your left you'll now spot a ruin: you'll later be passing a few metres from this building. It's possible to cut left down to the ruin but it's easier, if a little longer, to follow a clearer path which contours round the bowl of the valley, crosses a (dry) stream then climbs to the top of the ridge and another G.R. post 22.

Bear left along the ridge to a flat area then angle right and continue along the ridge top for 100m to another marker post. Here cut left down an eroded path to the ruin you could see earlier 23. Passing behind the ruin head to the southern end of the terraces which lie just beneath it to a large cairn. Here, bearing right, you pick up a path which runs down towards Sedella. Passing a stone ruin it arcs right then descends more steeply: it's loose and eroded so care should be taken. Following white paint splashes you reach the floor of the valley where you cross a Roman bridge 24. Bear left and follow the track up to the village where you reach a sign *Puente Romano 806m*. Here cut up right past house no. 17 then take the next left to reach house no. 4. Here bear right then left and continue past the town hall to the main square of the village 25. **(3 hrs 35 mins)**

Distance: 10 kms **Time Required:** 3.5 hours **Rating:** Easy/Medium

Total Height Gain: 525m **Map:** IGN 1:50000 Vélez-Málaga 1054 (18-44)

W **Water:** spring at waypoint 5 @ 1hr or at any bar in Corombela

4 Sayalonga and Corumbela Circuit

Overview

This easy half-day excursion links two of the prettier villages of the western Axarquía, Sayalonga and Corumbela. The walk leads you through the subtropical orchards of Sayalonga's terraced river valley where there's an astonishing variety of fruit trees: avocado, citrus, medlar, walnut, olive, almond and pomegranate are all cultivated on the valley's terraced slopes as well as the sweet moscatel grape for which the region has long been famous. A steep climb up past the Tres Fuentes spring brings you to Corumbela passing by several small farmsteads. On the return leg you're treated to sweeping views of the Sierra de Tejeda and south towards the Mediterrranean. Most of the walk is by way of farm tracks and this is an easy circuit to follow. There's a short section of tarmac road when you leave Corumbela but you'll see little passing traffic. It's worth taking a few minutes out at the beginning or end of the walk to visit Sayalonga's unusual circular cemetery, one of the few of its kind in Iberia.

The Walk

The walk begins in Sayalonga's pretty main square, Plaza Rafael Alcoba (1). From here take the street that cuts past the *Ayuntamiento* into Calle Cristo and follow signs for *Cementerio Redondo*. Branch right into Calle Rodríguez de la Fuente then at the end of the street turn left. *If you wish to visit the round cemetery and its mirador cut right here then later retrace your footsteps*. Pass beneath the Santa Catalina church then take the next right and descend to a sign for *Corumbela, 5kms* (2).

Bearing right for some 50m you reach a fork. Here bear right, passing beneath the cemetery, along a concreted section of track which descends through fertile groves of fruit trees. The route is occasionally waymarked with P.R. flashes. The track meets the river which it follows for a short distance then crosses it via an arched bridge 3. **(20 mins)**

Continuing along the river's left bank you shortly pass Casa El Molino. The track climbs through lush, irrigated terraces. There are now good views back to Sayalonga. Soon the track heads directly away from the river up a side valley then bears left, climbing steeply. A fence runs to the right of the track. Crossing a (dry) streambed the track continues climbing, now with the stream to your right. After a steep ascent the track loops hard right, crosses the streambed once more, then angles left and passes beneath a line of houses which straddle a ridge before angling right and descending for about 50m. The Mediterranean comes into view as you reach a fork in the track 4. **(45 mins)**

Here bear hard left and continue climbing. Cómpeta is visible over to the right and soon Corumbela comes into view. Having passed a number of small farms the track descends, crosses a gulley then runs up to the picnic area of *Las Tres Fuentes* (The Three Springs) W on your left 5. **(1 hr)**

From here the track winds up towards Corumbela, passes above a five-a-side football pitch then meets a tarmac road 6. **(1 hr 20 mins)** Cross the road and head up Calle Las Pitas into Corumbela. Bearing left past the bakery and you arrive at Bar Cantero, an excellent place for a drink after the long climb from Sayalonga. Here swing left past a small supermarket 7 into calle Las Pitas. At the end of this street bear slightly left and follow a track that runs just above the Corumbela/ Daimalos road, passing through groves of almonds, olives and medlars. The track climbs, passes Villa Almenara, then drops down past a ruin to meet the tarmac road. Bear right along the road and follow it to the top of the pass. Here, just as the road swings sharply right, turn left along a track 8. **(1 hr 45 mins)**

The track immediately passes by a farm with *secaderos* (glossary) for grapes. You soon reach a fork 9 from where there

are views down to the sea and across to the Sierra de Tejeda and its highest point, La Maroma (2068m). Here, bearing right, the track leads past several small farms before it runs down hill past two houses with wafer-bricked gate columns then runs on towards another house with a row of arches. Just before reaching this house swing left 10 on a track that cuts steeply downhill. With Sayalonga clearly visible on the other side of the valley the track passes two small farms, then a crumbling ruin.

Keep to the main track which continues to descend, looping left then right. The track passes just to the left of a ruin 11 then arcs right. You pass an odd-looking house with twin balconies and after a steep descent reach another track by a farm with twin palm trees next to its entrance, Cortijo Pepe y Angelina 12. Here turn left and continue your descent, passing a water tank then an ice cream kiosk (which now serves as a shed) to reach the river 13. **(2 hrs 15 mins)**

Cross the river (you may need to remove boots and socks in the wetter months) then bear right and follow a concreted road steeply upwards. After passing a pylon you come to a white building to the left of the track, home to an extended family of pigs. Immediately before this building 14 branch left and climb a stony path which runs between fences. It soon widens and meets with a concreted section of track. At the end of this track bear left then immediately right at a metal railing to reach the first village houses and Calle La Loma. At the end of this street bear left then right into Calle Morales. When you reach a sign *Cementerio Redondo* turn right along a narrow street to Plaza de la Constitución then angle left along Calle Cristo to arrive back in Plaza Rafael Alcoba 1. **(2 hrs 40 mins)**

Distance: 11 kms **Time Required:** 3.5/4 hours **Rating:** Medium
Total Height Gain: 300m **Map:** IGN 1:50000 Zafarraya 1040 (18-43)
Ⓦ **Water:** 300m beyond waypoint 11 @ 1 hr 45 mins

5 Canillas de Albaida: Cajulas valley Circuit

Overview

This shortish circuit numbers amongst the more seductive rambles of the western Axarquía. The walk leads out from Canillas de Albaida by way of an enchanting riverside path that meanders through thick stands of oleander, crossing back and forth across the Cájula river: it's easily passable unless there's been heavy rain. After a steep climb the middle section of the walk is mostly a via farm tracks and is quite different in feel. But this part of the hike is easy to follow and allows you to drink in the big views north towards the Sierras of Tejeda and Almijara without having to concentrate on where your feet are going. The final stretch of the walk leads you up an ancient cobbled path from where you're treated to more enchanting vistas of Canillas de Albaida and the Chapel of Santa Ana. The walk is particulary memorable when the oleander which line the river banks are in flower during the summer months. You push past a few prickly plants before you reach the forestry track so it's a good idea to slip a pair of long trousers into your day pack.

The Walk

The walk begins at a junction next to a shrine dedicated to the Virgin and Christ (1) set in a wall at the entrance of the village: you'll see it as you arrive from Cómpeta. With your back to the Virgin (no disrespect) turn left and pass along the edge of a square between a college and the village *Consultorio* (glossary). Exit the square down Calle Llano de la Fuente passing by a spring. At the bottom of the street turning right along Calle Poeta Migiñas you come to the pretty *plaza* of the village. Head straight across the square into Calle Málaga which after a few

metres becomes Calle Plazoleta. At the end of the street bear left and drop down Calle Axarquía. At the bottom of the street continue straight ahead to a green railing ❷ where you pick up a narrow cobbled path path which passes a pylon then zigzags down into the Cájula valley to meet with a road. Here rurn right, cross the river and immediately bear sharp right at a sign for *Río Turvilla* ❸ along a concrete track that runs towards an old mill.

The track soon narrows to become a path which follows the course of the river, crossing it several times but always sticking close to the river. The path eventually crosses the river once again **(25 mins)**, zigzags to a higher level, then passes beneath a steep cliff then a second overhanging rock face before descending and crossing the river once again ❹.

Careful! 200m (it's worth counting them out) after crossing the river you reach a fork in the path ❺. Here cut left through a gap in the oleander, cross the river once more via stepping stones then climb steeply up the other side with a fence now

running to your right. After about 75m the path broadens to become a track. You'll now see a small farm building up ahead of you. Before reaching it branch right off the track at a sign for *Camino Río* 6 along a narrow path which cuts through a grove of avocado trees. It shortly winds past the stumps of a line of poplars then continues on a rather serpentine course marked by cairns. About 300m beyond the line of poplar stumps the path crosses another which has a black plastic water pipe following its course. Having crossed the pipe bear left and wind down to the river which you cross via stepping stones 7 before ducking beneath a branch barrier marking the boundary of a farm.

The path climbs then loops left along the stream's east bank, sticking close to the water. A ruined farm comes into sight on the other side of the river. When you're almost opposite the ruin cross the river a final time and follow a path up to the house 8. Looping past the farm to its right climb steeply to the northwest, parallel to the valley of a tributary of the Cájula. As you climb you'll see a solitary modern house on the crown of a hill. Remember this landmark which you'll later pass by. The path swings right, descends, crosses the (dry) streambed 9 then bears once more right and loops uphill then crosses a series of terraces. Up to your right you'll now spot a small farm. Choose the easiest path up across the terraces to the east wall of the farm where, passing a metal post, you reach a dirt track. Here turn right 10 **(1 hr 15 mins)** and head down towards the solitary house you saw earlier.

Reaching the house the track bears left then once more right before adopting a course towards the head of the Cájula gorge and a cluster of houses. Descending it crosses El Arroyo de Luchina via a concrete bridge 11. Climbing again it runs past a pretty farm and, just beyond it, a line of cypress trees before descending to a point where several tracks converge. Ignore two tracks cutting right and one cutting up left: continue along the main track which passes just right of a water deposit where there's a tap W with drinking water. **(1 hr 45 mins)**

Bearing right the track climbs gently on a course parallel to the Cájula back towards Canillas. It eventually passes two pylons, then a water tank then a house with a line of cypresses marking its boundary. Beyond the house the track swings left where a track branches down to the right with a chain across it. Ignore this turning and continue for just 50m then angle right off the track 12 on a path which zigzags down to the river Llanada de Turvilla. Cross a bridge 13 over the stream, bear right, then wind up the other side of the valley towards the Santa Ana Chapel. After a steep climb, and passing beneath the chapel, the path merges with a track which passes beneath the village cemetery. Reaching a pylon bear left, right and left again then retrace the route you followed earlier back to the start point of the walk 1. **(2 hrs 45 mins)**

Distance: 16 kms **Time Required:** 6.5 hours **Rating:** Medium/Difficult
Total Height Gain: 625m **Map:** IGN 1:50000 Zafarraya 1040 (18-43)
W **Water:** spring at waypoint 18 @ 4 hrs 40 mins

6 Cómpeta: Puerto Blanquillo Circuit

Overview

This long loop out from Cómpeta makes for an unforgettable day of walking and takes in a stunning slice of the Sierra de Almijara. Be sure to get going early if planning to walk this route in the warmer months and be prepared for a rigorous start to the day: from the main square in Cómpeta to Puerto Blanquillo there's a height gain of 575m. Your efforts will be amply rewarded: the approach to Blanquillo climbs through wildly beautiful terrain and once you're over the pass the landscape changes dramatically as you drop down the lush, subtropical Cueva del Melero valley. You may encounter lorries on the section of road that leads from the quarry down to Canillas de Albaida so plan your walk so as to negotiate this section between 2pm and 4pm when work stops for lunch. Remember that you could shorten the walk by returning to Cómpeta from Canillas by taxi or knock 200m off the initial ascent by taking a taxi up to the football ground.

The Walk

The walk begins in the main square of Cómpeta, La Plaza de la Almijara ❶. Leave the square at its top, right-hand corner along Calle Carretería. The street climbs steeply then bears right. Pass a fountain then at house no. 60 turn left and up a narrow street with concrete steps. Take the higher option at any junction. Reaching a tarmac road turn left. Passing by Bar David you reach the Plaza del Carmen. Here bear right along Camino de Jata following a sign for *Campo de Fútbol*. At the top of the street bear left at a fork to reach the top road around the village ❷. Cross over the road and climb past a group of modern houses. The road zigzags up to the entrance of the village football ground. Just before its entrance cut right, then left and where the road ends drop down to a sandy path which cuts along to the right of a wall topped by a fence. The path climbs steeply, crosses a water pipe, then passes a water deposit before angling up right to a track 3. **(30 mins)**

Turn left along the track which climbs gently, passes through a swathe of pines, then reaches a junction by two metal posts. Here cut right and continue climbing. Looking ahead you'll see the track later makes a huge loop left where you'll spot a sandy path climbing steeply esatwards away from the track. Be ready to cut right right up this path at a cairn **(55 mins)** 4 which follows a line of pylons steeply upwards.

The path merges with a track 5 and runs on towards a stand of pines, now more level. Ahead you'll see an observation post with antennae atop a steep, convex hill. Views open out to the east as you contour round the base of the hill beneath the hut, passing by its concreted access road. The track descends, climbs again then once more runs downhill. Careful! At a point where the track arcs hard left cut right on a narrow path 6 which immediately passes a rock with a red circle. **(1 hr 45 mins)**

The path passes an abandoned farm then descends. Faint red arrows and dots mark the path which shortly passes a *calera* (glossary) 7. Eventually the path bears left, descends through pines then runs up to a second ruined farm. Here an arrow 8 directs you left past the farm and its threshing circle. The path runs parallel to a low wall, climbs past a second *calera* before reaching a third ruined farm daubed with the words *Casa de Donados*. Beyond the farm the path swings left and climbs up the left bank of the Arroyo de Pradillos.

Keep your eyes to the left of the path. At a point just 10m

before the path crosses the bed of the stream 9 angle left at cairn: it's easily missed. Follow cairns and red dots up to the Puerto Blanquillo pass 10 **(2 hrs 30 mins)**, the highest point of your walk @1202m. A few metres beyond the pass you reach a broad track. Turn left along the track for 250m. Reaching a cairn and marker post 11 cut right down a loose, sandy path. Zigzagging steeply down the path improves as it runs left of a (dry) stream. Crossing the stream it climbs steeply before dropping down to the stream of Arroyo de la Cueva del Melero where ahead of you is a farm.

Don't cross the stream but rather bear left 12 down its left bank for 60m then cross to the opposite bank to reach the terraces beneath the farm. Follow the path parallel to an old fence, descending more or less parallel to the right bank of the stream. Soon you pass through a rickety wooden gate 13 then go through a second gate made of an old bed base: you begin to see more waymarking posts. Beyond the gate a metal fence runs just right of the path. Where the fence angles right the path crosses a (dry) streambed then angles left, then right, and crosses a second (dry) streambed. The path, cobbled in parts, loops down to the Cueva del Melero stream which it crosses then runs up to another gate made from a bed base 14. Beyond the gate the path crosses back to the right bank before returning once again to the left bank where it widens to become a track 15. **(3 hrs 35 mins)**

After climbing for a short distance the path descends: a metal fence soon runs to your right. Passing a water tank you come to a fork. Here angle down to the right, still following the fence. After 150m you reach a gap in the fence marked by a post and a red arrow 16. Cut right through the gap then bear left at a red dot along a narrow path which loops back and forth across the streambed through clumps of oleander. Eventually you arrive at the Fábrica de Luz de Canillas **(4 hrs 5 mins)**. Here you cross the stream a final time 17. Passing directly beneath the Fábrica you come to a parking area. Head straight down the tarmac road which follows the left bank of the Río Llanada de la Turvilla. You soon pass a quarry. Passing the spring of Fuente El Chorillo W 18 head on down the valley to a junction where a road cuts up to the Chapel of San Antón 19. **(4 hrs 50 mins)**

Here angle left at a sign for *Cómpeta* with a walker icon and climb a section of steep, concreted track, passing by a water deposit to the left of the track. Continue up for 60m then cut right at a second sign for *Cómpeta* 20. The sandy track bears sharply left then passes above a house with a swimming pool. The track narrows to become a path which runs beside an irrigation channel. Reaching a three way fork take the lower path which shortly runs up to a tarmac road. Turn right along the road then after 300m cut left up the second of two concrete drives. Just before the gate, at a small cairn, 21 cut right along a narrow path which runs on through a beautiful swathe of irrigated terraces. The path arcs hard left and then once more right and reaches a fork. Take the higher path which has recently been widened and wooden railings added. Passing a builder's yard you reach a tarmac road at the outskirts of Cómpeta 22. Cut right, then left and head all the way along Calle de San Antonio to return to the square 1. **(5 hrs 45 mins)**

Costa Tropical: Eastern Sierra de Tejeda, Almijara & Alhama

Walks close to Frigiliana, Nerja, Maro & Almuñécar

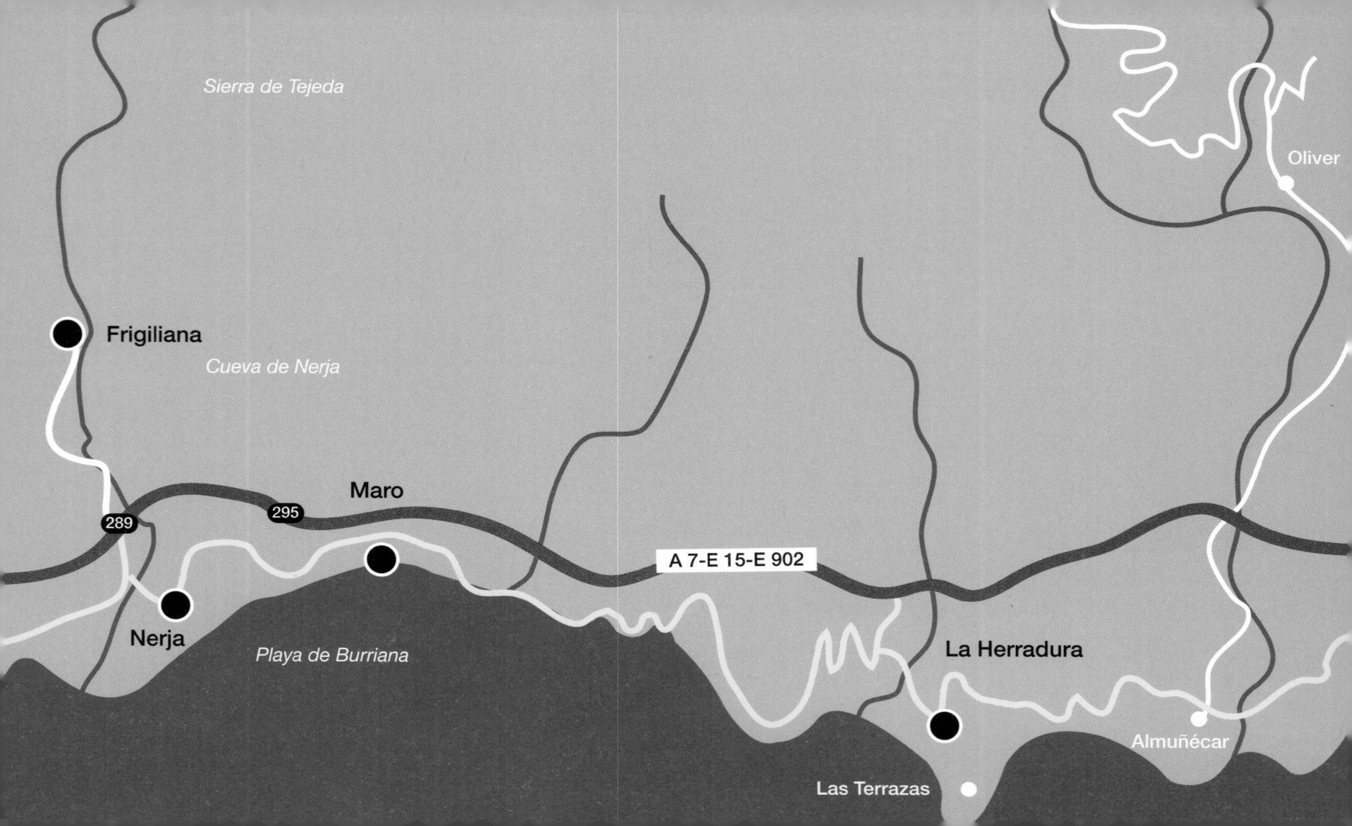
Sierra de Tejeda
Oliver
Frigiliana
Cueva de Nerja
Maro
295
289
A 7-E 15-E 902
Nerja
Playa de Burriana
La Herradura
Almuñécar
Las Terrazas

Costa Tropical: Eastern Sierra de Tejeda, Almijara & Alhama

At the western flank of the Parque Natural de Sierra de Tejeda, Almijara & Alhama a broad band of cultivated terrain separates the main massif from the sea. The topography of its eastern side is very different in nature. Here, just metres back from the Mediterranean, a line of cliffs rises steeply up to a narrow band of coastal plain beyond which the Almijara mountains rise precipitously upwards. This majestic swathe of limestone terrain is cut through by spectacular mountain gorges which have been hewn out over the millenia by the waters that run down from the high *sierra.* The walking possibilities in this extraordinary tract of land are limitless and when researching the routes in this area it was a tough decision as to which walks to include. Those I've chosen can be divided into three categories: cliffside walks, gorge walks and high mountain trails. Together they offer an enticing first taste of the eastern end of the Park.

The cliffside paths described fall within the *Paraje Natural de los Acantilados de Maro-Cerro Gordo.* Stretching east from Maro towards Almuñecar the sanctuary includes the Costa Tropical's most beautiful beaches as well as a line of 16th century watchtowers whose purpose was to give warning by smoke or fire when raids by North African corsairs appeared imminent. Vehicle access to some beaches is limited during summer whilst others can only be reached via steep paths which cut down from the clifftops: even in July and August you can stake a claim on the sand. The beauty of this area is not just on *terra firma*: the turquoise waters at the base of the cliffs are picture-perfect and offer some of the finest scuba diving on the Mediterranean coast.

The gorges of the Chillar and the Higuerón are amongst Andalucía's most magnificent inventions of Nature with waterfalls, rock pools and towering rock faces. To access the most spectacular sections of the gorges you'll need to wade and scramble over rocks but there are rich rewards for your efforts. The walks are best undertaken in summer when you can bathe in the rock pools and, given that these are there-and-back itineraries, you can decide how far you'd like to go. The four higher mountain walks explore the flank of the Almijara closest to the sea. Of these El Camino del Imán is a stunning roller-coaster walk which begins at the Nerja cave (it coincides with Day 1 of The Andalucían Coast to Coast Walk) and is not to be missed.

On all walks, including those close to the sea, you can expect to see groups of *Capra Hispánica* whose numbers have multiplied since they were declared a protected species whilst birdlife is astonishly varied thanks to the Park and *Paraje* encompassing marine, coastal and inland terrain.

Maro, Frigiliana and Nerja all had a moment of glory when the land here was planted with cane for sugar manufacture: the crop thrived thanks to the region's subtropical climate. This flourishing industry rapidly declined in the early 20th century when it proved unable to compete with sugar manufactured from beet. The ruins of a number of factories are all that remain of what once was a cornerstone of the local economy. All three villages have several places to stay whilst their large, resident ex-pat communities have spawned a number of excellent restaurants. Frigiliana has won numerous prizes for conservation and is amongst southern Spain's prettiest villages: it would be my first choice when looking for somewhere to stay in the area. Behind Maro lies the Cueva de Nerja. This complex of underground caverns and lakes, complete with ancient rock art, was discovered by a group of Maro schoolboys hunting for bats in 1959. A visit to the cave could dovetail nicely with both the Camino del Imán and Cortijo Almachares circuit.

BEST SLEEPS

Maro

Hotel Restaurante Playa Maro €–€€
Tel: 952 529 582 Email: playamaro@ hotelplayamaro.com
www.hotelplayamaro.com
Cheap-and-cheerful 3 star hostelry on the eastern side of the village with sauna and pool.

Nerja

Hotel Paraiso del Mar €€–€€€
Tel: 952 521 621 Email: info@hotelparaisodelmar.es
www.hotelparaisodelmar.es
Friendly, family-run hotel next to the Parador with great sea views.

Frigiliana

Hospedería El Caravansar €–€€
Tel: 952 533 586
Cosy B&B a short walk from Plaza del Ingenio with small, comfortable rooms.

Las Chinas €
Tel: 952 533 073
Basic *hostal* with home cooking, five minutes from Plaza del Ingenio.

Taxis: Nerja/Maro 952 520 537, Frigiliana 622 101 095

Distance: 8 kms **Time Required:** 3.5 hours **Rating:** Medium
Total Height Gain: 700m **Map:** IGN 1:50000 Vélez-Málaga 1054 (18-44)
Ⓦ **Water:** no springs along the way so take plenty

1 Frigiliana: Ascent of El Fuerte

Overview

Towering to almost 1000m the rugged massif of El Fuerte provides a stunning backdrop to pretty village of Frigiliana. The mountain played a dramatic role in the region's history at the time of the last *Morisco* uprisings. The Moslems who stayed on after the Reconquest knew they were living on borrowed time yet were loathe to abandon this exquisite swathe of *Al Andalus*. Taking refuge atop the rocky pinnacle of El Fuerte their last stand against de Zuarzo's troops is one of the most evocative incidents of the rebellion. When you get to the top of this dramatic pinnacle of rock you'll appreciate why they chose the mountain as a last refuge. The path that leads up from Frigiliana is well marked and easy to follow even if you have some 650m of fairly steep climbing to negotiate. But the extraordinary panorama that awaits at the top more than justifies the effort. There's a path down the mountain's southern flank that drops down to the track leading to El Acebuchal but it's steep and poorly waymarked. But returning by the same route is just as much of a treat: the vast views that you get at every point along the way make this itinerary an absolute must-walk.

The Walk

The walk begins in Frigiliana in the square at the entrance of the village, La Plaza del Ingenio (1) next to a round hut containing a puppet theatre. From here head up the cobbled road beneath El Ingenio passing a series of ceramic pictures. Continue along Calle Real then opposite house 9A cut right up a cobbled staircase at a sign *Barrio Morisco-Mudéjar*. At house 13 pass beneath an arch then bear right at a sign *Panoramicas*.

Reaching The Garden Restaurant the path divides 2. Carry straight ahead passing above the restaurant. After 100m the path narrows then loops steeply upwards. Reaching a tiled bench head straight on following a sign for *El Castillo* 3. You pass several sculptures, the work of a resident ex-pat. Zigzagging higher views open out across the village and east towards the Higuerón valley. Climbing through a swathe of young pines you pass a delapidated mirador 4. Passing a second mirador 5 you come to a bluff from where you'll see a large water tank down to the left. Cut left on a narrow path which zigzags down to a track 6 **(15 mins)** where angling right you pass the water tank.

Beyond the water deposit cut right up a cobbled staircase that passes an old mill then zigzags up to a pylon. Here bear left. You'll see marker posts. After climbing steeply the path angles left 7 into a group of pines, descends for a few metres, then resumes its ascent. The trees thin out as views open out towards the Mediterranean. The path runs on towards the northwest, parallel to a ridge which is now to your right. Bearing right it climbs more steeply as views briefly open out to the north. Soon the path adopts its former course to the left of the ridge before passsing an old *calera* (glossary) 8 **(55 mins)** then runs on towards the towering massif of El Fuerte. After descending for a short distance the path angles left then climbs again. Passing through a breach in the rocks angle left then continue to the summit of El Fuerte where you reach a trig point (976m) and a sign *Fin de Sendero* 9. **(1 hr 15 mins)** Return by the same route back to the start point of the walk 1.
(2 hrs 5 mins)

Distance: 15.5 kms **Time Required:** 5 hours **Rating:** Medium
Total Height Gain: 375m **Map:** IGN 1:50000 Vélez-Málaga 1054 (18-44) & Motril 1055 (19-44) Ⓦ **Water:** spring at waypoint 5 @ 35 mins

2 Frigiliana: The Río Higuerón Gorge

Overview

This there-and-back walk leads you north along the Higuerón river valley into a wild and beautiful swathe of the Sierra de Enmedio. Being a linear walk you can make this trail as long as you choose though if you're walking the route in the summer months you'll certainly want to get as far as the beautiful rock pools of the river's upper course. This adventurous hike might not be to everyone's taste as you are obliged to wade through the river at several points as well as clamber across boulders: think canyoning at this point rather than walking. But that's all a part of the fun and it's worth persevering to reach the rock face and waterfall at waypoint 10. As well as your walking boots it would be a good idea to have some kind of non-perishable footwear in your day pack along with your swimming gear: the large water tank you pass by near the beginning and end of the walk is as spectacular an outdoor bathing spot as you could hope to find.

The Walk

The walk begins in Frigiliana in the square at the entrance of the village, La Plaza del Ingenio (1) next to a round hut containing a puppet theatre. From the hut cross the road to the Unicaja bank then angle left at a sign for *Río Higuerón* then follow a concrete road that loops steeply down to the river (2). Cross to its eastern bank then angle left on a broad, pebbly track. You soon pass a large water deposit (3) just to the left of the track then a small white hut. Head straight on past a red and white marker post (where the GR-242 cuts east towards Maro) straight up the Higuerón Valley. The track leads past a *calera* (glossary) (4).

The track runs on to reach a picnic area where the river has been dammed and where there's a twin-spouted spring W 5. **(35 mins)** The vegetation now becomes denser and soon you're obliged to pick your way across the river, still following the rough track which loops to and fro across its bed: there are stepping stones at some crossings. Soon you pass by a white shrine to the right of the river bed 6. The valley widens **(1 hr)** as the river braids. At this stage the right side of the valley offers the easiest walking. Sticking to the main valley you pass two tributaries of the Higuerón, unmarked on the ING 1:50000 map. The river angles to the right at which stage a water channel runs over to your left. The going becomes tougher underfoot as you head on up the pebbly river bed before passing a small white hut with a green door 7 where the river angles left, adopting a more northerly course, as it leads past a weir. The valley soon narrows once again: you'll now see two black plastic pipes to the left of the river bed. Soon you reach the first of several rock pools 8. **(1 hr 30 mins)**

The gorge narrows to just 3m then widens once more. Here it's easier going along the river's right bank though soon you're obliged to drop back down into the water. Reaching a confluence 9 with another valley, El Barranco del Mármol, take the right fork which cuts towards the towering massif of the Cerro del Cisne. From this point the walk becomes more of a canyoning adventure: how far you continue will depend on how much you enjoy a hands-on, wet river experience, but a very exciting one at that. Climbing on past more pools the gorge again narrows down. Reaching a 4 metre high waterfall the adventure comes to an end for all but rock climbers 10. **(2 hrs 15 mins)** From here it's a question of retracing your (very wet) footsteps back to the start point of the walk 1. **(4 hrs 25 mins)**

Distance: 12 kms **Time Required:** 4.5 hours **Rating:** Medium
Total Height Gain: 475m **Map:** IGN 1:50000 Vélez-Málaga 1054 (18-44)
Ⓦ **Water:** no springs along the way so take plenty

3 Frigiliana: Cruz de Pinto via the Higuerón Gorge Circuit

Overview

This half day ramble has an astonishing variety of scenery considering that you're never more than 5 kilometres from Frigiliana. From the village you drop down into the spectacular gorge of the Río Higuerón. After cutting north along the river a steep path (the final section of Maro to Frigiliana trail which is also described in this book) leads up the gorge's eastern side before cutting south along the top of a ridge to La Cruz de Pinto, a hilltop shrine dedicated to La Virgen del Carmen. You then loop back down to the gorge where you follow a path through one of its narrowest sections before the final steep pull back up to Frigiliana. You could pack long trousers for the rather overgrown middle section of the walk. Remember that the path through the gorge on the walk's final section can be dangerous after heavy rain. If in doubt head straight across the river at waypoint 13, climb the track which arcs up the western side of the gorge then return to the Plaza del Ingenio along the Nerja to Cómpeta road.

The Walk

This walk begins in Frigiliana in the square at the entrance to the village, La Plaza del Ingenio (1). With your back to a series of tiled pictures head down the hill then cut left along the road that runs to the right of the Unicaja bank signposted *Río Higuerón.* This concreted road loops steeply down to the river (2). Cross to its eastern bank then swing left on a broad, pebbly track. You soon pass a large water deposit, just to the left of the track, then a small white hut. Just beyond the hut you reach a sign for *Sendero de la Fuente del Esparto, 5.5 kms* (3). Here cut right on

a narrow path which climbs steeply up the side of the gorge to the top of a pass 4. **(35 mins)**

Continue for just a couple of metres beyond the pass then cut right off the footpath at a small cairn: ignore the marker post pointing left for *Fuente del Esparto*. You pick up a narrow path which leads up to the highest point of the ridge 5. Here bear left and continue along the apex of the ridge. Ahead in the distance you should be able to spot a pylon and, just behind it, the narrow footpath that will later lead you up to the Cruz de Pinto. Faint red, blue and yellow waymarking, as well as cairns, help you to plot your course.

You reach a dip in the ridge where the path angles right 6 then runs on just to the right of the ridge's highest point. Soon you pass a massive circular cairn. Continuing along the ridge you reach a second large cairn 7 where the path divides. Take the

left fork and continue along the top of the ridge. Shortly you descend and pass immediately left of a pylon. The path angles right then reaches a fork where a path angles left, a track right 8. Cut left on the path which climbs up the left side of the ridge. After a steep ascent you arrive at La Cruz de Pinto 9. **(1 hr 5 mins)**

From this high vantage point there's a fine 360 degree panorama of the sea, the coastal villages, Frigiliana and, to the north, the crumpled massif of the Sierra de Almijara.

Facing the north side of the shrine, and the small black door protecting its votive offerings, cut east along the ridge for 40m then swing right and pick up a path which leads down the hill's southern side. After descending for about 100m it passes left of a rocky outcrop then cuts right through a small col 10. Beyond the col the path descends steeply back into the Higuerón valley

where after a 10 minute descent it reaches a track by a sign for *Parque Natural* 11. Here bear left and descend for 200m to a point where the track you're following converges with three more 12. Here loop sharply right onto the most westerly (lower) of the tracks which climbs slightly before levelling. A line of telegraph posts runs beside the track. Soon you pass Cortijo Floreana. The track begins to descend, passing by a number of small houses/farms and groves of olives and avocado, then finally a horse stable before it reaches the valley floor 13. **(1 hr 35 mins)**

Cut right just before you reach the Higuerón river and head along its right bank. You soon pass just left of a red-tiled building. The indistinct path loops back and forth across the river and then, as the gorge narrows down, climbs along the stream's east bank via a stone staircase beyond which it descends steeply for a short distance. The path, cobbled in parts, passes a spring (often dry) then continues to loop back and forth across the river. You eventually reach the point where you first crossed the Higuerón at the beginning of the walk. 2 Here cut left across the river and retrace your footsteps back up to your point of departure 1. **(2 hrs 20 mins)**

Distance: 14.5 kms **Time Required:** 5 hours **Rating:** Medium/Difficult
Total Height Gain: 875m **Map:** IGN 1:50000 Motril 1055 (19-44) & Vélez-Málaga 1054 (18-44) Ⓦ **Water:** tap at 55 mins @ waypoint 6

4 Maro to Frigiliana via the Camino del Imán

Overview

This mountain trail, known to locals as *El Camino del Imán*, is amongst the most spectacular walks of the eastern Axarquía. The itinerary begins in gentle mode as it heads along a broad forestry track which leads north from the Cueva de Nerja: the cave is well worth a visit before you set out. Once you've passed the picnic area of El Pinarillo things take on a different tempo as the trail roller-coasters its way west to Frigiliana across four deep gorges via a spectacular narrow path. It scarcely seems possible, when you behold such wild mountain scenery, that you're only a few kilometres from the urban sprawl of the coast. This is a walk to be savoured so get going early with a picnic and plenty of water: this will also ensure that you'll get some shade from the pines on the approach to El Pinarillo. There are regular buses between Frigiliana and Nerja but from there you'll need to take a taxi up to the Nerja cave. Or you could leave a car close to the square in Frigiliana then taxi to the beginning of the walk. If you're tackling the walk in summer be sure to leave time enough for a dip in one of the rock pools of the Chillar gorge.

Getting to the beginning of the walk

From the A7-E15 motorway exit for Maro then follow signs for Cueva de Nerja. Reaching the main gate into the Cueva car park turn left where there's plenty of space for parking beneath the pines.

The Walk

The walk begins just outside the car park of the Nerja Cave next to its green entrance gates 1. From here head north up a track following signs *Área Recreativa El Pinarillo* and *Fuente del Esparto* passing a signboard detailing the GR 242 footpath. Passing a barrier continue along the main track parallel to the Barranco de Maro. You'll see wooden marker posts with white arrows marking your way. You reach a fork where one sign points left for *Area Recreativa El Pinarillo* and another right for *Sendero* 2. **(35 mins)**

Here branch left. The track continues to climb and eventually arrives at El Pinarillo. Here the track divides again 3. Bearing left you pass a map of the park then head straight on through the picnic/camping area. You can replenish your water bottle about 50m past the map at taps next to a barbecue W. **(55 mins)** At the far end, after passing a threshing circle, you come to a green barrier 4. Beyond it drop down a broad track and cross the (dry) riverbed. 20m beyond the river the track divides. Take the narrower, left hand path which climbs steeply and shortly crosses the track that you have just left. Head on up a deeply eroded path. You reach a broader track where you'll see a marker post 5. Don't turn right here (this fork leads to the Fuente del Esparto) but rather cut left along a broad track which climbs to the top of a pass where it passes a *No Entry* sign 6. Magnificent views open out to the north and west. Continue along the track which arcs hard right and runs up to a chain across the track. **(1 hr 20 mins)**

Continue past the chain remembering that you'll be cutting left onto a narrow path after approximately 950m. You pass two marker posts to the left of the track then, at a point where the track cuts right, reach a third post and a large cairn 7. Here cut left on a narrow path which zigzags steeply down into the Chillar gorge. The path drops down past a small ruin, crosses a water

channel then continues down to the riverbed 8. Here bear right at a blue arrow on a rock along the river's east bank for 30m then cross to the opposite bank by way of stepping stones. Look for blue arrows. After running close to the river's west bank for 50m (where there are rock pools where you can cool off in the warmer months) the path angles left and begins to climb. You reach a point where the path divides by a marker post 9. Here turn left and continue to climb steeply. Eventually you reach the top of the second steep pass of the walk 10. **(2 hrs 20 mins)**

Beyond the pass the path, deeply eroded in parts, descends into the next valley, soon crossing a (dry) streambed 11. It then climbs for a short distance before descending and crossing another stream where there's a cairn and a marker post 12. After crossing two more (dry) streambeds it climbs to the top of a third pass where views open out into the next valley 13. Here the vegetation becomes sparser, the result of a forest fire. The path again descends and crosses another (dry) streambed 14 before climbing once again to the top of the fourth and final pass from where the Higuerón valley is now visible to the west 15. The path runs along the spine of the ridge and, after passing a marker post where there are views both east and west, runs gently downhill just east of the ridge for a short distance then reaches a divide by a marker post 16. **(3 hrs 10 mins)**

Here cut right by a rock with a large blue dot and drop down a beautiful narrow path which cuts through a stand of pines to reach the valley floor and a sign for *Frigiliana-Fuente del Esparto* 17. Swinging left and descending you pass a white hut then a large water tank. The track leads on down the valley then loops across to the river's west bank towards a large green water pipe where it becomes concreted 18. Follow the track steeply upwards. After a final steep climb you reach the Unicaja bank and, just beyond, the Plaza del Ingenio and the Frigiliana taxi rank 19. **(3 hrs 45 mins)**

Distance: 14 kms **Time Required:** 5.5/6 hours **Rating:** Medium/Difficult
Total Height Gain: 625m **Map:** IGN 1:50000 Motril 1055 (19-44) & Vélez-Málaga 1054 (18-44) Ⓦ **Water:** no springs along the way so take plenty

5 Nerja: The Río Chillar Gorge Circuit

Overview

The Chillar canyon is one of Andalucía's most spectacular natural events, a fabulous gorge that cuts a deep gash in the southern flank of the Sierra de Almijara that funnels down to little more than 2 metres at its narrowest point. It begs to be explored but this is no normal hiking trail: even during the Andalucían summer you're obliged to wade from bank to bank as you follow the river northwards, scrambling across boulders, ducking beneath tree trunks and climbing a series of waterfalls that feed several idyllic rock pools. Leaving the river the next part of the circuit follows the course of a narrow water channel which contours high above the river: you'll need a head for heights on this section. Finally, after a steep climb, you follow a path that hugs the spine of a high ridge back towards the sea before zigzagging back down to the Chillar. If the complete circuit sounds a little too adventurous you can turn this into an easier there-and-back walk or cut 30 minutes off the walking time by carrying on along the water channel at waypoint 12, thus avoiding the ridge walk. This isn't a circuit to be undertaken after heavy rain or when storms are predicted.

Getting to the beginning of the walk

Arriving in Nerja from Maro head along the N340 to a roundabout with palm trees. Turn left following a sign Cahorros del Río Chillar. Follow the road round to the right then cut left at a sign for 'Rastrillo' into Calle Cisne. Reaching a roundabout turn right. Head straight over the next roundabout into Calle Mirto. Reaching a junction turn left and follow the road down under the motorway to a Stop sign and the gates to a cement factory. There's space for parking 50m further on.

The Walk

From the parking area beyond the cement factory 1 head north along the river following a track that runs past a sign *Parque Natural Sierra Tejeda, Almijara & Alhama*. Soon you pass a graffiti-covered concrete hut 2. Continuing up the gorge you lose the pylons as you cross from one side of the river to the other. Passing a group of buildings and a sluice gate **(25 mins)** 3 the gorge narrows down: from this point on you'll be wading in sections. The gorge narrows to just arm's width **(45 mins)** beyond which you reach the first rock pools. The gorge widens once more as you head on up the river: you'll need to climb across tree trunks and scramble across boulders as you climb past a series of waterfalls with cliffs towering high above you.

Blue dots now mark your path as it threads through the rocks. Reaching a point where the valley has widened still further the river braids into a series of streams 4. Here plot a course along the river's right bank, being prepared to use hands as well as feet. You soon reach more fabulous rock pools, one fed by a high waterfall 5. **(1 hr 40 mins)** *This could be a point to turn back if you prefer an easier up-and-down walk.*

Continue up the river bed which adopts a northwesterly course, still marked by blue dots. After scrambling over rocks and pulling yourself up waterfalls the path becomes clearer as it threads its way on between oleander, pines and lentiscus, crossing from bank to bank. At a point where the path angles to the left side of the river you begin to see marker posts and more blue dots before you reach a red and white G.R. marker post pointing left 6. **(2 hrs 10 mins)**

Here a path cuts up the west side of the gorge, leading to Frigiliana. Ignoring this path retrace your footsteps down the gorge for some 80m. Reaching marker posts to either side of

the river 7 angle left through the oleander along a sandy path for 20m then angle left again, away from the river 8 along a path that loops steeply upwards. 350m from the river you reach a junction where a broad path (it is in fact a water channel) crosses your path 9.

Here cut right along the water channel. Passing through a breach in the rocks 10 drop down a flight of steps then follow a fenced walkway round another rocky outcrop before passing a sluice gate 11. **(2 hrs 30 mins)** Bearing right the channel crosses a (dry) streambed then passes through another breach in the rock where the path is fenced. Careful! Reaching a point where the old concrete slabs covering the channel have been replaced by newer ones, you reach a large cairn 12. **(2 hrs 40 mins)**

Here you have a choice. *The easiest option is to continue straight on along the water channel to waypoint 19. If you do so, deduct 30 mins from all subsequent timings.* If you're happy with a more challenging walk cut left up a sandy path which zigzags steeply up to reach a track on a hairpin bend 13 at El Collado de los Galgos. Here angle hard right, past a post indicating this isn't the course of the GR-242, to a three way junction 14. Take the middle option (the right branch would do just as well) and head along the ridge top which cuts towards the sea on a southwesterly course. The path runs up and down across a series of peaks, sticking to the spine of the ridge. Eventually the path drops down to a fence and gate 15.

Angle left along the fence, then right, to pick up the continuation of the path which climbs once again: it occasionally braids but taking the higher options you can't go wrong. Reaching twin cairns 16 **(3 hrs 20 mins)** cut right down a narrower path which descends southwest towards the Chillar sticking close to the spine of a ridge. Angling south for 200m the path reaches twin cairns where it arcs back right 17 then drops steeply back down to the water channel at a small reservoir feeding a black turbine pipe 18. **(3 hrs 55 mins)**

Leaving the reservoir head southwest to pick up the footpath which loops steeply down to the left of the turbine pipe. Crossing the race angle left then drop down a flight of steps to reach the buildings you passed at waypoint 3 3. Cut left then make your way back down the Chillar to the start point of the walk 1. **(4 hrs 30 mins)**

Distance: 14.5 kms **Time Required:** 5/5.5 hours **Rating:** Medium
Total Height Gain: 675m **Map:** IGN 1:50000 Motril 1055 (19-44)
Ⓦ **Water:** no springs along the way so take plenty

6 Maro: Cortijo Almachares Circuit

Overview

This averagely challenging walk explores the wild swathe of mountains that lie just to the north of the Costa Tropical: it seems unbelievable that such majestic scenery is only a few minutes away from the busy coastal roads and housing developments that fan out between Maro and Nerja. The walk begins just outside the Nerja Cave (it's well worth a visit) and at first follows the forestry track that leads up towards the Pinarillo picnic area. You then cut down a narrow path into the bed of the Barranco de Maro which you follow on to the north before cutting steeply up eastwards to the ruined farm of Cortijo de la Civilia (marked on the ING 1:50000 map as *La Sibilia*). Retracing your footsteps for a few hundred metres you pick up a narrow footpath which leads down to the Cortijo Almachares: this is a wonderful spot to break for a picnic with sweeping views south towards the Mediterranean. From here you continue down towards the sea before descending into the Arroyo del Romero which you follow on south towards Maro. The path is slightly overgrown beyond the Cortijo Almachares so be sure to have a pair of long trousers in your day pack.

Getting to the beginning of the walk

From the A7-E15 motorway exit for Maro then follow signs for Cueva de Nerja. Reaching the main gate into the Cueva car park turn left where there's plenty of space for parking beneath the pines.

The Walk

The walk begins outside the entrance gates to Cueva de Nerja (1). From here head north up a track following signs

Área Recreativa El Pinarillo and *Fuente del Esparto* passing a signboard detailing the GR 242 footpath. Passing a barrier continue along the main track parallel to the Barranco de Maro. After 1.15 kms, just before teaching a sign for *Parque Natural*, cut left at a cairn and wooden post 2 **(15 mins)** down a narrow path which leads into the pines, looking for cairns. Reaching a rocky area cut right then after 10m angle left and clamber down a slope marked by red dots to the bed of the *barranco* 3. Angling right continue up the river bed along a broad track. Reaching a point where the track ends 4 bear left on a path which angles up the left side of the gorge round a rockfall before returning to the riverbed. Continuing up the river for 350m cut right, away from the streambed, up a broad stony path which climbs, angles right then left, before meeting the track you left at waypoint 2 2. **(55 mins)**

Turn right. After 225m at a junction cut left following a sign *Sendero*. At a point where the track loops hard right, cut left 6 at a marker post up a path which soon meets the track once more. Bear left for 20m then cut right up another path. Meeting the track a third time angle left for a few metres then once again right and continue your ascent. The path angles right to reach a junction where cutting left you return to the track once again 7. Here bear left towards the Pico del Cielo: the cross at its summit is just visible in clear weather. Soon the Mediterranean comes into view. Passing through a bulldozed breach in the rocks 8 the track descends then arcs hard left. Crossing the (dry) streambed of the Arroyo Romero the track bears right then passes a concrete hut with a rusting iron gate 9. **(1 hr 35 mins)** *You could shorten the walk by angling right here and picking up instructions at the second waypoint 9 in these notes.*

Continue up the track with a deep barranco to your left. You'll now see the vestiges of the terraces that once were farmed

round Cortijo La Civilia which you'll soon spot up ahead. At this stage you may spot ibex on the lower reaches of Cerro Molinero. Soon you reach a track which cuts in to the ruined farm 10.
(2 hrs) This is a natural place to break journey. From La Civilia retrace your steps to the hut at waypoint 9 9. Cut round to the southern side of the hut to pick up a narrow path marked by blue dots which winds down through the rosemary and pines. Crossing a low rise the path again descends as Maro comes into view. The sparse vegetation at this stage is testimony of a forest fire. Reaching a swathe of pines the path crosses a dry stream before dropping down to a junction 11. Here cut right to the ruined buildings of the Cortijo Almachares 12. To its west is a flat area, a perfect spot to break journey: there are soaring views out along the Med' to Nerja and further west towards Málaga. **(2 hrs 40 mins)**

From the Cortijo retrace your footsteps for 60m back to

waypoint 11 then continue straight ahead. The path becomes more overgrown as it runs on high above the Arroyo del Romero. Careful! After descending for 900m from Cortijo Almachares be ready to cut right off the footpath you've been following at a point where there is faint yellow and purple waymarking on the rocks 13. The beach of Burriana comes into view as you descend. The path zigzags steeply down to a dry streambed 14 which you follow on down to the bed of the Romero 15. Here cut left and make your way down through the rocks. Sticking to the streambed you pass a cave 16 before the valley widens. Soon the path merges with a track by a green gate 17. **(4 hrs)**

The track runs past a number of smallholdings to a fork 18. Here angle right along a tarmac road which passes above a greenhouse before cutting through a tunnel beneath the A7 motorway 19. Reaching a roundabout head straight across following a sign *Playa Maro/Centro Ciudad* to reach a second roundabout 20. Take the first exit passing right of Hotel Apartamentos Playa Maro. A few metres past Bar Los Pinos turn right up Calle Virgen de las Maravillas 21 then cross the A7 via a newly-built footbridge. Beyond the bridge bear left up to the car park of the Nerja cave. Leaving the car park at its western end you return to the start point of the walk 1.
(4 hrs 20 mins)

Distance: 7 kms **Time Required:** 2.5 hours **Rating:** Easy
Total Height Gain: 225m **Map:** IGN 1:50000 Motril 1055 (19-44)
W **Water:** no springs along the way so take plenty

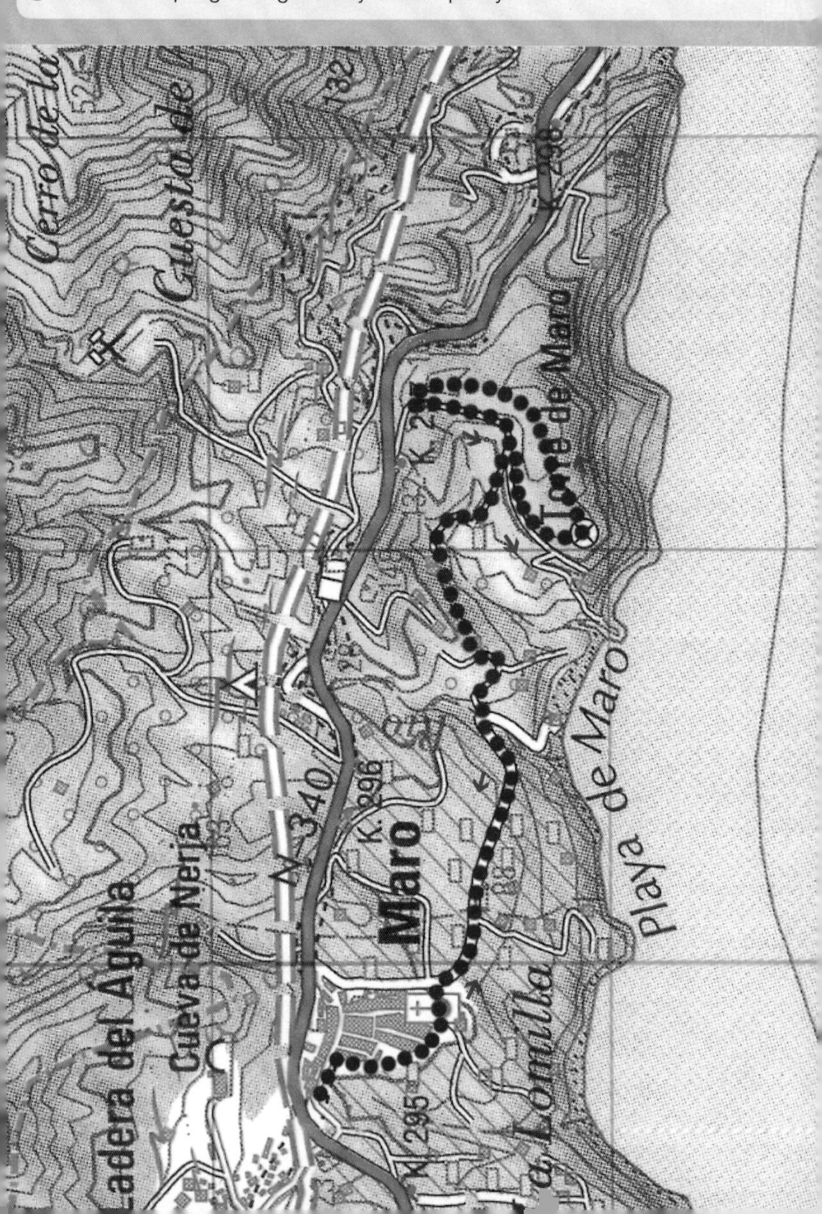

7 Maro: Cliff Circuit via Torre de Maro

Overview

This 7km walk is amongst the easiest listed in this book, a there-and-back ramble with a short loop beyond the Torre de Maro. The first part of the route leads round the edge of Maro: this is the prettiest village of this part of the Axarquía and one of the few to have escaped the development that has blighted so much of the Andalucían seaboard. After cutting down towards Maro's beach (it's worth a quick detour) you head on towards the *torre* through a swathe of irrigated terraces where banana, avocado, custard fruit and vines are cultivated as well as tomatoes, peppers and cucumbers in the plastic-covered greenhouses: you'll soon see why this part of Andalucía's coast is known as the *Costa Tropical.* A steep climb leads up through pine forest to the Torre de Maro. On a clear day, looking east and west along the coast, you'll spot other watch towers with which this one once communicated, signalling warnings by smoke or fire should a raid by North African corsairs appear imminent. From the tower a short loop to the north leads back to the track you followed earlier from where you return to the village past the old sugar cane factory.

The Walk

The walk begins just beyond the roundabout at the entrance to Maro, on the western side of the village, next to the Hogar y Centro Social de Maro (1). From here walk east. As you reach Bar La Entrada turn right (2) along Calle Virgen de las Maravillas. The road bears right then left as it skirts round the edge of the village. Passing Hotel Casa Romántica de Maro you reach an

esplanade. Here 3 cut right down a flight of steps. Passing the old sugar cane factory, El Ingenio, you reach the MA138 4. Turn right and follow the road down towards the Playa de Maro beach for 700m. At a point where the road loops hard right cut left up a dirt track 5. **(15 mins)**

Becoming concreted the track loops right and reverts to dirt. The Torre de Maro comes into view as the track loops hard back to the left for 75m then reaches a small brick water deposit to the right of the track 6. Here branch right along a narrow path which runs beneath a breeze block wall. Reaching a fork 7 take the higher, left branch which runs on between greenhouses before descending steeply to a track 8. Angling left you pass a ramshackle house with a cylindrical water deposit. **(25 mins)** Passing right of another house the track descends for a short distance between groves of avocado and custard fruit as it contours round a *barranco*.

Climbing once more you reach a sign *Paraje Natural* 9 and a junction. Carry straight on, climbing more steeply, to a point where a track angles up to meet yours from the right 10. Here angle hard back to the right and follow a track which gradually angles back towards the sea. Passing an area where the track broadens out cut left 11 up a path which leads steeply up to the Torre de Maro. **(40 mins)**

Leaving the tower head north along a rocky track until you reach a point where the pines to either side of you become denser. Here cut left at a cairn 12 along a narrow path which angles down through the trees to reach a track 13 that cuts down towards the N340. Here angle left along the track back to waypoint 10 10 then retrace your steps back to the top of the steps above El Ingenio. Here turn right along the esplanade then continue straight on along Calle Real. Reaching a junction and turning left 14 after 250m you return to the start point of the walk 1. **(1 hr 40 mins)**

Distance: 13 kms **Time Required:** 5 hours **Rating:** Medium/Difficult
Total Height Gain: 675m **Map:** IGN 1:50000 Motril 1055 (19-44)
Ⓦ **Water:** in the bars of the Cantarriján and Cañuelo beaches

8 La Herradura: Cliff Circuit via the beaches of El Cañuelo & Cantarriján

Overview

This figure of eight walk takes you past two of the nicest stetches of sand on the Costa Tropical, Cantarriján and the mesmersingly beautiful beach of El Cañuelo. Both beaches restrict vehicle access in summer meaning that even then you can stake a claim on the sand whilst the snorkelling and diving is amongst the best on the *Costa*. The walk leads past two watch towers which formed part of a line of communications that stretched all the way along Spain's southern seaboard. The middle section of the walk takes you along the spine of the Caleta ridge: this is walking at its dramatic best but not for anyone who suffers from vertigo. Here the path is less clear but waymarking and cairns make things much easier and the views from the Caleta's summit are breathtaking. There are two stretches of road walking and three steep ascents. Don't let these short sections of tarmac put you off: there's precious little traffic on the old coastal road and the views are stunning. If you're walking the route in July or August you can save a steep climb up from either of the beaches by taking a minibus up to the junctions at waypoints 19 and 24.

Getting to the beginning of the walk

From the A7-E15 motorway exit for La Herradura/Almuñécar. Reaching a roundabout at the bottom of the hill turn right on the N340A towards Maro then turn right again at km305 for Cerro Gordo. Continue along the old coastal road to a sign Mirador de Cerro Gordo. There's room to park on the left.

The Walk

The walk begins next to the Mirador de Cerro Gordo 1. From here follow a path signposted *Sendero* past the Mirador restaurant. Reaching a junction stick to the higher path. After 250m you reach the *Torre Vigía* 2. After visiting the tower return to the start point of the walk then turn left **(20 mins)** and follow a tarmac road past Casa Lupo y Lupita to a sign *Playa Naturista Cantarriján* 3. Here cut hard left past a *No Entry* sign.

After cutting beneath a delapidated building the road angles right then passes a barrier 4 and a number of houses before reaching the Cantarriján beach 5. **(50 mins)** Turn right and head along to the far end the beach then cut right at a sign *Prohibido Aparcar* along a track which passes left of a car park 6. After 100m angle left away from the track 7 and continue up a (dry)

streambed following G.R. waymarking.

Careful! Following the *barranco* north for 350m you'll see two large boulders flanking a path that cuts up to the road. Ignoring this path angle hard left 8 and leave the streambed via a path which loops up then runs towards the sea. At the top of a bluff you reach a junction 9 where a path cuts up to the right. Take the left option, maintaining your course. Soon a watch tower comes into view: to your right is the towering southern face of Cerro Caleta. Blue dots and G.R. flashes mark your way and lead to a fork 10. Here cut left for 200m to the Torre de Caleta 11. **(1 hr 30 mins)** After visiting the tower retrace your footsteps back to the junction at waypoint 10 10. Turn lefting for 25m you reach another junction.

To shorten the walk, which means not visiting El Cañuelo, angle right up a steep path which soon passes left of ruin 12 then

climbs directly north past a second ruin 13 before merging with a track that leads you to the access track of El Cañuelo beach 14. Here turn right then pick up these notes at waypoint 19 19.

If you wish to visit the beautiful beach of El Cañuelo bear left. The path runs close to the edge of a barranco, descends steeply through the pines, before cutting right at a small cairn 15 and angling down towards a ruin on a bluff above a tiny cove. The path is less distinct but G.R. waymarking guides you down. 40m before reaching the ruin 16 angle right across the hillside along a narrow path, on a northerly course. Cutting through thick vegetation the path drops down to the beach of El Cañuelo 17. **(1 hr 50 mins)**

Head northwest past Chringuito Las Piedras then cut right 18 beyond a bus stop (they only run in summer) and head on up a track. After climbing steeply the track angles right past two round water deposits then bears once more left. At the top of

the rise, looking right, you'll see a shrine 19. Cut right to the shrine dedicated to San Judas Tadeo 20 then angle right and pick up a narrow path which climbs steeply through the scrub. Reaching a carob tree loop left then right then head on parallel to the Caleta ridge. Following cairns and blue dots you pass a saddle 21 before reaching the highest point on the ridge (239m) 22. **(2 hrs 45 mins)**

Head down on the same course, just left of the ridge (there are steep drops on its sea-facing side) following cairns and blue dots. After cutting through thicker undergrowth you return to the junction at waypoint 9 9. **(3 hrs 10 mins)** Turn left and retrace the path back down into the streambed. Angling left between two boulders you reach the access track to Cantarriján 23. Follow this steep track up to the N340 24 and a barrier and car park. Turn right then after 200m branch right again at a sign *Cerro Gordo*. Follow this quiet road back to the start point of the walk 1. **(4 hrs 5 mins)**

GPS Coordinates

REGION 1

Vejer de la Frontera: Santa Lucía & El Abejaruco Circuit

1 30 S 232923 4017986
2 30 S 232653 4018134
3 30 S 232506 4018267
4 30 S 232256 4018564
5 30 S 232101 4018796
6 30 S 232639 4019128
7 30 S 233788 4018087
8 30 S 233956 4017931
9 30 S 234575 4018396
10 30 S 234934 4018549
11 30 S 235165 4018687
12 30 S 235612 4018613
13 30 S 235327 4018249
14 30 S 234827 4017800
15 30 S 234383 4017973
16 30 S 233807 4017920
17 30 S 233306 4017635
18 30 S 233306 4017635

Vejer de la Frontera: Las Marismas de Barbate Circuit

1 30 S 235055 4015031
2 30 S 235269 4014181
3 30 S 236025 4014309
4 30 S 237052 4013080
5 30 S 237523 4011556
6 30 S 237148 4011161
7 30 S 235319 4013139
8 30 S 235318 4014067

Vejer to Cape Trafalgar via El Palomar de la Breña

1 30 S 233901 4016348
2 30 S 233334 4016253
3 30 S 233274 4015912
4 30 S 233016 4015797
5 30 S 232753 4015134
6 30 S 232728 4014356
7 30 S 232747 4014030
8 30 S 232692 4013188
9 30 S 232843 4012703
10 30 S 232928 4012311
11 30 S 233096 4012045
12 30 S 233037 4011598
13 30 S 232790 4011546
14 30 S 232513 4010997
15 30 S 232020 4009525
16 30 S 231907 4008097
17 30 S 230820 4008386
18 30 S 230722 4008435
19 29 S 769800 4008623
20 29 S 769487 4008650
21 29 S 768777 4008844
22 29 S 768226 4008929
23 29 S 766784 4008510
24 29 S 767623 4009272

Caños de Meca: La Breña & Los Acantilados Cliff Circuit

1 29 S 768684 4008908
2 29 S 769084 4008884
3 29 S 769087 4009100
4 29 S 768217 4010299
5 29 S 769222 4010218
6 30 S 230742 4009831
7 30 S 230689 4010157
8 30 S 231784 4010270
9 30 S 232026 4010318
10 30 S 232487 4010988
11 30 S 234687 4010423
12 30 S 233772 4008997
13 30 S 234090 4008907
14 30 S 234310 4008900
15 30 S 234593 4008716
16 30 S 232927 4008179
17 30 S 230821 4008386
18 30 S 230202 4008626
19 29 S 769172 4009046

Caños de Meca: Cape Trafalgar to Conil via the Castilnovo Tower

1 29 S 767642 4009268
2 29 S 766961 4008559
3 29 S 766740 4008591
4 29 S 765857 4010008
5 29 S 765520 4010370
6 29 S 763286 4013866
7 29 S 762442 4016269
8 29 S 762059 4017618
9 29 S 761740 4018093
10 29 S 761845 4018267
11 29 S 761683 4018654

REGION 2

Bolonia: Laja de la Zarga Observatory Circuit

1 30 S 254092 3998770
2 30 S 254012 3999116
3 30 S 253864 3999829
4 30 S 253803 4000223
5 30 S 253561 4000755
6 30 S 253287 4000985
7 30 S 253197 4001373
8 30 S 252963 4001562
9 30 S 252824 4001761
10 30 S 252051 4001099
11 30 S 251921 4000746
12 30 S 251232 4000232
13 30 S 251103 4000126
14 30 S 251257 3999539
15 30 S 251993 3999340
16 30 S 252790 3999082
17 30 S 252842 3999109
18 30 S 253118 3998950

Tarifa to Bolonia via Los Lances & Valdevaqueros

1 30 S 265592 3988801

2 30 S 265140 3988243

3 30 S 264269 3989618

4 30 S 263467 3990811

5 30 S 261027 3993368

6 30 S 260755 3993530

7 30 S 260243 3993690

8 30 S 259562 3993889

9 30 S 258914 3994335

10 30 S 257149 3994831

11 30 S 256356 3994240

12 30 S 256184 3994137

13 30 S 255917 3994104

14 30 S 254429 3994699

15 30 S 253441 3995208

16 30 S 253333 3995240

17 30 S 252411 3995564

18 30 S 250937 3997181

Monte de la Torre to El Pelayo via Las Corzas

1 30 S 275987 4005203

2 30 S 276332 4004687

3 30 S 276410 4004314

4 30 S 276253 4004058

5 30 S 276310 4003907

6 30 S 276189 4003680

7 30 S 276271 4003593

8 30 S 276398 4003500

9 30 S 276167 4003391

10 30 S 275915 4002933

11 30 S 275599 4003080

12 30 S 274421 4002866

13 30 S 274275 4002905

14 30 S 274042 4002812

15 30 S 272574 4002590

16 30 S 273354 4002642

17 30 S 273218 4001857

18 30 S 273113 4001703

19 30 S 272706 3999909

20 30 S 272559 3999818

21 30 S 272524 3999424

22 30 S 273726 3997848

23 30 S 273977 3996850

24 30 S 273888 3996248

25 30 S 274094 3996239

26 30 S 274260 3996358

27 30 S 274445 3996179

28 30 S 274695 3996218

El Pelayo to Tarifa via Guadalmesí

1 30 S 274695 3996218

2 30 S 274425 3995777

3 30 S 275215 3995583

4 30 S 274612 3994282

5 30 S 274541 3993434

6 30 S 273753 3992937

7 30 S 272916 3991984

8 30 S 272855 3991876

9 30 S 273049 3991226
10 30 S 272162 3990950
11 30 S 271284 3990671
12 30 S 271177 3990549
13 30 S 271087 3990468
14 30 S 270749 3990343
15 30 S 270094 3989943
16 30 S 269924 3989862
17 30 S 268964 3989377
18 30 S 268568 3989212
19 30 S 268190 3989061
20 30 S 267867 3988903
21 30 S 267815 3988893
22 30 S 266596 3988673
23 30 S 266446 3988807
24 30 S 266081 3988647
25 30 S 265826 3988634
26 30 S 265592 3988801

Los Barrios: Prisioneros & Río de la Miel Circuit

1 30 S 277169 4000013
2 30 S 276405 3999776
3 30 S 275990 3999693
4 30 S 275910 3999217
5 30 S 276139 3998644
6 30 S 275950 3998464
7 30 S 275044 3998652
8 30 S 274366 3998728
9 30 S 273833 3998182
10 30 S 273738 3997853
11 30 S 272885 3998691
12 30 S 272527 3999421
13 30 S 272699 3999892
14 30 S 272762 3999885
15 30 S 273433 3999436
16 30 S 273771 3999331
17 30 S 273963 3999331
18 30 S 274334 3999366
19 30 S 274380 3999336
20 30 S 275099 3999430
21 30 S 275177 3999463
22 30 S 275349 3999504
23 30 S 275424 3999544
24 30 S 275617 3999528
25 30 S 275683 3999505

Gibraltar: High Rock Circuit via The Mediterranean Steps & Ingliss Way

1 30 S 288549 4002820
2 30 S 288388 4001672
3 30 S 288476 4001391
4 30 S 288569 4001251
5 30 S 288665 4001069
6 30 S 288769 4000660
7 30 S 288967 4000114
8 30 S 289333 4000288
9 30 S 289316 4000362
10 30 S 289210 4000548
11 30 S 289200 4000568

12	30 S 289200 4000513
13	30 S 289053 4000860
14	30 S 289081 4001106
15	30 S 289035 4001217
16	30 S 289011 4001347
17	30 S 289024 4001581
18	30 S 289035 4001454
19	30 S 289024 4001581
20	30 S 288818 4001364
21	30 S 288844 4001601
22	30 S 288842 4002068

REGION 3

Manilva: Utrera Gorge Circuit via the Río Manilva & the Hedionda Baths

1	30 S 297308 4030218
2	30 S 296494 4030218
3	30 S 295989 4030319
4	30 S 295585 4030512
5	30 S 295338 4030829
6	30 S 295255 4030985
7	30 S 295353 4032057
8	30 S 295530 4032160
9	30 S 295630 4032233
10	30 S 296571 4032564
11	30 S 296721 4032278
12	30 S 297027 4031789
13	30 S 297135 4031298
14	30 S 297100 4031168
15	30 S 297191 4030548
16	30 S 297290 4030501

Casares: Crestellina Circuit via the Mirador de Castillón

1	30 S 296361 4035813
2	30 S 296435 4036587
3	30 S 296705 4038801
4	30 S 296641 4038959
5	30 S 296368 4039056
6	30 S 295547 4037111
7	30 S 295525 4036912
8	30 S 295652 4037157
9	30 S 295977 4036811
10	30 S 295926 4036048
11	30 S 296127 4036377

Casares Eastern Circuit via Manga Celima & Arroyo del Tocón

1	30 S 296369 4035803
2	30 S 296610 4035992
3	30 S 296670 4036433
4	30 S 296996 4037286
5	30 S 297136 4037643
6	30 S 297246 4037713
7	30 S 297612 4036514
8	30 S 297541 4036115
9	30 S 297970 4036035
10	30 S 297802 4035653
11	30 S 298196 4034550

12 30 S 296663 4034060

13 30 S 296616 4034000

14 30 S 296499 4034088

15 30 S 296375 4034595

Casares Circuit via La Acedía & El Muladar

1 30 S 298609 4035698

2 30 S 299371 4036620

3 30 S 299720 4036528

4 30 S 299515 4036759

5 30 S 299778 4037234

6 30 S 300222 4037705

7 30 S 300764 4038738

8 30 S 300812 4038778

9 30 S 300655 4037523

10 30 S 300421 4036781

11 30 S 299414 4036070

12 30 S 298927 4036086

Pico Reales Circuit via the Pinsapo Path & Mirador de Salvador Guerrero

1 30 S 302974 4040891

2 30 S 302405 4040833

3 30 S 302172 4041085

4 30 S 302013 4040815

5 30 S 302278 4040143

6 30 S 302333 4040209

7 30 S 303006 4039994

8 30 S 302958 4039924

9 30 S 302987 4039662

10 30 S 302890 4039288

25 30 S 292807 4044670

REGION 4

Istán: Infierno Valley Circuit

1 30 S 325855 4050282

2 30 S 325893 4050300

3 30 S 325956 4050255

4 30 S 326169 4050069

5 30 S 326461 4050013

6 30 S 326649 4051506

7 30 S 327463 4051942

8 30 S 328576 4052254

9 30 S 328617 4051773

10 30 S 328406 4051761

11 30 S 328154 4051720

12 30 S 328194 4051658

13 30 S 328111 4051365

14 30 S 327930 4051423

15 30 S 327558 4051253

16 30 S 327405 4051415

17 30 S 327386 4051432

18 30 S 327163 4051015

19 30 S 327045 4050705

20 30 S 326443 4050255

21 30 S 326389 4050282

Istán to the Río Verde & Charco del Canalón

1 30 S 325861 4050247
2 30 S 325707 4050481
3 30 S 326113 4050393
4 30 S 326129 4050852
5 30 S 326318 4051403
6 30 S 326654 4051992
7 30 S 326828 4052617
8 30 S 326809 4053194
9 30 S 326762 4053461
10 30 S 326747 4053770
11 30 S 326768 4054020
12 30 S 326789 4054050
13 30 S 326821 4054106
14 30 S 326881 4054398
15 30 S 326857 4054448

Istán Reservoir Circuit via Camino de la Cuesta & San Miguel Chapel

1 30 S 325861 4050247
2 30 S 325703 4050448
3 30 S 325598 4050482
4 30 S 325056 4050167
5 30 S 325005 4050067
6 30 S 325029 4050073
7 30 S 325048 4049729
8 30 S 325265 4049430
9 30 S 325148 4049293
10 30 S 325675 4049148
11 30 S 325670 4049199
12 30 S 325809 4049323
13 30 S 326076 4049879
14 30 S 326170 4050070

Marbella to Istán via the Mirador del Macho Montés & Río Molinos

1 30 S 331625 4044424
2 30 S 331343 4044602
3 30 S 331424 4045778
4 30 S 331408 4046015
5 30 S 331311 4046322
6 30 S 331291 4046389
7 30 S 330858 4048763
8 30 S 330895 4048466
9 30 S 331068 4049068
10 30 S 330977 4049108
11 30 S 330639 4049342
12 30 S 330127 4049669
13 30 S 329429 4049581
14 30 S 329292 4049648
15 30 S 327668 4049521
16 30 S 327036 4049589
17 30 S 326588 4049846
18 30 S 326238 4049898
19 30 S 325893 4050297
20 30 S 325865 4050246

Ascent of La Concha from El Refugio de Juanar

1 30 S 331409 4050136

2	30 S 331478 4050057
3	30 S 331488 4049789
4	30 S 331069 4049072
5	30 S 330974 4049108
6	30 S 330644 4049347
7	30 S 330037 4048516
8	30 S 329144 4048499
9	30 S 328793 4048309
10	30 S 328165 4047699
11	30 S 328093 4047604
12	30 S 328064 4047430
13	30 S 327815 4047058
14	30 S 327786 4046994

Refugio de Juanar: Los Cuchillos Circuit

1	30 S 331413 4050132
2	30 S 331472 4050076
3	30 S 331667 4050597
4	30 S 331631 4050588
5	30 S 331641 4051450
6	30 S 331500 4051456
7	30 S 331067 4051521
8	30 S 330821 4051351
9	30 S 330628 4051665
10	30 S 330599 4051726
11	30 S 330720 4051705
12	30 S 330234 4051019
13	30 S 329903 4050744
14	30 S 330231 4050305
15	30 S 330569 4050311

Ojén to the Cruz de Juanar via El Puerto de Marbella

1	30 S 333965 4048386
2	30 S 333977 4048458
3	30 S 333962 4048758
4	30 S 333552 4048718
5	30 S 333500 4048803
6	30 S 333571 4048922
7	30 S 333369 4049313
8	30 S 332389 4049331
9	30 S 331602 4049636
10	30 S 330867 4048771
11	30 S 330270 4048435
12	30 S 330275 4048455
13	30 S 330042 4048511
14	30 S 330640 4049344
15	30 S 330970 4049115
16	30 S 331069 4049070

REGION 5

Mijas: Pico de Mijas Circuit via the Ermita del Calvario

1	30 S 353323 4051452
2	30 S 353426 4051566
3	30 S 353490 4051712
4	30 S 353399 4051664
5	30 S 353225 4051829
6	30 S 353047 4052167
7	30 S 353108 4052337

8 30 S 352710 4052855

9 30 S 352374 4052478

10 30 S 351901 4053414

11 30 S 351843 4053490

12 30 S 351711 4053467

13 30 S 352113 4053352

14 30 S 352021 4052204

15 30 S 352161 4052056

16 30 S 351922 4052197

17 30 S 351657 4052319

18 30 S 351346 4052080

19 30 S 351409 4051916

20 30 S 352387 4051834

21 30 S 352816 4051489

22 30 S 353183 4051638

Mijas: Puerto de Málaga & Los Arenales Circuit

1 30 S 353325 4051459

2 30 S 353433 4051563

3 30 S 353488 4051713

4 30 S 353383 4052188

5 30 S 353047 4052167

6 30 S 353110 4052335

7 30 S 353123 4052361

8 30 S 352714 4052854

9 30 S 352957 4053301

10 30 S 352939 4053552

11 30 S 353604 4053764

12 30 S 354472 4054001

13 30 S 354675 4054145

14 30 S 354637 4053809

15 30 S 354791 4053596

16 30 S 354861 4053505

17 30 S 355078 4053163

18 30 S 355168 4053319

19 30 S 355288 4053169

20 30 S 355290 4052717

21 30 S 355195 4052434

22 30 S 354173 4051902

Alhaurín El Grande: Puerto de la Encina Circuit via La Cañada de las Palomas

1 30 S 350285 4057306

2 30 S 350629 4056839

3 30 S 351171 4056034

4 30 S 351275 4055964

5 30 S 351745 4055678

6 30 S 351787 4055686

7 30 S 351830 4055655

8 30 S 351954 4055607

9 30 S 352160 4053983

10 30 S 351838 4053496

11 30 S 351726 4053464

12 30 S 352150 4053986

13 30 S 351938 4055241

14 30 S 351840 4055858

15 30 S 351424 4056387

16 30 S 351219 4056478

17 30 S 351053 4056492

Alhaurín de la Torre: Cortijo Jarapalos Circuit

1 30 S 357017 4056645
2 30 S 356962 4056231
3 30 S 356522 4055556
4 30 S 356182 4055009
5 30 S 355467 4054673
6 30 S 355333 4054848
7 30 S 355194 4054922
8 30 S 354968 4055069
9 30 S 354777 4055504
10 30 S 355416 4056145
11 30 S 355431 4056247
12 30 S 355530 4056334
13 30 S 356042 4056163
14 30 S 356245 4056459

Alhaurín de la Torre: Puerto del Viento Circuit via the Palomas peak

1 30 S 361721 4057598
2 30 S 361821 4057318
3 30 S 361939 4057102
4 30 S 362597 4056328
5 30 S 362662 4056240
6 30 S 362812 4056412
7 30 S 363038 4056284
8 30 S 361919 4055405
9 30 S 361689 4055151
10 30 S 360978 4054710
11 30 S 360978 4054710
12 30 S 360934 4054722
13 30 S 361018 4055128
14 30 S 360357 4057022
15 30 S 360210 4058255

Benalmadena: Puerto Viejo de Mijas Circuit via the Quejigal stream

1 30 S 360233 4052198
2 30 S 359994 4052445
3 30 S 359910 4052454
4 30 S 359630 4052545
5 30 S 358790 4052865
6 30 S 358713 4053089
7 30 S 358698 4053498
8 30 S 358578 4053611
9 30 S 360225 4053899
10 30 S 360420 4053309
11 30 S 360508 4053150
12 30 S 360507 4052906
13 30 S 360305 4052680
14 30 S 360420 4052398

REGION 6

Sedella to Alcaucín via El Collado de la Gitana

1 30 S 407972 4080261
2 30 S 407834 4080729
3 30 S 407787 4081094
4 30 S 407713 4081124

5 30 S 407639 4081274

6 30 S 407187 4081468

7 30 S 407357 4081783

8 30 S 407482 4082556

9 30 S 407367 4082803

10 30 S 407044 4082921

11 30 S 407047 4083442

12 30 S 406893 4083450

13 30 S 406474 4083453

14 30 S 405957 4083134

15 30 S 405990 4083441

16 30 S 405769 4083653

17 30 S 405706 4083773

18 30 S 405722 4083948

19 30 S 404942 4083565

20 30 S 404368 4084038

21 30 S 403514 4084236

22 30 S 402993 4084122

23 30 S 402452 4083945

24 30 S 402006 4084035

25 30 S 401589 4083773

26 30 S 401548 4083767

27 30 S 401324 4084045

28 30 S 401170 4083986

29 30 S 400737 4083711

30 30 S 400954 4084283

31 30 S 400858 4084840

Canillas de Aceituno: Maroma Ascent

1 30 S 403676 4081566

2 30 S 403482 4081852

3 30 S 403600 4082121

4 30 S 403672 4082365

5 30 S 403520 4082856

6 30 S 403615 4083071

7 30 S 403644 4083075

8 30 S 403955 4082983

9 30 S 404429 4083005

10 30 S 404616 4083469

11 30 S 404931 4083569

12 30 S 405703 4083787

13 30 S 405421 4084020

14 30 S 405095 4084401

15 30 S 405778 4084747

16 30 S 405852 4084745

17 30 S 406801 4084814

18 30 S 406949 4084788

19 30 S 406894 4084733

20 30 S 405957 4083131

21 30 S 405987 4083447

22 30 S 405032 4082458

23 30 S 405067 4082422

24 30 S 405032 4082449

25 30 S 403809 4081733

26 30 S 403785 4081768

Cómpeta to Sedella via La Cruz del Muerto

1 30 S 413182 4076989

2 30 S 412833 4077315

3 30 S 412657 4077918

4 30 S 412552 4078129
5 30 S 412452 4078531
6 30 S 412300 4078584
7 30 S 412025 4078483
8 30 S 411733 4078553
9 30 S 411516 4078690
10 30 S 411453 4078753
11 30 S 411511 4079682
12 30 S 411147 4079674
13 30 S 411263 4079836
14 30 S 410834 4080014
15 30 S 410640 4080054
16 30 S 410605 4080324
17 30 S 409985 4081057
18 30 S 409351 4080777
19 30 S 409319 4080421
20 30 S 408944 4080484
21 30 S 408919 4080885
22 30 S 408701 4081182
23 30 S 408640 4081036
24 30 S 408640 4081036
25 30 S 408292 4080960

Sayalonga & Corumbela Circuit

1 30 S 409843 4073127
2 30 S 409739 4073247
3 30 S 409902 4073960
4 30 S 410238 4074591
5 30 S 409938 4075557
6 30 S 410259 4075783
7 30 S 410351 4075767
8 30 S 409702 4075690
9 30 S 409460 4075482
10 30 S 408823 4075042
11 30 S 409418 4073937
12 30 S 409324 4073765
13 30 S 409509 4073430
14 30 S 409122 4073297
15 30 S 409843 4073127

Canillas de Albaida: Cajulas Valley Circuit

1 30 S 412229 4078391
2 30 S 411929 4078522
3 30 S 411770 4078609
4 30 S 411620 4079120
5 30 S 411698 4079272
6 30 S 411709 4079347
7 30 S 411798 4079635
8 30 S 411738 4079925
9 30 S 411451 4080095
10 30 S 411429 4080238
11 30 S 412176 4080488
12 30 S 411993 4079066
13 30 S 412356 4078989

Cómpeta: Puerto Blanquillo

1 30 S 413199 4076992
2 30 S 413332 4077203
3 30 S 413649 4077371
4 30 S 413997 4077804

5 30 S 414314 4077832

6 30 S 415328 4078845

7 30 S 416534 4079785

8 30 S 416731 4079903

9 30 S 417379 4080615

10 30 S 417464 4080923

11 30 S 417259 4081050

12 30 S 416308 4081348

13 30 S 415775 4081354

14 30 S 415423 4081202

15 30 S 415104 4081098

16 30 S 414541 4080831

17 30 S 413652 4080472

18 30 S 413565 4079050

19 30 S 412292 4078590

20 30 S 412452 4078527

21 30 S 412713 4077823

22 30 S 412822 4077313

REGION 7

Frigiliana: Ascent of El Fuerte

1 30 S 420268 4072253

2 30 S 420159 4072391

3 30 S 420224 4072451

4 30 S 420225 4072526

5 30 S 420134 4072569

6 30 S 420131 4072656

7 30 S 420155 4073068

8 30 S 419512 4073970

9 30 S 418568 4074850

Frigiliana: The Río Higuerón Gorge

1 30 S 420268 4072253

2 30 S 420409 4072325

3 30 S 420505 4072775

4 30 S 420606 4073341

5 30 S 420347 4073600

6 30 S 420187 4074288

7 30 S 420824 4075765

8 30 S 420658 4076334

9 30 S 420307 4076879

10 30 S 420568 4077454

Frigiliana: Cruz de Pinto Circuit

1 30 S 420261 4072283

2 30 S 420412 4072326

3 30 S 420621 4072788

4 30 S 421035 4072940

5 30 S 420973 4072692

6 30 S 420968 4072374

7 30 S 420951 4071671

8 30 S 420931 4071528

9 30 S 420992 4071045

10 30 S 421061 4070955

11 30 S 420789 4070635

12 30 S 420770 4070490

13 30 S 420419 4070939

Maro to Frigiliana via El Camino Imán

1 30 S 424479 4068976
2 30 S 424382 4071312
3 30 S 424229 4072821
4 30 S 424204 4072965
5 30 S 424208 4073217
6 30 S 423860 4073211
7 30 S 423630 4073805
8 30 S 422937 4074150
9 30 S 422983 4074226
10 30 S 422569 4073943
11 30 S 422381 4073816
12 30 S 422161 4073675
13 30 S 421726 4073295
14 30 S 421525 4073367
15 30 S 421140 4073251
16 30 S 421036 4072940
17 30 S 420629 4072796
18 30 S 420427 4072331
19 30 S 420268 4072253

Nerja: The Río Chillar Gorge Circuit

1 30 S 421652 4070109
2 30 S 421548 4070841
3 30 S 421302 4071673
4 30 S 423362 4073516
5 30 S 423361 4073558
6 30 S 423006 4074253
7 30 S 422944 4074187
8 30 S 422938 4074135
9 30 S 423135 4074010
10 30 S 423349 4073741
11 30 S 423502 4073633
12 30 S 423439 4073305
13 30 S 423833 4073208
14 30 S 423825 4073190
15 30 S 423518 4072728
16 30 S 423417 4072576
17 30 S 423161 4072345
18 30 S 422442 4071868
19 30 S 421802 4071825

Maro: Cortijo Almachares Circuit

1 30 S 424478 4068977
2 30 S 423919 4069883
3 30 S 423905 4069775
4 30 S 424110 4070945
5 30 S 424213 4071408
6 30 S 424666 4071370
7 30 S 424976 4071293
8 30 S 425338 4071695
9 30 S 425496 4071802
10 30 S 426314 4072109
11 30 S 425821 4071191
12 30 S 425753 4071175
13 30 S 426143 4070768
14 30 S 425660 4070526
15 30 S 425537 4070473
16 30 S 424982 4069404

17	30 S 425119 4069172
18	30 S 425085 4068982
19	30 S 425013 4068827
20	30 S 424974 4068737
21	30 S 424750 4068712

Maro: Cliff Circuit via Torre de Maro

1	30 S 424639 4068722
2	30 S 424742 4068707
3	30 S 424858 4068422
4	30 S 424939 4068394
5	30 S 425590 4068322
6	30 S 425751 4068307
7	30 S 425809 4068328
8	30 S 425875 4068386
9	30 S 426057 4068322
10	30 S 426244 4068242
11	30 S 426009 4068179
12	30 S 426348 4068306
13	30 S 426316 4068504
14	30 S 424852 4068679

La Herradura Cliff Circuit via El Cañuelo, Cantarriján and the Caleta Ridge

1	30 S 431566 4065941
2	30 S 431582 4065662
3	30 S 431301 4066397
4	30 S 431053 4066231
5	30 S 430799 4066274
6	30 S 430694 4066339
7	30 S 430898 4067199
8	30 S 430702 4066650
9	30 S 430570 4066466
10	30 S 430076 4066756
11	30 S 430037 4066549
12	30 S 430009 4066950
13	30 S 430057 4067131
14	30 S 430051 4067303
15	30 S 430037 4066746
16	30 S 429904 4066758
17	30 S 429827 4066890
18	30 S 429589 4067119
19	30 S 430160 4067438
20	30 S 430183 4067436
21	30 S 430356 4066962
22	30 S 430362 4066805
23	30 S 430716 4066658
24	30 S 430895 4067204
25	30 S 431088 4067113

Andalucían Bird Checklist

LEGEND

IUCN Red List Category

LC	Least Concern
NT	Near Threatened
VU	Vulnerable
EN	Endangered
CR	Critically Endangered
EX	Extinct
DD	Data Deficient

Andalucía Status

A	Observed since 1950
B	Observed prior to 1950 but not since
C	Introduced, established breeding
D	Unknown origin
E	Escape / Introduced
*	Rarity description required by ABS
	Considered race to scare in Andalucía

The order of birds used in this list follows the IOC World Bird List 2008. English names used are those most commonly in use and therefore recognisable by the majority of birdwatchers. The list has been compiled by Peter Jones, a nature guide based close to Ronda, who leads groups and individuals throughout the province. He also leads guided tours to other parts of Spain, Morocco and many other destinations worldwide. The author can not speak too highly of Peter's birding excursions. A natural communicator, Peter has that rare ability of conveying specialist knowledge in a way that's accessible to one and all. A day in his company offers a unique insight into the extraordinarily diverse birdlife of southern Spain and would dovetail perfectly if you were walking in the mountains in the Ronda or the Grazalema Sierra (see my companion guide Walking in Andalucía). To contact Peter either email pr.p.jones@gmail.com or visit **www.spanishnature.com**

Andalucia Bird Society is a great resource for exchanging and or getting information on many aspects of birding here in southern Spain. If you intend visiting this area, then an open and free forum allows you to contact locals on specific site or species information. Contibute to their database and conservation efforts by submitting your vacation trip reports or sightings to the society. www.andaluciabirdsociety.org

References: BirdLife International www.birdlife.org, IOC World Bird List 2008 version 1.7

Species	Category	Status	Seen
Red-legged Partridge *Alectoris rufa*	LC	C	
Common Quail *Coturnix coturnix*	LC	A	
Common Pheasant *Phasianus colchicus*	LC	CE	
Greylag Goose *Anser anser*	LC	A	
Mute Swan *Cygnus olor*	LC	CE	
Shelduck *Tadorna tadorna*	LC	A	
Gadwall *Anas strepera*	LC	A	
Wigeon *Anas penelope*	LC	A	
Mallard *Anas platyrhynchos*	LC	A	
Shoveler *Anas clypeata*	LC	A	
Pintail *Anas acuta*	LC	A	
Garganey *Anas querquedula*	LC	A	
Teal *Anas crecca*	LC	A	
Marbled Teal *Marmaronetta angustirostris*	VU	A	
Red-crested *Pochard Netta rufina*	LC	A	
Pochard *Aythya ferina*	LC	A	
Ferruginous Duck *Aythya nyroca*	NT	A*	
Tufted Duck *Aythya fuligula*	LC	A	
White-headed Duck *Oxyura leucocephala*	EN	A	
Little Grebe *Tachybaptus ruficollis*	LC	A	
Red-necked Grebe *Podiceps grisegena*	LC	A	
Great Crested Grebe *Podiceps cristatus*	LC	A	
Black-necked Grebe *Podiceps nigricollis*	LC	A	
Greater Flamingo *Phoenicopterus roseus*	LC	A	
Lesser Flamingo *Phoeniconaias minor*	NT	A	
Black Stork *Ciconia nigra*	LC	A	
White Stork *Ciconia ciconia*	LC	A	
Northern Bald Ibis *Geronticus eremita*	CR	E*	
Glossy Ibis *Plegadis falcinellus*	LC	A	
Spoonbill *Platalea leucorodia*	LC	A	
Little Bittern *Ixobrychus minutus*	LC	A	
Night Heron *Nycticorax nycticorax*	LC	A	
Squacco Heron *Ardeola ralloides*	LC	A	
Cattle Egret *Bubulcus ibis*	LC	A	
Grey Heron *Ardea cinerea*	LC	A	
Purple Heron *Ardea purpurea*	LC	A	
Great (White) Egret *Ardea alba*	LC	A	
Little Egret *Egretta garzetta*	LC	A	
Great Cormorant *Phalacrocorax carbo*	LC	A	
Lesser Kestrel *Falco naumanni*	VU	A	
Common Kestrel Falco tinnunculus	LC	A	

Species	Category	Status	Seen
Red-footed Falcon *Falco vespertinus*	NT	A	
Eleonora's Falcon *Falco eleonorae*	LC	A	
Merlin *Falco columbarius*	LC	A	
Eurasian Hobby *Falco subbuteo*	LC	A	
Lanner Falcon *Falco biarmicus*	LC	D*	
Peregrine Falcon *Falco peregrinus*	LC	A	
Osprey *Pandion haliaetus*	LC	A	
Honey Buzzard *Pernis apivorus*	LC	A	
Black-winged Kite *Elanus caeruleus*	LC	A	
Red Kite *Milvus milvus*	NT	A	
Black Kite *Milvus migrans*	LC	A	
Lammergeier *Gypaetus barbatus*	LC	A	
Egyptian Vulture *Neophron percnopterus*	EN	A	
Rüppell's Vulture *Gyps rueppellii*	NT	A*	
Griffon Vulture *Gyps fulvus*	LC	A	
Black Vulture *Aegypius monachus*	NT	A	
Short-toed Eagle *Circaetus gallicus*	LC	A	
Western Marsh-harrier *Circus aeruginosus*	LC	A	
Hen Harrier *Circus cyaneus*	LC	A	
Montagu's Harrier *Circus pygargus*	LC	A	
Sparrowhawk *Accipiter nisus*	LC	A	
Goshawk *Accipiter gentilis*	LC	A	
Common Buzzard *Buteo buteo*	LC	A	
Long-legged Buzzard *Buteo rufinus*	LC	A*	
Greater Spotted Eagle *Aquila clanga*	VU	A*	
Spanish Imperial Eagle *Aquila adalberti*	VU	A	
Golden Eagle *Aquila chrysaetos*	LC	A	
Bonelli's Eagle *Hieraaetus fasciatus*	LC	A	
Booted Eagle *Hieraaetus pennatus*	LC	A	
Great Bustard *Otis tarda*	VU	A	
Little Bustard *Tetrax tetrax*	NT	A	
Water Rail *Rallus aquaticus*	LC	A	
Corncrake *Crex crex*	NT	A	
Little Crake *Porzana parva*	LC	A	
Baillon's Crake *Porzana pusilla*	LC	A	
Spotted Crake *Porzana porzana*	LC	A	
Purple (Swamphen) Gallinule *Porphyrio porphyrio*	LC	A	
Moorhen *Gallinula chloropus*	LC	A	
Red-knobbed Coot *Fulica cristata*	LC	A	
Common Coot *Fulica atra*	LC	A	
Common Crane *Grus grus*	LC	A	

Species	Category	Status	Seen
Red-footed Falcon *Falco vespertinus*	NT	A	
Eleonora's Falcon *Falco eleonorae*	LC	A	
Merlin *Falco columbarius*	LC	A	
Eurasian Hobby *Falco subbuteo*	LC	A	
Lanner Falcon *Falco biarmicus*	LC	D*	
Peregrine Falcon *Falco peregrinus*	LC	A	
Osprey *Pandion haliaetus*	LC	A	
Honey Buzzard *Pernis apivorus*	LC	A	
Black-winged Kite *Elanus caeruleus*	LC	A	
Red Kite *Milvus milvus*	NT	A	
Black Kite *Milvus migrans*	LC	A	
Lammergeier *Gypaetus barbatus*	LC	A	
Egyptian Vulture *Neophron percnopterus*	EN	A	
Rüppell's Vulture *Gyps rueppellii*	NT	A*	
Griffon Vulture *Gyps fulvus*	LC	A	
Black Vulture *Aegypius monachus*	NT	A	
Short-toed Eagle *Circaetus gallicus*	LC	A	
Western Marsh-harrier *Circus aeruginosus*	LC	A	
Hen Harrier *Circus cyaneus*	LC	A	
Montagu's Harrier *Circus pygargus*	LC	A	
Sparrowhawk *Accipiter nisus*	LC	A	
Goshawk *Accipiter gentilis*	LC	A	
Common Buzzard *Buteo buteo*	LC	A	
Long-legged Buzzard *Buteo rufinus*	LC	A*	
Greater Spotted Eagle *Aquila clanga*	VU	A*	
Spanish Imperial Eagle *Aquila adalberti*	VU	A	
Golden Eagle *Aquila chrysaetos*	LC	A	
Bonelli's Eagle *Hieraaetus fasciatus*	LC	A	
Booted Eagle *Hieraaetus pennatus*	LC	A	
Great Bustard *Otis tarda*	VU	A	
Little Bustard *Tetrax tetrax*	NT	A	
Water Rail *Rallus aquaticus*	LC	A	
Corncrake *Crex crex*	NT	A	
Little Crake *Porzana parva*	LC	A	
Baillon's Crake *Porzana pusilla*	LC	A	
Spotted Crake *Porzana porzana*	LC	A	
Purple (Swamphen) Gallinule *Porphyrio porphyrio*	LC	A	
Moorhen *Gallinula chloropus*	LC	A	
Red-knobbed Coot *Fulica cristata*	LC	A	
Common Coot *Fulica atra*	LC	A	
Common Crane *Grus grus*	LC	A	

Species	Category	Status	Seen
Stone Curlew *Burhinus oedicnemus*	LC	A	
Oystercatcher *Haematopus ostralegus*	LC	A	
Black-winged Stilt *Himantopus himantopus*	LC	A	
Avocet *Recurvirostra avosetta*	LC	A	
Lapwing *Vanellus vanellus*	LC	A	
Golden Plover *Pluvialis apricaria*	LC	A	
Grey Plover *Pluvialis squatarola*	LC	A	
Ringed Plover *Charadrius hiaticula*	LC	A	
Little Ringed Plover *Charadrius dubius*	LC	A	
Kentish Plover *Charadrius alexandrinus*	LC	A	
Woodcock *Scolopax rusticola*	LC	A	
Jack Snipe *Lymnocryptes minimus*	LC	A	
Common Snipe *Gallinago gallinago*	LC	A	
Black-tailed Godwit *Limosa limosa*	NT	A	
Bar-tailed Godwit *Limosa lapponica*	LC	A	
Whimbrel *Numenius phaeopus*	LC	A	
Curlew *Numenius arquata*	LC	A	
Spotted Redshank *Tringa erythropus*	LC	A	
Redshank *Tringa totanus*	LC	A	
Greenshank *Tringa nebularia*	LC	A	
Green Sandpiper *Tringa ochropus*	LC	A	
Wood Sandpiper *Tringa glareola*	LC	A	
Common Sandpiper *Actitis hypoleucos*	LC	A	
Ruddy Turnstone *Arenaria interpres*	LC	A	
Knot *Calidris canutus*	LC	A	
Sanderling *Calidris alba*	LC	A	
Little Stint *Calidris minuta*	LC	A	
Temminck's Stint *Calidris temminckii*	LC	A	
Curlew Sandpiper *Calidris ferruginea*	LC	A	
Purple Sandpiper *Calidris maritima*	LC	A	
Dunlin *Calidris alpina*	LC	A	
Ruff *Philomachus pugnax*	LC	A	
Wilson's Phalarope *Steganopus tricolor*	LC	A*	
Red-necked Phalarope *Phalaropus lobatus*	LC	A	
Collared Pratincole *Glareola pratincola*	LC	A	
Common (Mew) Gull *Larus canus*	LC	A	
Audouin's Gull *Larus audouinii*	NT	A	
Yellow-legged Gull *Larus michahellis*	LC	A	
Lesser Black-backed Gull *Larus fuscus*	LC	A	
Black-headed Gull *Larus ridibundus*	LC	A	
Slender-billed Gull *Larus genei*	LC	A	

Species	Category	Status	Seen
Mediterranean Gull *Larus melanocephalus*	LC	A	
Little Gull *Larus minutus*	LC	A	
Gull-billed Tern *Sterna nilotica*	LC	A	
Caspian Tern *Sterna caspia*	LC	A	
Sandwich Tern *Sterna sandvicensis*	LC	A	
Common Tern *Sterna hirundo*	LC	A	
Arctic Tern *Sterna paradisaea*	LC	A	
Little Tern *Sterna albifrons*	LC	A	
Whiskered Tern *Chlidonias hybrida*	LC	A	
Black Tern *Chlidonias niger*	LC	A	
Pin-tailed Sandgrouse *Pterocles alchata*	LC	A	
Black-bellied Sandgrouse *Pterocles orientalis*	LC	A	
Rock Pigeon *Columba livia*	LC	A	
Feral Pigeon *Columba.l.domestica*	LC	DE	
Stock Dove *Columba oenas*	LC	A	
Wood Pigeon *Columba palumbus*	LC	A	
Turtle Dove *Streptopelia turtur*	LC	A	
Collared Dove *Streptopelia decaocto*	LC	A	
Rose-ringed Parakeet *Psittacula krameri*	LC	C	
Monk Parakeet *Myiopsitta monachus*	LC	C	
Great Spotted Cuckoo *Clamator glandarius*	LC	A	
Cuckoo *Cuculus canorus*	LC	A	
Barn Owl *Tyto alba*	LC	A	
Scops Owl *Otus scops*	LC	A	
Eagle Owl *Bubo bubo*	LC	A	
Tawny Owl *Strix aluco*	LC	A	
Little Owl *Athene noctua*	LC	A	
Long-eared Owl *Asio otus*	LC	A	
Short-eared Owl *Asio flammeus*	LC	A	
Red-necked Nightjar *Caprimulgus ruficollis*	LC	A	
Nightjar *Caprimulgus europaeus*	LC	A	
Alpine Swift *Tachymarptis melba*	LC	A	
Common Swift *Apus apus*	LC	A	
Pallid Swift *Apus pallidus*	LC	A	
Little Swift *Apus affinis*	LC	A	
White-rumped Swift *Apus caffer*	LC	A	
Roller *Coracias garrulus*	NT	A	
Kingfisher *Alcedo atthis*	LC	A	
Bee-eater *Merops apiaster*	LC	A	
Hoopoe *Upupa epops*	LC	A	
Wryneck *Jynx torquilla*	LC	A	

Species	Category	Status	Seen
Lesser Spotted Woodpecker *Dendrocopos minor*	LC	A	
Great Spotted Woodpecker *Dendrocopos major*	LC	A	
Green Woodpecker *Picus viridis*	LC	A	
Great Grey Shrike *Lanius excubitor*	LC	A	
Southern Grey Shrike *Lanius meridionalis*	LC	A	
Woodchat Shrike *Lanius senator*	LC	A	
Golden Oriole *Oriolus oriolus*	LC	A	
Jay *Garrulus glandarius*	LC	A	
Azure-winged Magpie *Cyanopica cyanus*	LC	A	
Magpie *Pica pica*	LC	A	
(Red-billed) Chough *Pyrrhocorax pyrrhocorax*	LC	A	
Jackdaw *Corvus monedula*	LC	A	
Rook *Corvus frugilegus*	LC	A	
Carrion Crow *Corvus corone*	LC	A	
Common Raven *Corvus corax*	LC	A	
Coal Tit *Periparus ater*	LC	A	
Crested Tit *Lopophanes cristatus*	LC	A	
Great Tit *Parus major*	LC	A	
Blue Tit *Cyanistes caeruleus*	LC	A	
Penduline Tit *Remiz pendulinus*	LC	A	
Sand Martin *Riparia riparia*	LC	A	
Barn Swallow *Hirundo rustica*	LC	A	
Crag Martin *Hirundo rupestris*	LC	A	
House Martin *Delichon urbicum*	LC	A	
Red-rumped Swallow *Hirundo daurica*	LC	A	
Long-tailed Tit *Aegithalos caudatus*	LC	A	
Calandra Lark *Melanocorypha calandra*	LC	A	
Short-toed Lark *Calandrella brachydactyla*	LC	A	
Lesser Short-toed Lark *Calandrella rufescens*	LC	A	
Dupont's Lark *Chersophilus duponti*	NT	A	
Crested Lark *Galerida cristata*	LC	A	
Thekla Lark *Galerida theklae*	LC	A	
Wood Lark *Lullula arborea*	LC	A	
Skylark *Alauda arvensis*	LC	A	
Zitting Cisticola *Cisticola juncidis*	LC	A	
Cetti's Warbler *Cettia cetti*	LC	A	
Grasshopper Warbler *Locustella naevia*	LC	A	
Savi's Warbler *Locustella luscinioides*	LC	A	
Great Reed Warbler *Acrocephalus arundinaceus*	LC	A	
Sedge Warbler *Acrocephalus schoenobaenus*	LC	A	
Reed Warbler *Acrocephalus scirpaceus*	LC	A	

Species	Category	Status	Seen
Western Olivaceous Warbler *Hippolais opaca*	LC	A	
Melodious Warbler *Hippolais polyglotta*	LC	A	
Willow Warbler *Phylloscopus trochilus*	LC	A	
Common Chiffchaff *Phylloscopus collybita*	LC	A	
Iberian Chiffchaff *Phylloscopus ibericus*	LC	A	
Bonelli's Warbler *Phylloscopus bonelli*	LC	A	
Blackcap *Sylvia atricapilla*	LC	A	
Garden Warbler *Sylvia borin*	LC	A	
Orphean Warbler *Sylvia hortensis*	LC	A	
Common Whitethroat *Sylvia communis*	LC	A	
Dartford Warbler *Sylvia undata*	NT	A	
Spectacled Warbler *Sylvia conspicillata*	LC	A	
Subalpine Warbler *Sylvia cantillans*	LC	A	
Sardinian Warbler *Sylvia melanocephala*	LC	A	
Bearded Reedling *Panurus biarmicus*	LC	A	
Firecrest *Regulus ignicapilla*	LC	A	
Wren *Troglodytes troglodytes*	LC	A	
Nuthatch *Sitta europaea*	LC	A	
Short-toed Treecreeper *Certhia brachydactyla*	LC	A	
Starling *Sturnus vulgaris*	LC	A	
Spotless Starling *Sturnus unicolor*	LC	A	
Ring Ouzel *Turdus torquatus*	LC	A	
Blackbird *Turdus merula*	LC	A	
Fieldfare *Turdus pilaris*	LC	A	
Redwing *Turdus iliacus*	LC	A	
Song Thrush *Turdus philomelos*	LC	A	
Mistle Thrush *Turdus viscivorus*	LC	A	
Robin *Erithacus rubecula*	LC	A	
Bluethroat *Luscinia svecica*	LC	A	
Nightingale *Luscinia megarhynchos*	LC	A	
Rufous-tailed Scrub Robin *Erythropygia galactotes*	LC	A	
Black Redstart *Phoenicurus ochruros*	LC	A	
Redstart *Phoenicurus phoenicurus*	LC	A	
Whinchat *Saxicola rubetra*	LC	A	
Stonechat *Saxicola rubicola*	LC	A	
Northern Wheatear *Oenanthe oenanthe*	LC	A	
Black-eared Wheatear *Oenanthe hispanica*	LC	A	
Black Wheatear *Oenanthe leucura*			
(Rufous-tailed) Rock-thrush *Monticola saxatilis*			
Blue Rock-thrush *Monticola solitarius*			
Spotted Flycatcher *Muscicapa striata*			

Andalucian Flower Checklist

LIST OF SOME COMMON SPECIES OCCURING IN ANDALUCÍA
(List kindly provided by Martin Jacoby)

Plants: (reference numbers in Mediterranean Wild Flowers by Blamey & Grey-Wilson, Harper/Collins 1993)

Species		Date	Place
0058	Birthwort *Aristolochia bætica*		
0130c	Snow in Summer *Cerastium gibraltaricum* (boissieri)		
0157	Bladder Campion *Silene vulgaris*		
0191c	Wood Pink *Dianthus sylvestris*		
0197c	Spanish Barberry *Berberis hispanica*		
0208	Virgin's Bower *Clematis cirrhosa*		
0243	Spiny-fruited Buttercup *Ranunculus muricatus*		
0258c	Dwarf Lark's-spur *Delphinium nanum/gracile*		
0276	Peony *Pæonia broteroi*		
0283	Corn Poppy *Papaver rhœas*		
0310c	Hedge Mustard *Sisymbrium officinale*		
0313	Sand Stock *Malcolmia littorea*		
0336	Sweet Alison *Lobularia maritima*		
0337c	Shepherd's Purse *Capsell bursa-pastoris*		
0354c	Purple Cabbage *Moricandia moricandioides*		
0354c	Wall Rocket *Diplotaxis catholica*		
0355c	Black Mustard *Brassica nigra*		
0376	Wild Mignonette *Reseda lutea*		
0377	Dyer's Rocket *Reseda luteola*		
0382	Stonecrop *Sedum sediforme*		
0396	Navelwort *Umbilicus rupestris*		
0404	Evergreen Rose *Rosa sempervirens*		
0416c	Wild Pear *Pyrus bourgæna*		
0420c	Hawthorn *Cratægus monogyna*		
0428	Bramble *Rubus sp.*		

Species		Date	Place
0431	Carob *Ceratonia siliquae*		
0446	Bean *Trefoil Anagyris foetida*		
0453	Spiny Broom *Calycotome villosa*		
0454	Hairy Broom *Cytisus villosus*		
0475	Gorse *Ulex europæus*		
0478	Yellow Broom *Retama (= Lygos) sphærocarpa*		
0480	White Broom *Retama (= Lygos) monosperma*		
0481	Spanish Broom *Spartium junceum*		
0483	Yellow Lupin *Lupinus luteus*		
0508	Pitch Trefoil *Psoralea bituminosa*		
0525	Yellow Vetch *Vicia lutea*		
0536	Tangier Pea *Lathyrus tingitanus*		
0550	Pea *Lathyrus clymenum*		
0556	Large Yellow Restharrow *Ononis natrix*		
0572	Small-flowered Melilot *Melilotus indica*		
0596	Lucerne *Medicago sativa*		
0625	Common Bird's-foot Trefoil *Lotus corniculatus*		
0640	Orange Bird's-foot *Ornithopus pinnatus*		
0642	White Clover *Trifolium repens*		
0644	Hare's-foot Clover *Trifolium arvense*		
0645	Red Clover *Trifolium pratense*		
0662	Star Clover *Trifolium stellatum*		
0682	Asparagus Pea *Tetragonobolus purpureus*		
0684	*Scorpiurus muricatus*		
0690	Kidney Vetch *Anthyllis vulneraria*		
0696	Rush-like Scorpion Vetch *Coronilla juncea*		
0708	Horseshoe Vetch *Hippocrepis multisiliquosa*		
0710	Italian Sanfoin *Hedysarum coronarium*		
0735	Bermuda Buttercup *Oxalis pes-caprae*		
0743	Round-leaved Crane's-bill *Geranium rotundifolium*		
0748	Little Robin *Geranium purpureum*		
0761	Common Stork's-bill *Erodium cicutarium*		
0763c	Ivy *Hedera helix*		
0787c	Yellow Flax *Linum tenue*		
0799	Sun Spurge *Euphorbia helioscopia*		
0813	Sea Spurge *Euphorbia paralias*		

Species		Date	Place
0820	Annual Mercury *Mercurialis annua*		
0824	Castor Oil Plant *Ricinus communis*		
0850	Common Milkwort *Polygala vugaris*		
0865	Mastic Tree *Pistacia lentiscus*		
0885	Mediterranean Buckthorn *Rhamnus alaternus*		
0893c	Spanish Mallow *Malva hispanica*		
0897	Small-flowered Mallow *Malva parviflora*		
0910	Small Tree Mallow *Lavatera cretica*		
0917	*Stegia (= Lavatera) trimestris*		
0936	Mediterranean Mezereon *Daphne gnidium*		
0953	Perfoliate St John's-wort *Hypericum perfoliatum*		
0961	Grey-leaved Cistus *Cistus albidus*		
0971	Gum Cistus *Cistus ladanifer*		
0975	*Halimium halimifolium*		
1017	French Tamarisk *Tamarix gallica*		
1032	Squirting Cucumber *Ecballium elaterium*		
1033	White Bryony *Bryonia cretica*		
1052	Myrtle *Myrtus communis*		
1073	Sea Holly *Eryngium maritimum*		
1074	Eryngo *Eryngium aquifolium*		
1087	Alexanders *Smyrnium olosatrum*		
1097	Shepherd's Needle *Scandix pecten-veneris*		
1101	Rock Samphire *Crithmum maritimum*		
1105	Water Dropwort *Oenanthe fistulosa*		
1108	Fennel *Fœniculum vulgare*		
1134	Corn Caraway *Rhidolfia segetum*		
1136	False Bishop's Weed *Ammi visnaga*		
1141	Giant Fennel *Ferula communis*		
1161	Spreading Hedge Parsley *Torilis arvensis*		
1168	Wild Carrot *Daucus carota*		
1176	Strawberry Tree *Arbutus unedo*		
1178	Tree Heath *Erica arborea*		
1198	Scarlet Pimpernel *Anagallis arvensis*		
1245c	Narrow-leaved Ash *Fraxinus angustifolia*		
1248	Olive *Olea europæa*		
1251	Common Centaury *Centaurium erythræa*		

Species		Date	Place
1256	Oleander *Nerium oleander*		
1289c	Cleavers *Galium aparine*		
1305	Wild Madder *Rubia peregrina*		
1305c	Field Madder *Sherardia arvensis*		
1316	Bindweed *Calystegia sepium*		
1331	Mallow-leaved Bindweed *Convolvulus althæoides*		
1338	Dwarf Convolvulus *Convolvulus tricolor*		
1341	Heliotrope *Heliotropium europæum*		
1355c	Gromwell *Lithodora prostrata*		
1367	Honeywort *Cerinthe major*		
1383	Purple Viper's Buglos *Echium plantagineum*		
1395	Borage *Borago officinalis*		
1429	Tree Germander *Teucrium fruticans*		
1445	White Horehound *Marrubium vulgare*		
1465	Jerusalem Sage *Phlomis purpurea*		
1469c	Horehound *Ballota hirsuta*		
1485c	Woundwort *Stachys ocymastrum*		
1499c	Wood Calamint *Calamintha sylvatica*		
1524	Pennyroyal *Menta puligeum*		
1526	Rosemary *Rosmarinus officinalis*		
1528	French Lavender *Lavandula stœchas*		
1545	Wild Clary *Salvia verbenaca*		
1563	Black Nightshade *Solanum nigrum*		
1573	Mandrake *Mandragora autumnalis*		
1589	French Figwort *Scrophularia canina*		
1601	Mullein *Verbascum sinuatum*		
1609	Snapdragon *Antirrhinum majus*		
1626c	Sad Toadflax *Linaria tristis*		
1636	Woolly Fluellen *Kickxia lanigera*		
1645	Ivy-leaved Speedwell *Veronica hederifolia*		
1646	Pale Speedwell *Veronica cymbalaria*		
1651	Yellow Bartsia *Parentucellia viscosa*		
1655	Branched Broomrape *Orobanche ramosa*		
1693	Greater Plantain *Plantago major*		
1706	Plantain *Plantago afra*		
1711	Laurustinus *Viburnum tinus*		

Species		Date	Place
1713c	Honeysuckle *Lonicera periclymenum*		
1720	Fedia *Fedia cornucopiae*		
1725	Red Valerian *Centranthus calcitrapa*		
1732	Wild Teasel *Dipsacus fullonum*		
1749c	Drumstick Scabious *Scabiosa simplex*		
1759	Rampion Bellflower *Campanula rapunculus*		
1783	Throatwort *Trachelium cæruleum*		
1793	Southern Daisy *Bellis sylvatica*		
1824	Everlasting Flower *Helichrysum stœchas*		
1842	Aromatic Inula *Dittrichia (= Inula) viscosa*		
1843	Common Fleabane *Pulicaria dysenterica*		
1848	Yellow Sea Aster *Asteriscus maritimus*		
1858	Corn Chamomile *Anthemis arvensis*		
1879	Yellow Milfoil *Achillea ageratum*		
1890	Anacyclus *Anacyclus radiatus*		
1894	Corn Marigold *Chrysanthemum segetum*		
1895	Crown Daisy *Chrysanthemum coronarium*		
1908	Corn Marigold *Calendula arvensis*		
1916	Common Groundsel *Senecio vulgaris*		
1920	Flat-topped Carline Thistle *Carlina corymbosa*		
1935c	Globe Thistle *Echinops strigosus*		
1960	Giant Thistle *Cirsium scabrum*		
1960c	Stemless Thistle *Cirsium acaule*		
1966	Syrian Thistle *Notobasis syriaca*		
1970	Spanish Thistle *Chamæpeuce (=Ptilostemon) hispanica*		
1971	Galactites *Galactites tomentosa*		
1979c	Humble Artichoke *Cynara humilis*		
1982	Milk Thistle *Silybum marianum*		
1988	Mantisalca *Mantisalca salmantica*		
1990	Red Star-thistle *Centaurea calcitrapa*		
2006	Knapweed *Centaurea pullata*		
2020	Spanish Oyster Plant *Scolymus hispanicus*		
2023	Chicory *Cichorium intybus*		
2030	Bearded Tolpis *Tolpis barbata*		
2032	False Dandelion *Hyoseris radiata*		
2046	Ox-tongue *Picris echioides*		

Species		Date	Place
2059	Meadow Goat's Beard *Tragopogon pratensis*		
2067c	Hawk's-beard *Crepis vesicaria*		
2073	Sow-thistle *Sonchus tenerrimus*		
2076	Prickly Lettuce *Lactuca serriola*		
2081	Rabbit's Bread *Andryala integrifolia*		
2090	Branched Asphodel *Asphodelus ramosus agg.*		
2096	Blue Leafless Lily *Aphyllanthes monspeliensis*		
2113c	Autumn Crocus *Colchicum lusitanum*		
2163	Sea Squill *Urginea maritima*		
2171c	Star of Bethlehem *Ornithogallum orthophyllum*		
2183	Peruvian Squill *Scilla peruviana*		
2191	Spanish Bluebell *Hyacinthoides hispanica*		
2201	Tassel Hyacinth *Muscari comosum*		
2215	Leafless Asparagus *Asparagus aphyllus*		
2222	Smilax *Smilax aspera*		
2224	Rosy Garlic *Allium roseum*		
2229	Three-cornered Leek *Allium triquetrum*		
2265	Hair-leaved Snowflake *Leucojum trichophyllum*		
2270	Sea Daffodil *Pancratium maritimum*		
2278	Paper-white Narcissus *Narcissus papyraceus*		
2282	Black Bryony *Tamus communis*		
2290	Yellow Flag *Iris pseudacorus*		
2305	Barbary Nut *Gynandiris sisyrinchium*		
2307	Field Gladiolus *Gladiolus italicus (= segetum)*		
2314	Romulea *Romulea bulbocodium*		
2357	Dwarf Fan Palm *Chamærops humilis*		
2361	Large Cuckoo Pint *Arum italicum*		
2378	Friar's Cowl *Arisarum simorrhinum*		
2380	Broad-leaved Helleborine *Epipactis helleborine*		
2397	Heath Spotted Orchid *Dactylorhiza maculata*		
2416	Early Purple Orchid *Orchis mascula ssp. olbiensis*		
2422	Mirror Orchid *Ophrys ciliatum (= speculum)*		
2423	Yellow Bee Orchid *Ophrys lutea*		
2442	Sawfly Orchid *Ophrys tenthredinifera*		
2444	Bumblebee Orchid *Ophrys bombyliflora*		
2451	Tongue Orchid *Serapias lingua*		

Glossary & Useful Phrases

Glossary

área recreativa	picnic/camping area
alberca	tank for water storage
ayuntamiento	town hall
barranco	gorge or gully
calera	lime kiln
canuto	small gorge with humid microclimate
casa forestal	forestry hut
colegio público	secondary college
correos	post office
coto	designated hunting area
huerta	vegetable garden
ingenio	a factory for processing sugar cane
mirador	viewing area
mudéjar	architectural style that was copied from Moors
monte bajo	low growing scrubby vegetation
parador	state-owned hotel
sierra	mountain range
venta	roadside inn

Tracks & Paths

vereda	footpath
via pecuaria	drover's path
sendero	footpath
calzada	cobbled or paved footpath or track
camino	footpath
cañada real	drover's path

collado	drover's path
carretera	road
carril	dirt track
puerto	mountain pass
subida	ascent/way up
bajada	descent/way down

Directions

¿Vamos bien para...x?	Is this the way to...x?
¿Cuánto tiempo hay hasta...x?	How long will it take to...x?
¿Qué distancia hay hasta...x?	How far is it to...x?
A la derecha	Right
A la izquierda	Left
Todo recto	Straight ahead
Todo seguido	Straight ahead
Hacía en frente	Straight ahead

Signs you may encounter

Animales Sueltos	Grazing livestock
Prohibido al Paso	No Entry
Coto Privado de Casa	Hunting area (not necessarily private property)
Colmenas	Beehives
Peligro	Danger
Finca/Carril/Entrada Privada	Private farm/track/entrance
Cierran/Cerrar La Puerta	Please close the gate

Hoja de pedido de mapas
Maps Order Form

Atención de: *To:* ....

Email/Fax: ....

De Parte de: *From:* ....

Email/Fax: ....

Fecha: *Date:* ....

Estimados Señores/Señoras,
Dear Sir/Madam,

Les ruego mandarme los siguientes mapas, contra reembolso:
Please send me the following maps, to be paid on receipt of order:

No(s) de Mapa(s): Map reference(s):

....

....

....

....

....

El pedido va en nombre de: *Please send order in the name of:*

....

A esta dirección: *To this address:*

....

....

....

....

Les agradezco su amable cooperación
Many thanks for your help